CAMBRIDGE
UNIVERSITY PRESS

Cambridge
Global English

COURSEBOOK 10

Katia Carter & Tim Carter

CAMBRIDGE
UNIVERSITY PRESS

Shaftesbury Road, Cambridge CB2 8EA, United Kingdom

One Liberty Plaza, 20th Floor, New York, NY 10006, USA

477 Williamstown Road, Port Melbourne, VIC 3207, Australia

314–321, 3rd Floor, Plot 3, Splendor Forum, Jasola District Centre, New Delhi – 110025, India

103 Penang Road, #05–06/07, Visioncrest Commercial, Singapore 238467

Cambridge University Press is part of the University of Cambridge.

It furthers the University's mission by disseminating knowledge in the pursuit of education, learning and research at the highest international levels of excellence.

www.cambridge.org
Information on this title: www.cambridge.org/9781009364621

© Cambridge University Press & Assessment 2024

First published 2024

20 19 18 17 16 15 14 13 12 11 10 9 8 7 6 5 4 3 2 1

Printed in Malaysia by Vivar Printing

A catalogue record for this publication is available from the British Library

ISBN 978-1-009-36462-1 Coursebook with Digital Access (2 Years)
ISBN 978-1-009-36463-8 Digital Coursebook (2 Years)
ISBN 978-1-009-36464-5 Coursebook eBook

Additional resources for this publication at www.cambridge.org/go

Cambridge University Press has no responsibility for the persistence or accuracy
of URLs for external or third-party internet websites referred to in this publication,
and does not guarantee that any content on such websites is, or will remain,
accurate or appropriate. Information regarding prices, travel timetables, and other factual information
given in this work is correct at the time of first printing but Cambridge University Press does not
guarantee the accuracy of such information thereafter.

This text has not been through the Cambridge International endorsement process.

....

› Contents

Contents

Practise and prepare	Use of English	Vocabulary	Cross-curricular links	21st-century skills
Speaking Reading Writing	Multi-word verbs Comparative forms Suffixes and syllable stress in nouns Present simple or present continuous?	Education	Psychology and education	**Critical thinking:** Analysing results and making conclusions **Critical thinking:** Collecting and presenting information
Speaking Writing Listening	Dependent prepositions Comparing and contrasting ideas The passive	Animals in the wild or in captivity	Science	**Critical thinking:** Evaluating resources for your research **Critical thinking:** Supporting your research findings
Reading Writing Speaking	Zero and first conditionals Reporting survey results – expressing statistics	Science	Science	**Communication:** Giving polite suggestions **Critical thinking:** Analysing and understanding links between events
Speaking Writing Listening	The passive Using suffixes to make different words Modal verbs and other phrases of probability	Types of art	Music and psychology	**Communication:** Using your voice and body language when giving a talk **Communication:** Reading a conclusion **Communication:** Expressing your views for and against
Speaking Writing Reading	Superlative forms Short questions to show surprise in conversations Past simple, past continuous and past perfect simple used in storytelling	Animal migration	Geography	**Critical thinking:** Carrying out research on public opinion
Speaking Writing Listening	Multi-word verbs Expressing probability and certainty Linking words and phrases (contrast and addition)	Technology	Technology	**Critical thinking:** What can impact your survey results **Communication:** Giving written instructions **Creativity:** Designing slides for a presentation

Contents

Contents

Practise and prepare	Use of English	Vocabulary	Cross-curricular links	21st-century skills
Speaking Writing Reading	Compound nouns and adjectives First and second conditional structures Verb forms	Environmental activism	Environmental science	**Communication:** Taking turns during discussions **Social responsibility:** Understanding a global issue and its effects **Communication:** Being a good public speaker
Speaking Writing Listening	The third conditional Verb forms to talk about past events, recent news and future plans and decisions	Role models	History and science	**Communication:** Improving your speaking fluency
Speaking Writing Listening	Narrative verb forms – past simple and past continuous	Types of books	Sociology and education	**Communication:** Contributing effectively to a group discussion and reaching a conclusion **Creative thinking:** Brainstorming and trying out new ideas
Speaking Writing	Time adverbials used with the past simple and present perfect Indirect questions	Employment	Psychology and social science	**Social responsibilities:** Being culturally aware **Social responsibilities:** Gaining useful life skills

> How to use this book

In this book you will find lots of different features to help your learning.

What you will learn in the unit.

Big questions to find out what you know already.

GETTING STARTED

"What you learn without joy, you forget without grief."
(an old Finnish saying)

What do you think this saying means?

Key vocabulary for the unit.

Bachelor's degree · compulsory education · further education · graduate · half-term holiday · higher education · Master's degree · post-graduate · primary education · secondary education · semester · undergraduate · vocational course

Language that will help with your wider studies.

ACADEMIC LANGUAGE

Psychology and education

aural learner · be in tune with · brainstorm ideas · collaborate · excel in · flashcards · hands-on · kinaesthetic learner · logical learner · reasoning · social learner · solitary learner · strategies · verbal learner · visual learner

Glossaries to support texts.

thread: a long thin string often used for sewing or to make materials like wool or cotton · electrical current: the movement of electricity in a particular direction

Use of English boxes and accompanying questions present the main grammar points in a unit.

USE OF ENGLISH

Present simple or present continuous?

We can use either the present simple or the present continuous to talk about different present situations.

The **present continuous** is used here to describe a current situation that is in progress.

You're probably busy preparing for your exams this month…

The **present simple** is used here to describe a situation that repeats.

…and I know you sometimes get a bit worried about your exams.

Strategies you can use to help you with your learning.

SPEAKING TIP

Talking about preferences

To express your preference, you can say:

- *I prefer playing games to doing grammar exercises.*
- *I enjoy doing scientific experiments much*

Suggestions to help develop the 21st-century skills: creativity, collaboration, communication, critical thinking, learning to learn and social responsibilities.

CRITICAL THINKING

Analysing results and making conclusions

Look at the results of the quiz. What do you think they mean? How good is the student's study–life balance? What changes do you think they need to make in their lives, and why? How important do you think these changes are?

Group activities to create pieces of work.

PROJECT OPTION 1

A video clip or a presentation to promote mental health

As part of the mental health awareness week, your class want to prepare some activities to help students feel happy. You also want to make a short video or presentation to promote your activities.

Step 1: Recent research shows that the following situations improve people's happiness: being outdoors, talking to other people, making things.

In small groups, choose one of the situations and discuss:

• what activities your classmates could do for each situation

First, decide what information you need to include in your video or presentation, and other things to consider. For example, how long it will be and who will say what in your video or presentation.

Step 3: In your group, decide what each member is good at and what they should be in charge of (for example, filming).

A: You're quite good at _____, so how would you feel about being in charge of _____?

Step 4: Write a short script of what people will say in the video or presentation.

Step 5: Film the video or practise your presentation. Then decide whether anything needs to be edited or if you want to add anything, such as music.

Criteria to help you assess your own or another student's progress.

SELF-AND PEER ASSESSMENT

Think about how well you and your group did in the project. Then complete the statements below in your notebook.

• Our group worked particularly well in the following activities:…

• I really enjoyed working with… because he/she…

• While doing this project, I learnt that I'm really good at… and I enjoy…

• However, I need to practise… a bit more.

• I learnt…, and in the future this will help me…

Strategies to help you with exams.

EXAM TIP

Task completion – covering all the points from the task

In speaking and writing exams, read the task very carefully first and find all the points you should cover in your answer. If you don't answer all the points, you could lose marks. Task completion is one of the most important aspects the examiners will be looking for when marking your work.

REFLECTION

1 Look at the quotation by Albert Einstein at the start of this unit. Answer the following questions about it in pairs.

• Do you agree with the quotation? Why or why not?

• What do you think the quotation says about Albert Einstein as a person?

• Will anything that you learnt in this unit help you in your own life? Give examples.

2 Reflect on your progress as a learner while working on this unit. Discuss these questions

d Do you think that researching topics helps you learn? Why?

e In the Improve your writing lesson, you learnt a lot of new skills, including how to engage the reader, how to plan your review and how to give feedback to other students about their review. Which of these three skills do you feel most or least confident about? Why? How can you improve this skill?

f In the Project lesson, you worked as part of a team. What did you enjoy about working with other students? What did you learn

Questions to help you think about how you learn.

A checklist to use to check your understanding of the unit.

SUMMARY CHECKLIST

I can…

☐ listen to an interview and choose the correct answer from a list of options.
☐ read an article and find examples of animals' communication.
☐ match definitions to the correct words in a text.
☐ select relevant information for a presentation and deliver the presentation to an audience.
☐ use the passive confidently in appropriate situations.
☐ plan a review of a TV documentary and write it in an engaging way.
☐ select the best resources for my research.

Audio is available with the Digital Coursebook, Teacher's Resource or Digital Classroom.

Videos and grammar activities are available with Digital Classroom.

The **Think about it** lesson introduces the topic through topic vocabulary activities.

Engage with the topic of the unit and generate discussion using the image, the video and the big question.

This lesson develops students' listening skills.

The **cross-curricular** lesson prepares students to learn in English across the curriculum.

In this lesson you'll find Academic language boxes.

A non-fiction text exposes students to cross-curricular language.

There will be opportunities to think critically about the information in the text.

The **Talk about it** lesson develops students' speaking skills.

Listening models and speaking tips help provide scaffolding for speaking.

The **Improve your writing** lesson supports students to write effective texts.

Model texts support the writing process.

Step-by-step tasks support students in their planning, writing and editing.

Sample answers can be found in the Teacher's Resource.

Use of English boxes focus on important grammar points.

The **Project challenge** lesson provides a choice of projects and an opportunity to consolidate learning from the unit.

Projects encourage 21st-century skills such as research, collaboration, and creativity.

A final activity supports students to assess their own or their peer's work.

The **Practise and prepare** lesson provides opportunities to practise answering exam-style tasks.

At the end of the unit, a Reflection box contains questions to prompt students to think about their learning process.

A Summary checklist box supports students to check their progress with the unit content.

The Literature section at the end of the book includes extracts from five different literary texts. The accompanying activities help students to explore the different genres.

An About the author box provides biographical information about the author.

1 Learning and discovering

IN THIS UNIT YOU WILL...

- **listen** to two talks about schools in Finland and **make** comparisons

- **read** about different types of learners and **express** your preferences

- **interview** classmates about their study–life balance and **give** advice

- **review** and **practise** the present simple and continuous when talking about your daily life

- **write** an email to persuade someone to do something

- **make** a video clip or a presentation to promote mental health or **make** a diary about your own progress and **produce** a poster with tips

- **participate** in a group discussion.

GETTING STARTED

> *"What you learn without joy, you forget without grief."*
> (an old Finnish saying)

What do you think this saying means?

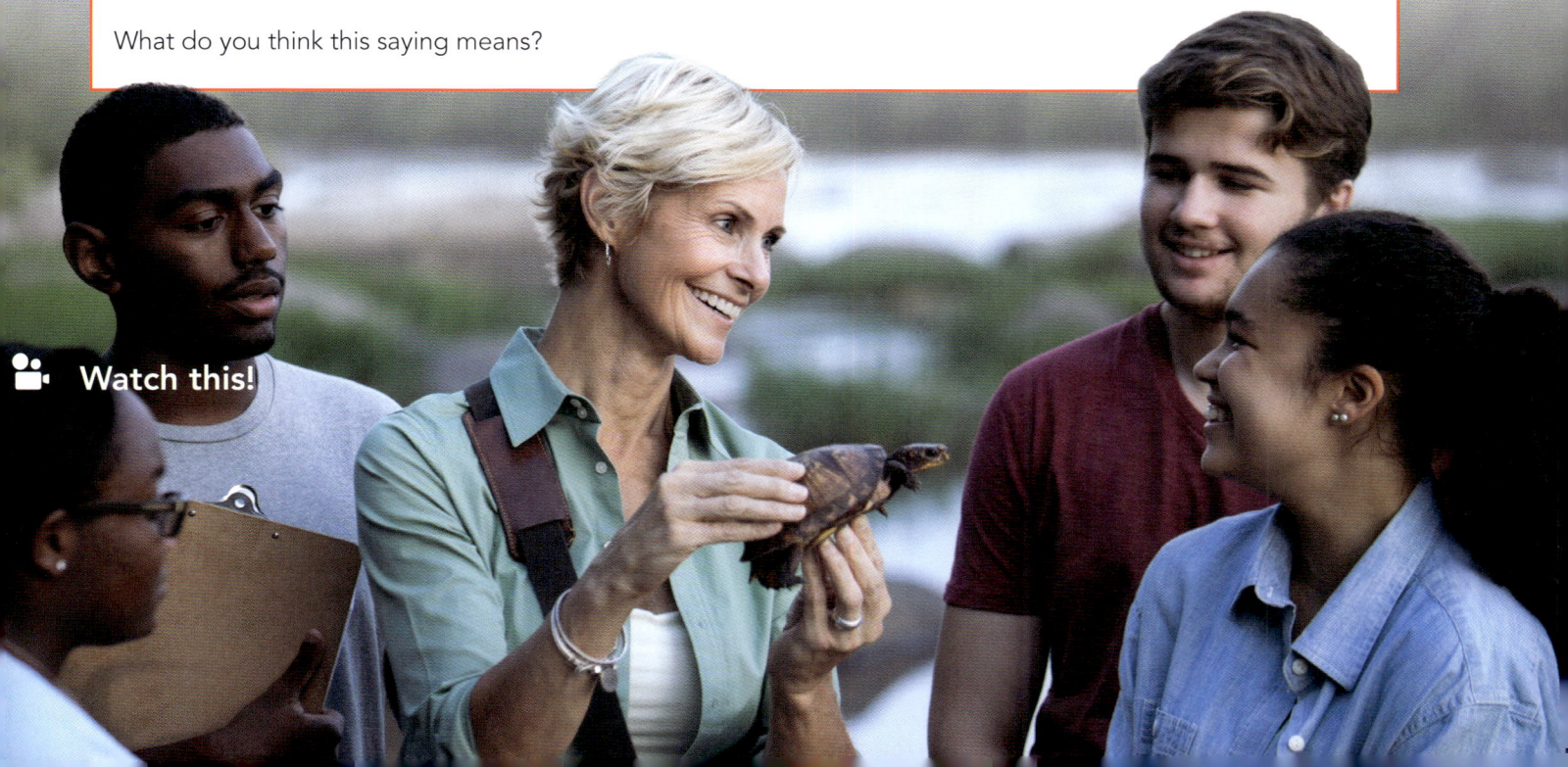

▶ **Watch this!**

Think about it: What is it like to be a student in Finland?

• **What do you think makes learning enjoyable for students?**

Vocabulary

1   Look at the vocabulary box and check the meaning of the unknown vocabulary in a reliable dictionary. Then work in pairs and tell each other about:

• **your journey as a student so far**

• **what you are planning to do after you finish this school.**

Use your own words and the vocabulary from the box.

Bachelor's degree	Master's degree
compulsory education	post-graduate
	primary education
further education	secondary education
graduate	semester
half-term holiday	undergraduate
higher education	vocational course

Listening

2   Listen to Olavi from Finland talking about what it is like to be a student in Finland. What aspects of studying does he mention?

USE OF ENGLISH

Multi-word verbs

Multi-word verbs are phrases that are made of a verb (such as *come, get, go*) and one or two particles (such as *up, over, off*). The meaning of these phrases is normally very different from the individual words they are made of.

Everything we needed to know we just ***got through*** *in our lessons.*

The multi-word verb *to get through* means 'to successfully complete or finish'.

Some multi-word verbs such as *to get through* can have more than one meaning. It is important to look at the whole sentence the multi-word verb is used in. This will help you understand the exact meaning of the multi-word verb.

---

3   Olavi uses some multi-word verbs in his talk. Listen again and write down the multi-word verbs you hear. Compare your answers with a partner.

For example: *got through*

4   Look at the definitions of the multi-word verbs from Exercise 3. In pairs, match them to the correct multi-word verbs.

For example: *to get through – to successfully complete or finish*

a   to learn something (for example, a skill) by chance and quite easily

b   to manage to do a task or an activity with difficulty, using only the limited knowledge or skill that you have

c   to start or continue doing a task

d   to try to find the information you need, for example on the internet or in a book

e   to become awake and leave your bed

f   to progress more slowly than other students

5 Choose three multi-word verbs from Exercise 4 and use them to make sentences about yourself. Then swap your sentences with another student and check if they used their multi-word verbs correctly.

6 Look at your answers from Exercise 2. You are now going to listen for more detail about each of them. Listen to Olavi's talk again and write down at least one extra detail about each answer.

> ## STUDY TIP
>
> **Taking notes**
>
> When you are listening to a talk and taking notes, don't write in full sentences. Instead, only write down short phrases and use abbreviations and symbols.

Speaking

> ## SPEAKING TIP
>
> **Speculating**
>
> When you want to express your opinion about something that you have very little information about, you can speculate.
>
> *I suppose this could be true because I read the same about other countries.*
>
> *I think it's unlikely that students would get so much time in between lessons.*

7 Look at the sentences about schools in Finland. In pairs, discuss which ones you think are true or false. Try to explain why you think this is.
   a Only primary and secondary schools in Finland are free, paid for by the government.
   b Children start going to school when they are seven years old.
   c Primary school students get about 120 minutes of break-time every day.
   d On average, the school week in Finland is 10 hours long.
   e The same teacher stays with a class for about five years, or more.
   f Over 90% of students go on to graduate from a high school and over 40% from a university.

Listening

8 Look at the sentences in Exercise 7. Then listen to Karolina, a student from Mexico who's studying in Finland, talking about Finnish schools. Are the sentences true or false?

9 Look at the sentences that you marked as false. What is the correct information? Listen again to check.

> ## USE OF ENGLISH
>
> **Degrees of comparison**
>
> When we use adjectives to compare two things, we use the comparative forms of these adjectives (such as *longer, more relaxed*). To show a big difference between two things, we can use *much* before the comparative form. To show only a small difference, we can use *a bit*.
>
> *Our school week is **much longer than** in Finland.*
>
> *Finnish students seem to be **much more relaxed than** students in other countries.*
>
> *Finnish children are **a bit older** when they start school **than** children in our country.*
>
> *The Finnish summer holiday is **a little shorter than** the summer break we get in our country.*
>
> We can also use the two structures below to compare two things:
>
> *Our breaks **aren't as long as** the school breaks in Finland.* (There is a difference between the two breaks.)
>
> *Our school day is **as long as** a school day in Finland.* (There is no difference between the two school days.)
>
> Look at the forms of the adjectives in each sentence. Do you need to use the adjective only (such as *small, exciting*) or the comparative form of the adjective (such as *smaller, more exciting*)?

Speaking

10 Work in pairs. Use the information from Karolina's talk and compare Finnish schools with schools in your country. Try to use a range of comparative forms.

Psychology and education: What type of learner are you?

• **What do you think helps you learn? What makes it difficult for you to learn?**

Reading

04

1 **Read this introductory paragraph about learning styles, then answer the questions that follow.**

> There is no doubt that we all have different abilities. While some of us are good at maths and science, others excel at music or the visual arts. This also means that we sometimes prefer to learn in a certain way and will enjoy some activities more than others. According to one theory, students respond to different types of activities better because they have a preferred way of learning. This theory also categorises learners into different groups. However, the same learner usually has more than one preferred learning style and we can even change the way we like to learn, over time. It's best for learners to experience a variety of different ways of learning. But the bottom line is – we all learn better when we enjoy what we do.

a Why does the writer use the first person 'we'? What effect on the reader does the writer want to achieve?

b The writer uses the phrase 'the bottom line is'. What does the writer tell us with this phrase?

c What is the best summary of the first paragraph?

   A Everybody should try to be good at all school subjects and we can only do that if we know our learning style.

   B It isn't important what the theories say, as long as students have fun while learning.

   C We can only understand how we should learn most effectively when we get older.

2 **Look at the Academic language box and check the meaning of the words and phrases in pairs. Use a reliable dictionary to help you.**

ACADEMIC LANGUAGE

Psychology and education

aural learner	logical learner
be in tune with	reasoning
brainstorm ideas	social learner
collaborate	solitary learner
excel in	strategies
flashcards	verbal learner
hands-on	visual learner
kinaesthetic learner	

---

3 **Read the descriptions of the seven types of learners, according to the learning theory from Exercise 1. Match each description to the correct learner from the Academic language box. Then check your answers in pairs.**

A Learning in groups and working with others is favoured by these learners. These learners know how to communicate effectively and enjoy collaborating with others, for example by brainstorming and discussing ideas and concepts. They are generally good listeners and are thoughtful and understanding.

B These learners prefer using words, both in speech and writing. They can easily express themselves and usually love to read and write. These learners tend to have a large vocabulary and excel in activities that involve speaking and debating.

C Some learners prefer learning by observing things. They use pictures, images, diagrams, whiteboards and more to help understand information better. These learners can easily visualise information, have a good sense of direction and usually like to draw things.

D These learners do well when there is logic, reasoning and numbers involved in an activity. They can solve complex problems by employing strategies and their scientific way of thinking. Maths and science are usually favoured by this type of learner.

E Sound and music work well for some learners, who typically have a good sense of rhythm. These learners are good listeners who normally learn best through verbal presentations like lectures and speeches.

F These learners prefer to use self-study and work alone. They are independent, very self-aware and are in tune with their thoughts and feelings. These learners prefer being away from the crowds and learn best in a quiet place where they can focus on their task.

G Whether it's by using their body or hands, these learners are all about the sense of touch. Physical activities and sports play a big part in these learners' lives. Getting hands-on is a must – they love to experiment and learn best when they can do rather than see or hear.

Speaking

4 **Look at this list of jobs. In pairs, discuss what job each type of learner might be good at, and why.**

- musician
- teacher
- freelance editor
- computer programmer
- journalist
- architect
- car mechanic

5 **Work in pairs. Think about the activities you enjoy in your lessons and how you prefer to learn. Discuss with your partner what type of learner you think you are, according to the theory. Why?**

> **SPEAKING TIP**
>
> **Talking about preferences**
>
> To express your preference, you can say:
>
> - *I **prefer** playing games **to** doing grammar exercises.*
>
> - *I **enjoy** doing scientific experiments **much more than** giving presentations.*
>
> - *I **find** using pictures **really helpful, more than anything else**.*

6 **Look at the cartoon. In pairs, discuss these questions.**

a What do you think the main message of the cartoon is?

b What is it trying to criticise?

c Think about what you have learnt in this lesson. What is the connection between the cartoon and the title of this lesson?

Talk about it: Do you have the right study–life balance?

- **Do you spend more time studying or doing your hobbies?**

Watch this!

Speaking

1   **Look at these activities, then answer the questions in pairs. When you finish your discussion, comment on how similar or different your study–life balance is to your partner's.**

> revising for exams   talking on the phone
>
> listening to music   doing homework
>
> meeting up with friends
>
> playing video games
>
> checking your social media accounts

   a   How often do you do these activities?

   b   How do you feel when you do these activities?

   c   Do you think you have a good study–life balance? Why or why not?

   d   Do you think you need to improve anything about your study–life balance?

SPEAKING TIP

When you take part in a conversation or a discussion, you should react to what others say. You can do this by:

- making a comment about something they have said

- agreeing or politely disagreeing with their opinion

- asking questions to find out more.

Listening

2   **Listen to a podcast where the speaker gives tips to high school students on keeping the right study–life balance. What advice does the speaker give? Put the tips below in the order you hear them.**

   a   You need to look after your mental health as well as your physical health.

   b   Make a timetable with all the tasks you have to do.

   c   Remember, it's fine to turn things down if necessary.

   d   It's important that you also have quality time with your friends.

   e   Decide how important each task is and do the more important ones first.

   f   You should take advantage of the support your school offers.

USE OF ENGLISH

Suffixes and syllable stress in nouns

You can make nouns by adding suffixes to verbs and adjectives. When you pronounce nouns, sometimes the stressed syllable is different to the one in the verb or adjective.

responsible (adj.) – responsibi**li**ty (n.)

invite (v.) – invi**ta**tion (n.)

weak (adj.) – weak**ness** (n.)

aware (adj.) – aware**ness** (n.)

3 **Which advice in Exercise 2 do you think is the most important? Give reasons for your opinion. Have you already tried any of the advice mentioned in the podcast? Was it useful? Why or why not?**

4 **Look at these phrases the speaker uses to give advice. Choose the correct verb form to complete each phrase. Then listen to the podcast again and check your answers.**

a it's a good idea *to draw / draw / drawing* up a weekly plan

b try *to highlight / highlight / highlighting* your priorities

c always remember *to get / get / getting* enough sleep

d *to spend / spend / spending* enough time with the people who are close to you is an absolute must

e make sure you *to reach / reach / reaching* out for help

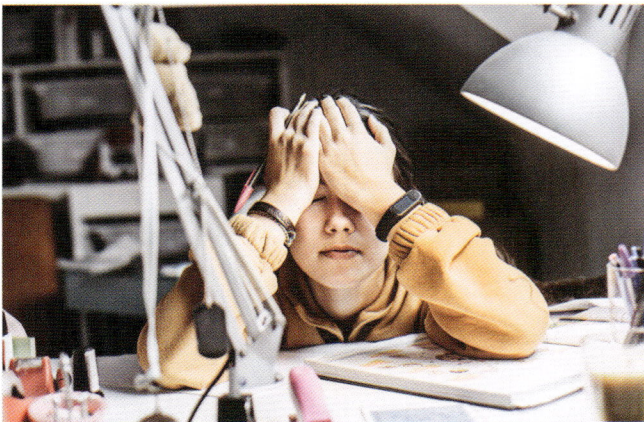

Speaking

5 **You are going to interview another classmate about their study–life balance. Look at the eight statements in the quiz below. Can you make the statements into questions?**

1	It feels like I spend all my time doing homework.	Yes / No
2	I hardly ever have time to catch up with my friends.	Yes / No
3	I often feel exhausted.	Yes / No
4	I tend to be in a bad mood.	Yes / No
5	I can't remember the last time I spent the whole time doing the things I like.	Yes / No
6	I sometimes forget to do things I've promised I'd do.	Yes / No
7	I've had to turn down invitations to go out because of other commitments.	Yes / No
8	I often agree to do things for others and end up being too busy.	Yes / No

6 **Interview another student and write down their answers. Give feedback to the other student about their study–life balance based on their answers to the quiz. The box below explains how to give a score for their answers. Remember to use the phrases from Exercise 4. Suggest what else they can do to have a good study–life balance, or what they should do to improve it.**

Results

Give one point for each yes. Each yes also shows the area of life where people should make some changes. The more answers with yes people have, the less study–life balance they have achieved.

CRITICAL THINKING

Analysing results and making conclusions

Look at the results of the quiz. What do you think they mean? How good is the student's study–life balance? What changes do you think they need to make in their lives, and why? How important do you think these changes are?

Improve your writing: A persuasive email

anxious: adjective – worried and nervous /ˈæŋk.ʃəs/

My brother always gets a bit *anxious* before flying.

anxiety: noun – a feeling of worry and nervousness /æŋˈzaɪ.ə.ti/

The first day at school can create a bit of *anxiety* in some students.

1   **The four pictures on this page represent four techniques that people can use to stop feeling anxious.**

   a   What do you think the techniques might be?

   b   How do you think they can help fight anxiety?

   c   Compare your ideas in small groups. Give reasons for your opinions.

2 Now read the email to find out what the four techniques are.
Were your predictions correct?

From: amir@email.com

To: ollie@email.com

Hi Ollie,

1 How are you? I haven't heard from you for ages! You're probably busy preparing for your exams this month and I know you sometimes get a bit worried about your exams. That's why I wanted to give you a few tips to help you.

2 I went to a presentation, organised by our school, about keeping anxiety under control. Well, I went because our teacher said we had to, but I learnt loads of interesting things. The first technique the speaker suggested was putting ice cubes on your wrists. The nerves controlling anxiety levels end in the wrists, and by placing cold ice there, you slow down everything, including your anxious thoughts. You should keep the ice there for 10–15 minutes and do something calming like listening to music or doing breathing exercises. It does sound like it might work.

3 Then the speaker mentioned the 'peeling an orange' technique. As you'd expect, the essential oils from citrus have a calming effect, but it's also combining this with doing an easy task with your hands that makes your brain forget your worries and you feel calmer. So next time you go shopping, definitely buy some oranges! And get some bananas too! Eating bananas is a good idea. They're rich in vitamin B and magnesium, both of which are needed to calm you down and boost your mood. So why not give them a try? You've got nothing to lose.

4 My personal favourite, though, was the '1 for 1' question technique. I think it's really worth a try and it'll also help you with your confidence. Basically, when you think of a worst-case scenario like 'What if I fail the test?', you immediately think of the best-case scenario like 'What if I get the best results I've ever got?' So you replace a negative thought with a positive one. And if you practise this, in a while you'll start doing it without even realising. The message was that we shouldn't focus on fear that isn't real. I'll definitely be trying that one myself!

5 Anyway, I hope you'll like one of these techniques. Remember to let me know how you get on! The speaker is back next month to talk about time management, and I can't recommend him enough. In the meantime, let me know if you have some time to meet. Remember, you need to switch off and have fun as well.

Speak to you soon,

Amir

3   Read the email again, then answer these questions.

a   Who is Amir writing to? Do you think they know each other well? Give examples to support your opinion.

b   Why did Amir go to the presentation?

c   What did Amir think about the techniques to help with anxiety before he went to the presentation?

d   Did his opinion about the techniques change at the end of the presentation? How do you know?

e   Do you think Amir might go to a similar event again? Why or why not? Give reasons.

4   The email is divided into paragraphs. Why do you think it's important to use paragraphs? What is the purpose of each paragraph (1–5) in Amir's email?

5   Amir is trying to persuade his friend to try one of the techniques. He does that by:

•   **giving him interesting facts about the techniques**

•   **directly encouraging him to try them out.**

Read Amir's email again and find what interesting facts he includes in it. Then read it again and find the phrases that Amir uses to encourage his friend to do something.

READING TIP

When you look for answers in a text, highlight the information you are looking for. For example, you can use different colours to highlight different types of information. This will make it easier for you to see the answers in the text or to find them quickly again if you need to check anything later.

6   Your teacher will divide the class into three groups. Each group will research what advice or techniques there are for students who have problems with different aspects of their studies.

Group 1: Issues with memorising facts and revising for lessons

Group 2: Issues with time management

Group 3: Issues with concentration for longer periods of time

Each group should:

•   find useful material online

•   make notes of the relevant advice/techniques

•   compare notes together with other students in their group and decide on the three most useful tips or techniques

•   complete a mind map with their selected ideas.

WRITING TIP

Before you start writing, you should plan what you want to write about. Brainstorm ideas and write them down. You can organise the ideas into a diagram such as a mind map to see how many paragraphs you need and which ideas should go in the same paragraph.

7   Imagine one of your friends is having problems with one aspect of their studies. It is the same aspect that you researched in Exercise 6. Write your friend an email to tell them about the advice/techniques that might be helpful and encourage them to try out the techniques. Write about 120–160 words.

USE OF ENGLISH

Present simple or present continuous?

We can use either the present simple or the present continuous to talk about different present situations.

The **present continuous** is used here to describe a current situation that is in progress.

You're probably busy **preparing** for your exams *this month…*

The **present simple** is used here to describe a situation that repeats.

…and I know **you** sometimes **get** a bit worried about your exams.

8   **Look at the sentences below. Do they use the present simple or continuous? Match each sentence to the correct situation.**

a   This week I'm revising for my maths exam.

b   I do a work-out every morning before I go to school.

c   I live close to my school.

d   I can't meet you right now – I'm helping my brother with his homework.

e   I sometimes feel nervous before presentations.

permanent situation
personal routine
temporary situation
situation that repeats
situation happening at the moment

9   **Read an extract from an email giving advice about the best place to do schoolwork. Complete the gaps with either the present simple or present continuous. Use the verbs in brackets. Then explain why you need the form using the situations from Exercise 8.**

I _____[1] (revise) for my final exams this week and I always _____[2] (find) it hard to concentrate when there's too much noise around, so I know how you feel. For example, right now my brother _____[3] (practise) his guitar next door, so it's absolutely impossible for me to do any revision at home. That's why I normally _____[4] (go) to the library. Also, our neighbours' kids are very noisy – they _____[5] (play) football in the garden while I _____[6] (write) this email to you. So this is another reason why I rarely _____[7] (do) my homework at home. I know that you _____[8] (not live) anywhere near the city library, so why don't you use your school library instead? I often _____[9] (see) my classmates in our school library, but personally I _____[10] (prefer) the one in the city centre because it has more resources.

10   **Read through your email from Exercise 7 again and underline any examples of the present simple or the present continuous that you used. Then check that you used them correctly.**

11   **Work in pairs. Exchange your email with your partner. Proofread your partner's email and complete the checklist. Which things did they do well? Which things do you think they need to improve? Then give feedback to your partner.**

The email:

✓   gives some advice

✓   gives some information about at least one technique

✓   is persuasive

✓   is written in a style that is appropriate when writing to a friend

✓   is divided into paragraphs

✓   uses the present simple or present continuous correctly.

12   **Now rewrite your email based on your partner's feedback.**

Project challenge

PROJECT LEARNING OBJECTIVES

In your project you will…

- take part in a group discussion
- work on your own as well as part of a team
- compare your work with other groups.

PROJECT OPTION 1

A video clip or a presentation to promote mental health

As part of the mental health awareness week, your class want to prepare some activities to help students feel happy. You also want to make a short video or presentation to promote your activities.

Step 1: Recent research shows that the following situations improve people's happiness: being outdoors, talking to other people, making things.

In small groups, choose one of the situations and discuss:

- what activities your classmates could do for each situation
- how they would benefit from taking part in these activities
- how easy or difficult the activities would be to organise
- which activity you would like to organise, and why.

Step 2: Your group is going to prepare a short video or presentation to promote your chosen activity and explain how it can improve students' mental health.

First, decide what information you need to include in your video or presentation, and other things to consider. For example, how long it will be and who will say what in your video or presentation.

Step 3: In your group, decide what each member is good at and what they should be in charge of (for example, filming).

A: You're quite good at _____, so how would you feel about being in charge of _____?

Step 4: Write a short script of what people will say in the video or presentation.

Step 5: Film the video or practise your presentation. Then decide whether anything needs to be edited or if you want to add anything, such as music.

Step 6: Show your video or give your presentation to your class.

Step 7: Watch the videos or presentations made by other groups. Was there any information missing? Ask questions to find out about the missing information.

Step 8: Discuss in groups which video or presentation was your favourite, and why.

CRITICAL THINKING

Collecting and presenting information

When doing research, always try to use more than one source of information. It is important to have a range of ideas and opinions to compare and choose from. When giving a talk or a presentation, use visual aids. These will make your talk or presentation more interesting for others.

PROJECT OPTION 2

A diary about your own progress and a poster with tips

You have decided to learn something new (such as a new skill) and provide advice for others who might be learning the same.

Step 1: In small groups, decide what each of you wants to learn, and how. For example:

- learn from a relative how to repair something

- learn something online about a new topic (for example, gardening, childcare)

- learn the basics of a foreign language from a friend.

Step 2: Spend one week learning your chosen topic or skill. Keep a video or written diary of what you do every time, what helps you learn and what you find difficult.

Step 3: When you finish your learning experience, complete these sentences in your notebook.

- I've been learning _____ for a week.

- I wanted to learn this skill / about this topic because…

- I chose to learn with my _____ / online because…

- I really enjoyed…

- What helped me learn the most was/were…

- I found _____ quite difficult because…

- Next time I would / I wouldn't _____ because…

Step 4: Give a short talk about your learning experience to others in your group. Use the sentences from step 3 to help you. To support your points, use clips from your video diary if you made one.

Step 5: After you have heard from everybody in your group, compare your experiences. Focus on:

- what students learnt, and why

- who they learnt with, and why

- what helped them learn, and why

- what they enjoyed most about the experience, and why.

Step 6: In your group, make a poster for other students about the best way to learn something new. Include five tips based on the experiences of your group. Present your poster to the class.

SPEAKING TIP

Comparing your own experience with other people's

Useful phrases:

- *Just like you, I preferred… for the same reason.* (similar experience)

- *Unlike you, I really enjoyed learning to… because…* (different experience)

SELF AND PEER ASSESSMENT

Think about how well you and your group did in the project. Then complete the statements below in your notebook.

- Our group worked particularly well in the following activities:…

- I really enjoyed working with… because he/she…

- While doing this project, I learnt that I'm really good at… and I enjoy…

- However, I need to practise… a bit more.

- I learnt…, and in the future this will help me…

Practise and prepare

Speaking

1 **Work in pairs. Answer these questions as fully as possible.**

   a What do you do to relax after your lessons?

   b When did you last work on a school project, and what happened?

   c Do you think students should be allowed to decide when they want to have lessons? Why or why not?

EXAM TIP

In most speaking exams, students do the test on their own, not in pairs. However, to prepare for your speaking exam, it's a good idea to practise in pairs. Ask a friend or a classmate to act as the examiner and read out questions to you. They can also give you feedback on:

- how fully you answered the question

- the range of grammatical structures and vocabulary you used

- how clear your answer was.

Then you can swap roles and you can be the examiner.

Reading

2 **Read the article on the opposite page about a group of students taking part in a reality show, and then answer the questions.**

   a When was the reality show filmed?

   b Why did some schools have to stop providing combined lessons for girls and boys?

   c What did the group of students enjoy most about their lessons in the 1980s?

   d What did the modern-day students find difficult during the reality show? Give **three** details.

Writing

3 **You recently did a project at school. Write an email to a friend about the project. Write about 120–160 words.**

In your email you should:

- describe what the project was

- say what you did to participate in the project

- explain why you enjoyed the project.

Have you ever imagined what school life was like 100 years ago? Would you like to travel back in time to find out? A group of teenagers from the United Kingdom didn't have to travel back in time, even though they felt like they had. They were chosen to be part of a reality show in which they experienced school life in different eras, from the late Victorian times at the end of the 19th century, through the whole of the 20th century, ending in recent times. They covered over 100 years of education history and were given the chance to see what each era was like for students. For the filming, the group had to give up their time during the summer holidays and the October half-term break to be part of the series, but no one regretted it in the slightest.

In the first episode, they found themselves in a classroom from 1895. Only about 4% of young teenagers were in education back then, and some strict rules had to be obeyed, like having neatly combed hair or only writing with your right hand, which is fine if you're right-handed, but not so much if you're left-handed! This strict rule proved really challenging for the few left-handed students, who were relieved when they could move onto another era after this rule was abolished in the UK. And while it was the norm at the time for girls and boys to be taught separately, there was a brief period between 1895 and 1902 when they were taught maths and science together at some schools, until school inspectors found out and put a stop to it. After that, girls had to go back to learning skills like bed-making while boys learnt Latin. The very limited options for girls lasted all the way to the 1970s, which came as a real shock for the participants and was one aspect they really struggled with. The different treatment of male and female students came through even in things like gender specific worksheets in maths lessons.

Some of the skills students were taught throughout the 20th century may seem very odd nowadays, such as bricklaying or needlework, but they meant students left school with some practical skills. However, the modern-day students didn't always like their choice being made for them. Also, not many secondary school students went on to study at university. In the 1960s, for example, only one in 22,000 students achieved this.

During the entire filming period, the students had to put their phones away, but, as they're not allowed to have phones at school anyway, they didn't mind this, unlike the food they had to eat at lunchtime. The government introduced free school meals in the early 20th century, but the food didn't always look very appetising.

It wasn't until the 1980s era that the modern-day students started to feel comfortable with their lessons, as the teaching styles started to resemble what they were familiar with from their own schools. They couldn't hide their excitement when the first computers were installed in the classroom, although they were very basic by current standards.

As the series reached the final stage – the present day – the group had a school reunion to share the highlights and low points and they wondered what their era would be remembered for.

REFLECTION

1   Look at the Finnish saying at the start of this unit. What do you think it means now? What information from this unit helped you with the explanation? Give examples. Compare your ideas in small groups.

2   Reflect on your progress as a learner while working on this unit. Discuss these questions with your partner.

a   In the Think about it lesson, did you find taking notes while listening to the talk easy or difficult? Will you do something differently next time you take notes? Why or why not?

b   In the Psychology and education lesson, what did you find most interesting in the article about how some people prefer to learn? Would you like to try some of the techniques in the future? In what subjects do you think some of the techniques might help you? Give examples and reasons.

c   In the Talk about it lesson, you explored the topic of study–life balance. What surprised you most about your, or other students', study–life balance? Give examples. What changes do you think you will make to your study–life balance? Why?

d   In the Improve your writing lesson, what helped you most in writing your email? Give examples and explain why. What was challenging for you when writing your email? What can you do to make this easier next time?

e   Think about yourself before you did the Project challenge lesson and after you finished it. What do you think you learnt from doing this project? Do you think this will help you in other subjects?

f   In the Practise and prepare lesson, which skill did you find the most difficult to practise? What can you do to improve this skill in the future?

SUMMARY CHECKLIST

I can…

- [ ] follow a talk about education systems and understand most of the information.
- [ ] read short texts about different types of learners and understand the main ideas.
- [ ] work out the meaning of unknown vocabulary from the context.
- [ ] lead an interview and ask clear questions.
- [ ] give appropriate advice about problems related to learning.
- [ ] use the present simple and present continuous confidently to talk about my daily life.
- [ ] write an email to a friend and use persuasive language.
- [ ] take part in group discussions.

2 Into the wild

- **listen** to a podcast and an interview about orangutans
- **read** an article about how animals communicate
- **give** a presentation about a conservation success story
- **learn** more about the passive
- **write** a review of a TV documentary
- **use** a range of resources for your research.

GETTING STARTED

"Look deep into nature and you will understand everything better."
(Albert Einstein, physicist)

What do you think you can learn from being in and observing nature?

Watch this!

Think about it: What can we do to help other living creatures?

• **Why do you think we need to protect other creatures on Earth?**

Listening

1 **Look at the picture of an orangutan. How much do you know about these animals? First do the quiz in pairs. Then listen to a short podcast about orangutans to check if you were right. Note: the answers in the podcast do not come in the same order as the questions.**

1 On which islands do most orangutans live?
   A   Borneo and Sumatra
   B   Marshall Islands
   C   Grenadines
2 The name orangutan comes from the Malay language and it means:
   A   orange king
   B   king of the jungle
   C   human of the forest
3 What do orangutans eat most of the time?
   A   fruit and leaves
   B   nuts and birds' eggs
   C   bark and insects
4 Orangutans can live up to _____ years in the wild.
   A   20   B   40   C   60

Vocabulary

2 **Look at the vocabulary box of words and phrases taken from the podcast. Then listen to the podcast again to see how this vocabulary is used. Can you guess the meaning of each word?**

average lifespan	nests
fully stretched arms	predators
in captivity	somebody's territory
in the wild	swing in trees
mammals	trespass

3 **Now compare your ideas in pairs. Then check the meanings in a reliable dictionary to see if you were right.**

Speaking

4 **In small groups, discuss what information about orangutans you found interesting, and why.**

5 **You are going to listen to an interview about a school for orangutans. In pairs, discuss what you think the answers are to the following questions.**
   a   Why do some young orangutans have to go to school?
   b   What do orangutans learn at their school?
   c   When are orangutans ready to leave their school?

> **SPEAKING TIP**
>
> When you don't know what the answer is to a question, you can say the following:
>
> • *Sorry, I have no idea what the answer is.*
>
> • *Sorry, but I don't really know anything about orangutan schools.*
>
> • *I haven't a clue – sorry.*

6 Work in groups of 4–6. Half of each group should look at set 1 and the other half at set 2. Write definitions for the words and phrases in your set on a piece of paper in a random order. Use a reliable dictionary to help you.

Set 1	Set 2
surrogate mothers	pet trade
an orphan	working ecosystems
plantations	to reverse a situation
timber	to become extinct
illegal	to raise awareness of an issue

7 Now look at the definitions made by the other half of your group. Can you match their definitions to the correct words? Check your answers together.

8 Read the questions and incomplete statements below. Then listen to the interview from Exercise 5 again to find the answers.

   a What is the main purpose of the orangutan school?

   b Budi says that the biggest threat to orangutans is…

   c What is the first thing that orangutans are taught at the school?

   d How does Budi feel on the day the orangutans are released back into the wild?

   e Budi believes that if we want to stop orangutans becoming extinct, we need to…

USE OF ENGLISH

Dependent prepositions

Many nouns, adjectives and verbs in English are followed by a preposition.

*The huge **advantage** of the orangutan school is that it teaches them how to survive.* (noun + preposition)

*Orangutans are really **good** at climbing trees.* (adjective + preposition)

*I want to **learn** more **about** orangutans because they're so fascinating.* (verb + preposition)

Remember, some nouns, adjectives and verbs can take more than one preposition, for example *thankful **for** something, thankful **to** someone.* Very often the meaning of the phrase changes too.

9 Look at the following phrases taken from the interview. They each have a missing preposition. What are the missing prepositions? Then listen to the interview again to check your answers.

   a acts _____ a babysitter

   b learn new skills _____ copying

   c they're listed _____ critically endangered

   d many factors that have contributed _____ this

   e make room _____ fields

   f they socialise _____ the other babies

   g start proper school lessons _____ how to get

   h we're a bit anxious _____ what the future holds

   i are aware _____ the issues

   j to get involved _____ various conservation projects

   k if we can succeed _____ this

   l have a positive impact _____ climate change

10 In groups, discuss the following questions. When answering the questions, try to use some of the words and phrases you have learnt in this lesson.

   a Do you think the orangutan school is a good idea?

   b Would you like to work as a volunteer at this school? Why or why not?

   c Do you know about any other wild animals that need protection? Give examples.

Science: Can animals talk to each other?

- **How do animals communicate?**

Reading

1 **Work in pairs and answer the following questions.**

   a   When and where did you last see an animal?

   b   How did the animal behave?

   c   Did you notice how it communicated with other animals? If so, give examples.

2 **Quickly skim-read the whole article and find the different types of communication that are mentioned.**

READING TIP

Skimming is a type of reading technique we use when we read a text quickly to get the general idea (for example, the main topic or subtopics). We don't focus on the details with this type of reading.

Animals cannot use speech like us, but they have other ways of communicating. Without any form of communication, animals couldn't indicate how they were feeling or what their intentions were. The simplest forms of communication allow animals to display dominance, alert others to danger or keep other creatures out of their territory. Communication is also vital to attract a mate. A mother couldn't bond with her young without some form of communication.

Body language is used by many species, the tail being especially important. How it is held and how it moves can signal many different things. For dogs and wolves, for example, a tail held upright signals dominance or interest, whereas a loose, wagging tail is used during play or to interact when grooming.

Cats will move their tails quickly from side to side when they feel annoyed or threatened. They will also use eye contact to communicate their intentions. Looking directly into each other's eyes for a long time is considered a warning. To signal a greeting, cats will narrow their eyes or slow blink at one another.

Rabbits and hares will use movements such as hitting their leg against the ground in order to alert other group members to potential danger. Male rabbits also show the white underside of their tail to attract a female.

Bees will use visual communication to show other bees the location of food sources. This is called the waggle dance. The bee performs a series of circular movements repeatedly. Its body moves quickly from one side to the other.

Sounds carry much further in water than in air, so it makes sense that sound is absolutely essential for animals that live in water. Dolphins are famous for having a complex vocabulary of sounds. Dolphins even give each other names in the form of a sound and they use these sounds to call to each other.

Many of us have heard birds sing. Every bird species produces different songs, depending on what they are trying to communicate. To warn others of danger, birds use songs that are loud and sharp, and some species even have different songs for air and land predators. In contrast, songs with more of a tune are used when males are trying to attract females. Birds also use songs to communicate the boundaries of their territory. These songs are used more frequently by males as a warning to others.

Animals also produce pheromones, which are a type of chemical communication. These are commonly used by insects, amphibians and reptiles. Snakes, for example, produce pheromones throughout their life, and the pheromones change as the snake ages. A snake can identify if another snake is male or female by investigating the scent that is left behind. Other animals can use pheromones to defend themselves or to attract a mate.

So next time you see an animal, look more carefully to see if you can understand what they're trying to say.

ACADEMIC LANGUAGE

Science: Animals and their behaviour

alert someone to danger	intruder
amphibians	marine animals
body language	pheromones
display dominance	reptiles
groom each other	scent
interact with each other	signal something
	wag

3   **Look at the words and phrases in the Academic language box and match them to the correct definitions.**

   a   animals that live on land and in water

   b   when an animal cleans the fur or skin of another animal

   c   an animal that enters a territory without permission

   d   animals that live in the sea

   e   why animals behave in this way to show they are the most powerful one

   f   animals that are cold-blooded and have no fur

   g   a chemical substance that is produced by an animal to attract a partner

   h   to make a sound or movement to give some sort of information

   i   to move something repeatedly (such as a tail) from side to side

   j   the natural smell of something

   k   when movements or facial expressions tell others how an animal might feel or be thinking

   l   to warn someone about a situation that can cause harm

   m   to make contact or to communicate with someone else

🎧 08   4   **Read the introductory paragraph. Find examples of why animals use communication.**

🎧 09   5   **Read the rest of the text and find specific examples of communication for the animals below.**

dogs and wolves	cats	rabbits
bees	dolphins	birds	snakes

Speaking

6   **In small groups, discuss how animals communicate in the following situations. Use the information from the article or what you have noticed yourself in everyday life. Try to use some of the words and phrases from the Academic language box.**

- show interest in something
- show they're feeling irritated
- signal to someone to leave them alone
- attract the attention of someone else
- alert someone to danger
- greet others

7   **In the same groups, discuss what people do in the same situations. Are there any similarities between how people and animals communicate? Did you find anything surprising?**

USE OF ENGLISH

Comparing and contrasting ideas

To compare two similar things or to contrast two different things, we can use the words or phrases in bold below. Study the examples. Are the words or phrases in bold followed by a noun or by a complete sentence?

Phrases used to compare two things that are similar:

Just like cats, people also use eye contact to show their feelings.

*Wolves, **as well as** dogs, use their tails to show their dominance.*

Words that are used to contrast two things that are different:

Unlike bees, people use words to communicate important information.

*People might use their hands to signal danger. **However**, birds use songs to do the same thing.*

*To attract attention, rabbits show the white part of their tail, **while** people would probably put on colourful clothes.*

8   **Write four sentences about the similarities and differences between animal and human communication. Use the ideas you discussed in Exercise 7. To link your ideas, use the words and phrases from the Use of English box.**

Talk about it: Conservation success stories

- How can wolves change the environment they live in?

Watch this!

Listening

1 Read the information about wolves in Yellowstone National Park. Then look at photos A–F and discuss the questions in pairs.

> **Can wolves change rivers?**
>
> In 1995, wolves were reintroduced into Yellowstone National Park in the USA. The reintroduction was very successful, with an unexpected outcome. The wolves even had an effect on the rivers.

a What do you think each photo shows?

b What do you think happened before and after wolves were reintroduced into Yellowstone National Park?

c The wolves indirectly changed the rivers in the park. How do you think this happened?

2 Listen to part of a presentation about the reintroduction of wolves into Yellowstone National Park. Check your answers to the questions from Exercise 1. What do you think is the most surprising fact about the reintroduction? Why?

Speaking

5 Work in small groups. Each group should research the conservation success story of one of the animals below and make notes for a short presentation.

bald eagle	humpback whale
mountain gorilla	tiger

You should include the following information in your presentation:

- general information about the animal
- how low the numbers were before the conservation efforts
- the main reasons the animal became endangered
- what has been done to help the animal
- the current situation.

Use at least two different websites to find the necessary information and make notes.

SPEAKING TIP

You can use the following phrases when something surprising happens. These phrases are more suitable when you talk to someone you know (such as a friend).

- *Wow! That's really amazing!*
- *I didn't know that was possible.*
- *This is so incredible, isn't it?*

3 Look at the fact file below. Some facts are missing. Copy the fact file into your notebook and then listen to the whole presentation. Add the missing facts.

Reintroduction of wolves in Yellowstone National Park

Species: grey wolf

Habitat:

Diet:

Role in the ecosystem:

Reasons for becoming endangered in the past:

Main concerns before the reintroduction:

Direct impact of the reintroduction on the ecosystem:

Other indirect impacts of the reintroduction:

CRITICAL THINKING

Evaluating resources for your research

When you use more than one website for your research and you want to evaluate them, you can consider the following questions.

- Were the websites easy to use?
- What did you like about each website?
- Was it easy to find the necessary information on each website?
- Was there anything you didn't like about the websites?
- How did you check if each website was reliable to use?

4 Listen to the presentation again. What phrases does the speaker use to do the following? Listen again to check.

a introduce the main topic
b say how the presentation is divided and what each part is
c introduce individual parts of the presentation
d end the presentation
e invite the audience to ask questions

6 Compare your notes with other students in your group and use the information to create your presentation. Remember to use the phrases from Exercise 4. Deliver your presentation to the class.

Improve your writing: A TV documentary review

1   **Read the review of a TV documentary about trees, then answer these questions.**

a   This review was written to: (select two answers)

   A   educate the reader

   B   raise concerns about the environment

   C   persuade the reader to watch the documentary

   D   to entertain the reader

b   Who is this review for?

   A   the wider public

   B   university students

   C   children

   D   adults only

c   What is the register of this review?

   A   very informal

   B   semi-formal

   C   formal

   D   very formal

d   The review is divided into three paragraphs, 1, 2 and 3. What is the main aim of each paragraph? Match the correct aim A–D to each paragraph. (There is one extra aim that you do not need to use.)

   A   to compare the documentary with other similar programmes

   B   to explain why the writer watched the documentary

   C   to express personal opinions and to give a recommendation

   D   to provide some facts about the documentary

e   The writer tries to engage the reader by: (select two answers)

   A   using strong adjectives

   B   providing a lot of details

   C   talking to the reader directly

   D   asking questions and providing answers

The Cycle of Life: Trees

1 *The Cycle of Life* is a series of documentaries covering a range of subjects, from human life to the life of trees and plants. Last night, the programme was about the life cycle of trees. I really enjoyed all the previous episodes so decided to give this one a go too. Even though I'm not a big fan of documentaries about plants, I really wanted to find out more about trees, as it has been proven just how important trees are for our planet and us.

2 The documentary was filmed in three stunning locations: Daintree Forest in Australia, Sagano Bamboo Forest in Japan and Jiuzhaigou Valley in China. It was narrated by William Peterson – an environmentalist who is passionate about trees and their conservation. His passion certainly came through in the documentary. And the soundtrack, which was specifically composed for this documentary by Franz Host, just added to the magical experience.

3 The information that was provided felt like just the right amount, and the way Peterson gave us all the information wasn't boring or too academic; quite the opposite, in fact. It was very interesting and enjoyable. The documentary also contained interviews with experts as well as people who made forests their home, and both groups shared fascinating facts about trees and their lives. For example, did you know that mature trees take care of their young or that they warn each other of danger? And if you want to find out how that's possible, you'll have to watch the episode for yourself! It'll be repeated on TV4U next Friday or you can watch it on the TV4U catch-up service right now. I cannot recommend it highly enough. You won't be disappointed and next time you go to the park or the forest, you'll never look at trees the same way again.

2 Quickly read the review again. Is the review all positive, all negative or mixed? Find some examples of words and phrases to support your opinion.

3 Look at some more useful phrases you can use in reviews. Would you use them to praise and recommend something or criticise and not recommend? Copy the mind maps and put the phrases into the correct category.

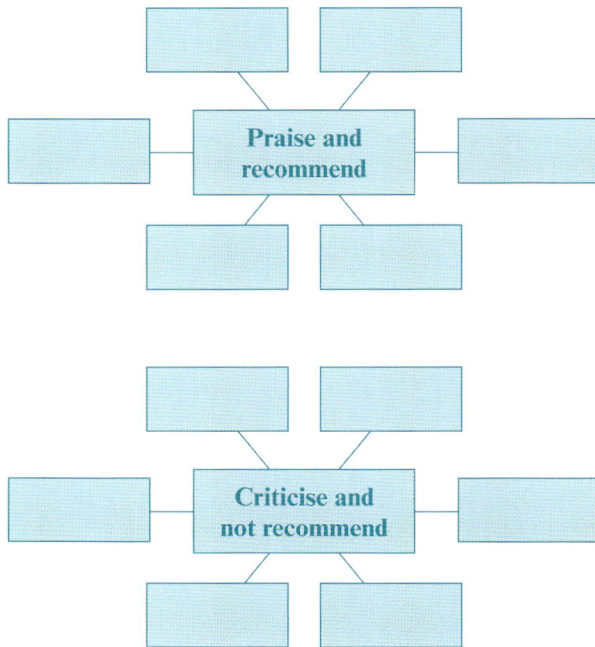

```
                    ┌──────────┐   ┌──────────┐
                    └──────────┘   └──────────┘
        ┌──────────┐                        ┌──────────┐
        └──────────┘      Praise and        └──────────┘
                          recommend
                    ┌──────────┐   ┌──────────┐
                    └──────────┘   └──────────┘


                    ┌──────────┐   ┌──────────┐
                    └──────────┘   └──────────┘
        ┌──────────┐                        ┌──────────┐
        └──────────┘      Criticise and     └──────────┘
                          not recommend
                    ┌──────────┐   ┌──────────┐
                    └──────────┘   └──────────┘
```

> breathtaking location
>
> the pace was a bit slow for my liking
>
> was out of this world
>
> the soundtrack was a bit of a let-down
>
> the makers of this film really exceeded themselves
>
> spectacular scenes of
>
> I must admit my expectations were very low and I was proven right.
>
> I lost my interest half way through
>
> highly original plot
>
> the camerawork was lagging behind
>
> the ending was very predictable
>
> If you're looking for something to cheer you up, this is it.

4 Work in pairs. Think of a TV programme you've seen recently (a film, documentary, interview, reality show, etc.). Tell each other whether you liked it or not and whether you'd recommend it and why. Use some of the phrases from the review and Exercise 3.

USE OF ENGLISH

The passive

Look at these examples of the passive used in the review.

It **has been** *proven* just how important trees are for our planet and us.

The documentary **was** *filmed* in three stunning locations.

It'll **be** *repeated* on TV4U next Friday.

We use the passive when we want to:

- focus on what happened rather than who did what

- to sound a little bit formal when we're talking to someone we don't know very well

- to sound less direct and more polite.

To use the passive structure in a different form, for example the past simple, we change the verb *to be* (for example, *was/were*), not the past participle verb form (for example, *filmed*).

5 Look at the sentences and identify the main verb. What form is the verb? Then rewrite each sentence using the correct passive structure. The first one has been done for you.

   a Apparently, people <u>cut</u> down around 40 million trees every day.

   Apparently, around 40 million trees <u>are cut</u> down every day.

   b Globally, people only plant about 5 million trees each day.

   c Since the 18th century, humans have destroyed about 64% of the world's tropical rainforests.

   d In the past, people mainly used wood for construction and as firewood.

   e Nowadays, people are also destroying forests to get more land for their animals and to grow more crops.

f   One environmentalist told me that we might lose all our rainforests within the next 100 years.

g   Filmmakers have made a lot of documentaries to raise the issue of deforestation.

h   We're going to plant 100 new trees in our local park this year.

i   This month they are making a wildlife documentary about frogs in our local nature reserve.

6   **Work in pairs. Think of a nature documentary you have seen and give each other some details about the documentary. Try to use some passive structures. Use the second paragraph from the review as a model for your answers.**

STUDY TIP

Watching documentaries

There are a lot of documentaries online or shown on TV. These programmes can give you a lot of information that can help you with your school work (for example, in science, geography and history). Many online documentaries are in English, so while you are learning new facts, you can also practise your English listening skills.

---

7   **You are going to write your own review of a nature documentary. Before you start writing, it is important to plan what information you want to include. Decide on the following:**

- the nature documentary you want to review
- how many paragraphs you need
- the information you will include in each paragraph
- what you liked about the documentary
- what you disliked about the documentary
- whether other people should watch it and why
- who is going to read your review
- what style and register you should use.

8   **Now write your review. Remember to use the language you have learnt in this lesson.**

9   **Work in pairs. When you finish your review, swap it with your partner's. Read your partner's review and focus on how engaging the writing is.**

- Did the review contain all the information you expected to find? Give details.
- Was the review interesting to read? Why or why not?
- Was the recommendation convincing? Why or why not?

10 **Give feedback to your partner. Then listen to their feedback. Rewrite your review based on the feedback.**

SPEAKING TIP

Giving feedback

Always start with something positive and then add something that can be improved next time.

Your review was very interesting to read, but how about adding…?

I really enjoyed reading your review, but perhaps next time you could…

I learnt a lot of interesting things from your review, but personally I'd…/I wouldn't…

Project challenge

PROJECT LEARNING OBJECTIVES

In your project you will…

- carry out research and share your findings with others

- select the most important information

- persuade others to do something.

PROJECT OPTION 1

A presentation about a local wildlife project

You and your classmates would like to volunteer with a local wildlife project. You want to prepare a presentation to encourage other students to join you.

Step 1: Work in three small groups. Each group will research a different topic.

- Group 1: a wildlife project available in your local area or in your country (for example, working with endangered animals), who organises it and what it involves

- Group 2: benefits of volunteering on wildlife projects for young people (for example, the skills you learn)

- Group 3: what you need to know when working with animals or in the countryside (for example, safety rules to follow).

Step 2: Decide what resources you will use for your research. Then do your research to find the necessary information. Make notes of your findings.

Step 3: Plan your presentation to encourage other students to join a local wildlife project. Include the information that you collected in step 2. You should also decide on:

- how many sections the presentation will have

- what information you will include in each section

- who will present each section

- how long the whole presentation and individual sections should take

- photos or video clips you would like to include.

Step 4: Practise your presentation. Time yourself to see how long your section takes to deliver. If it takes too long, review it and edit it.

Step 5: Deliver your presentation. Then ask if other students have any questions and whether they would like to join the wildlife project.

CRITICAL THINKING

Supporting your findings

When you present your findings, support them with examples of research or what experts say about the topic. This will support what you say.

- *According to the latest research,…*

- *Many experts support this opinion,…*

SPEAKING TIP

Expressing your opinion about which option to choose

When you're discussing several options and deciding what to choose, you can say:

I really feel that… would be best because…

In my view… would probably be the best activity to include, because…

PROJECT OPTION 2

Take part in a discussion and design a poster

Our modern way of life means that many wildlife habitats have been lost or reduced. Are you passionate about animals? Do you want to do something to stop the destruction of their habitats? Then help us encourage others to make changes to their lifestyles. Even a small change can make a huge difference.

Step 1: Read the social media post above. In groups, discuss how important it is to raise awareness of this issue.

Step 2: In your same groups, look at the diagram below about the causes and consequences of deforestation. Explain what human activities lead to deforestation, and how. Then explain what changes people can make to their lifestyles and how these can improve the issue.

Deforestation

demand for timber/ land (e.g. for animals and crops)		fragmented habitats
frequent consumption of meat	→	reduction in food/ shelter for animals
		changing climate, increasing CO_2
		risk of soil erosion, droughts

Reducing deforestation

smart buying choices (e.g. sustainable sources)		improving biodiversity/ preventing extinction
reducing red meat in your diet	→	reversing the effects of global warming/ protecting local communities
growing your own vegetables		

Step 3: Now research what everyday human activities lead to different types of pollution (such as soil, noise and light pollution) and how this affects the wildlife and their habitats. Make notes of your findings. Using your notes, make diagrams similar to the diagrams in step 2.

Step 4: Now design a poster to raise awareness of how pollution affects wildlife. Use the information and diagrams from step 3. Discuss how other features of the poster can affect how powerful your message is. Consider the following: the title, font, visual features, colour and layout.

Step 5: Present your poster to your class.

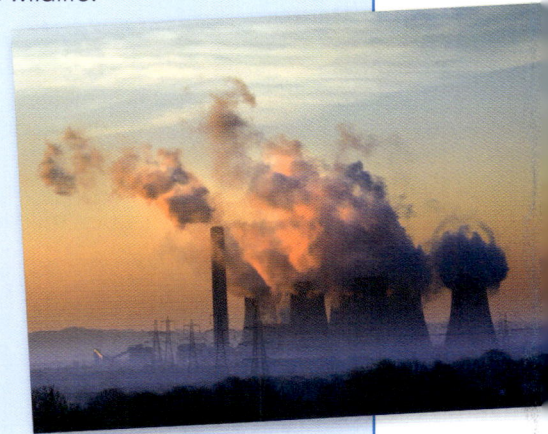

SELF AND PEER ASSESSMENT

Think about how well you and your group did in the project. Then copy and complete the statements below.

a   Our group worked particularly well in the following activities:…

b   I really enjoyed working with… because he/she…

c   While doing this project, I learnt that I'm really good at… and I enjoy…

d   However, I need to practise… a bit more.

e   I learnt… and, in the future, this will help me…

Practise and prepare

Speaking

1   **Work in pairs. Read the task below. Spend one minute preparing what you want to say. Then give your talk.**

> **You and your family have decided to spend more time outdoors together. You are considering the following options:**
>
> • **having picnics in the local park**
>
> • **going for a swim at a local outdoor pool.**
>
> **Talk about how easy or difficult each option would be for your whole family to do. Say which option you would prefer and why.**

EXAM TIP

Task completion – covering all the points from the task

In speaking and writing exams, read the task very carefully first and find all the points you should cover in your answer. If you don't answer all the points, you could lose marks. Task completion is one of the most important aspects the examiners will be looking for when marking your work.

Writing

2   **Your class recently went on a one-day school trip to a local nature reserve. You have decided to write a review of the trip for the school website. In your review, give more information about the school trip and say whether it was enjoyable and why. The comments below may give you some ideas, and you should also use some ideas of your own. Write about 120–160 words.**

Here are some comments from other students who went on the same trip:

Now I know what job I want to do.

One day wasn't long enough.

We learnt so much.

I was too cold to enjoy it.

EXAM TIP

Multiple-choice listening exercises

In multiple-choice listening exercises, you will hear all the options from the question mentioned in the recording. However, only one option is the correct answer. The other options are there to distract you as they test your ability to listen for specific detail. This means you need to listen very carefully to all the details (such as who, when, where) to determine which option fully answers the question and is, therefore, the correct response.

Listening

3 **You will hear three short recordings. For each question, choose the correct answer, A, B, C or D.**

a What did the boy enjoy most about his recent holiday to the mountains?

A

B

C

D

b What animals do the students decide to do their next presentation about?

A

B

C

D

c Where does the girl suggest going for a walk this afternoon?

A

B

C

D

REFLECTION

1   Look at the quotation by Albert Einstein at the start of this unit. Answer the following questions about it in pairs.

- Do you agree with the quotation? Why or why not?

- What do you think the quotation says about Albert Einstein as a person?

- Will anything that you learnt in this unit help you in your own life? Give examples.

2   Reflect on your progress as a learner while working on this unit. Discuss these questions with your partner.

a   In the Think about it lesson, you listened to two different recordings, a short talk and an interview. Which recording did you find harder to follow? Why? What are you going to do to improve your listening to this type of recording?

b   In the Science lesson, you read an article about animal communication. What helped you learn new words from the article? Do you have any tips for memorising new vocabulary? Can you think of other ways you could try to remember new words?

c   In the Talk about it lesson, you researched a conservation success story with your classmates. What did you enjoy most about this activity? Why?

d   Do you think that researching topics helps you learn? Why?

e   In the Improve your writing lesson, you learnt a lot of new skills, including how to engage the reader, how to plan your review and how to give feedback to other students about their review. Which of these three skills do you feel most or least confident about? Why? How can you improve this skill?

f   In the Project lesson, you worked as part of a team. What did you enjoy about working with other students? What did you learn from working in a group?

g   In the Practice and prepare lesson, did you use any of the information or skills you learnt in this unit? Which ones? How did they help you to answer the questions?

SUMMARY CHECKLIST

I can…

- [ ] listen to an interview and choose the correct answer from a list of options.
- [ ] read an article and find examples of animals' communication.
- [ ] match definitions to the correct words in a text.
- [ ] select relevant information for a presentation and deliver the presentation to an audience.
- [ ] use the passive confidently in appropriate situations.
- [ ] plan a review of a TV documentary and write it in an engaging way.
- [ ] select the best resources for my research.

3 Everyday science

IN THIS UNIT YOU WILL...

- **listen** to young people talking about science
- **read** an article about whether people can live without science
- **participate** in a discussion and solve a problem
- **report** survey findings using approximate and exact numbers
- **carry out** a survey about a school science laboratory and **write** a report
- **extract** relevant information from various sources.

GETTING STARTED

"Somewhere, something incredible is waiting to be known."
(Carl Sagan, scientist and author)

Where and what do you think this could be?

Watch this!

Think about it: We need more young scientists!

• Why do some young people like science and others don't?

Vocabulary

1   In small groups, look at the words and phrases in the vocabulary box. Check the meaning of the vocabulary you don't know in a reliable dictionary.

> analyse
> bone defects
> compare and contrast
> carry out experiments
> CO_2 levels
> collect data
> (dis)prove theories
>
> experimental medicine
> infectious diseases
> make predictions
> microbiology
> mix chemical solutions
> school field trip
> stem cells

2   Now look at the questions below and think about the answers. Make two answers true about yourself and one answer wrong. Try to use some of the words and phrases from the vocabulary box.

a   What's your favourite subject at school? Would you include science as one of them?

b   What do you enjoy about your science lessons?

c   Would you like to get a job in science in the future?

3   In your group from Exercise 1, share your answers. Do the other students know which answer is wrong?

Listening

4   Listen to the introduction of an interview with students who like science and answer the questions below.

a   What has made young people more interested in science in recent years? Why do you think this is?

b   How does one school hope to make more students interested in science? Why do you think the students might be more interested in science after doing this?

5   Read the questions below. Then listen to the interviews and decide which question each student is answering. There is one extra question that you don't need to use.

a   You've recently won the Science Challenge competition. How did it feel to win?

b   Are there enough role models for young people in science?

c   Do you think it's good for young people to take part in science competitions?

d   What would you like to do in the future?

e   Can you tell us a bit about your project?

f   How did you become interested in science?

6   Now listen to the interviews again and write down some details from the students' answers that helped you decide on the correct question for each from Exercise 3. The answers from Speaker 1 have been done for you as an example.

Speaker 1: *show what you can do | come up with new ideas | meet people | make new friendships | include this experience on my university application | represent your school | a thank you present to our teachers*

LANGUAGE TIP

Verbs in longer expressions

Some common verbs (for example, *get*) are frequently used in longer expressions. Some of these expressions are fixed and never change (for example, *to get along with*). Other expressions are semi-fixed and other verbs can be used too (for example, *to get bored* or *to become bored*). There are no rules for which verb to use. You can check which expressions you can form with particular verbs in an English learner's dictionary. It is also a good idea to keep a list of the expressions you have learnt so that you can refer back to it when necessary.

7 Look at the expressions from the interviews and the list of verbs. In pairs, match the correct verb to each expression. Then listen to the interviews again and check your answers.

become	get	go
come	give	make

a   _____ me a lot of confidence
b   _____ an interview
c   _____ up with new ideas
d   it has _____ a cool thing to do
e   the CO_2 levels _____ up
f   _____ famous
g   _____ to meet people
h   _____ new friends
i   _____ my favourite subject
j   _____ to show what you can do

8 Look at the questions in Exercise 5 and listen to how each one is pronounced. Does the speaker's voice go up or down at the end of each question? Based on the examples from this exercise, what do you think the rule is for the intonation in questions?

9 Work in pairs. You are going to interview another pair about how much they like science. Prepare six questions you want to ask. You can use some of the questions from Exercise 5 or think of your own. Then practise saying your questions with the correct rising or falling intonation.

10 Interview two of your classmates. Then share your findings with the rest of the class and say what you found surprising about the answers, and why. Try to use some of the vocabulary you have learnt in this lesson.

Science: We can't live without science

- Does science only happen in a lab?

Vocabulary

> **ACADEMIC LANGUAGE**
>
> **Science: Types of sciences**
>
> | | |
> |---|---|
> | chemistry | ornithology |
> | dermatology | physics |
> | ecology | physiology |
> | meteorology | zoology |
> | microbiology | |

1   Look at the different sciences in the Academic language box. In small groups, discuss what you think is studied in each science.

2   Now match each science from the Academic language box to one of the areas of study below. Then check your answers in a reliable dictionary.

> animals
>
> very small organisms (e.g. bacteria)
>
> birds
>
> living things
>
> skin
>
> natural forces, such as energy, heat, light
>
> how organisms react with the environment around them
>
> the weather and the climate
>
> the basic characteristics of substances and the ways in which they react or combine

3   Work in groups to discuss these two questions.

a   When you hear the word science, what do you imagine?

b   What type of science do you think of?

Speaking

4   Look at the following problems. In pairs, discuss whether you know what to do in these situations. Which sciences might help us to solve each problem, and why?

a   I bought a cardigan and after the first wash it started bobbling – it had tiny bits of wool stuck to it, which made it look quite worn.

b   I pulled a muscle in my calf when I was working out.

c   I got caught in a storm this afternoon. First it was just raining, but then a thunderstorm came. It gave me such a fright – it was so loud.

d   My favourite T-shirt has sweat stains and they won't come out in the wash!

e   After wearing newly bought clothes, I came out in a rash. It's so itchy!

Reading

5   Read the article on the next page. What does the writer suggests doing for each of the situations from Exercise 4? Is there anything that you might try yourself? Why or why not?

6   In small groups, discuss the following questions.

a   What information from the article did you find most surprising, and why?

b   What science are you most fascinated by, and why?

c   How can this science help people in their everyday lives?

Do we need science?

The human race wouldn't be where we are today without scientific discoveries. Science helps us understand the world around us. But it can also help us stay safe and teach us to look more critically at things and make useful connections. So, if you
5 think you don't need science, just think again!

What about people who love fashion and shopping for new clothes? Can they benefit from scientific knowledge? The answer is yes. For instance, you should know that after buying new clothes, you should always wash them before the first
10 use. This is because in some newly bought items it reduces the amount of chemicals left on the clothes from manufacturing processes. When these chemicals touch your skin, you might have an allergic reaction and develop itchy red spots on your skin, such as dermatitis.

15 Some people may argue that if you wash your clothes too often, the friction created inside the washing machine may damage the clothes and develop tiny balls of thread called bobbles. This type of damage is a particular problem in clothes made from materials like cotton or wool. So, how do you wash your
20 clothes and stop them from developing bobbles? Research suggests putting them in a plastic bag in your freezer for about two days. The cold temperature tightens the fibres, which means they become much stronger and less likely to get damaged in the wash.

25 People who go to the gym should also remember a few simple scientific rules. If you're planning a work-out, you should remember to warm up first. A good warm-up will raise your body temperature, helping your muscles to warm up. This will allow them to contract and relax more easily, making it easier

30 for you to perform physically demanding tasks more easily. Your heart is also given a chance to prepare, meaning it won't be too strained during your workout.

And, what do you do with sweat stains on your favourite gym T-shirt? Treat them with vinegar. Vinegar is an effective stain
35 remover, especially when it comes to acidic stains caused by sweat. The acid in vinegar reacts with the weaker acid in the stain, causing it to break up. Simply mix two tablespoons of vinegar in a cup of water and apply it to the stain for up to an hour. Then wash the T-shirt in cold water.

40 What if you love spending time outdoors and there is a sudden thunderstorm? Thunderstorms are often accompanied by lightning, sometimes even very strong winds and heavy rain. If you hear thunder, you are already within range of lightning. Lightning can strike as far as 15 kilometres away from the
45 centre of a storm, so you should find shelter as quickly as you can, for example in a car. The car's metal body will protect you, as it redirects the energy from the lightning around the vehicle and safely into the ground. But you need to remember that things inside the car, such as GPS systems and metal handles,
50 can also conduct electrical current, so you mustn't touch them during thunderstorms. If you're too far away from any shelter, you shouldn't panic. Just sit on your heels close to the ground, with your hands on your knees and your head between them. Try to touch as little of the ground as possible, as lightning
55 generates electrical currents along the ground in all directions – the fewer potential points there are for your body to get hit, the better.

As you can see, science can be both interesting and fun once we realise how scientific knowledge can be applied in our
60 everyday lives.

---

[17] **thread:** a long thin string often used for sewing or to make materials like wool or cotton

[50] **electrical current:** the movement of electricity in a particular direction

---

USE OF ENGLISH

Zero and first conditionals

Zero conditional

The zero conditional is used to talk about something that is a general truth or a rule. Both parts of the sentence use the present tense.

*If you **hear** thunder, you **are** already within range of lightning.*

First conditional

The first conditional is used to talk about one particular situation that will happen in the future. The *if* part of the sentence uses the present tense. The other part uses a future form (for example, *will*). We can also use modal verbs in this part (such as *can*, *may*) to show how certain we are about the situation.

*If you **have** too much contact with the ground, you **may be** more likely to get electrocuted.*

You should put a comma after the *if* part.

Talk about it: Who's coming to dinner?

● **What do you have to consider when you are planning to cook for other people?**

📹 **Watch this!**

Speaking

1 **What is important for you when you choose what to eat? Look at the list and rank the items in order of importance. Then work in pairs. Say how important the items from the list are for you, and why. Use the words in the vocabulary box to help you.**

> nutritious food   food allergens
> seasonality   vegan food
> ingredients

- how healthy and nutritious the food is
- the taste
- the cost
- the seasonality
- where the food comes from
- the ingredients
- the food allergens
- if it's suitable for a range of diets (e.g. vegan)
- how easy it is to make
- how long it takes to make.

SPEAKING TIP

Reacting to what others say

When you're having a conversation with someone, you should react to what they say to show that you're listening. You can do this by:

● sounding interested, for example *That's a very interesting choice.*

● showing surprise, for example *Oh, really?*

● asking questions to find out more, for example *Where did you learn all this?*

● agreeing or disagreeing, for example *Me too!* or *I feel a bit differently about this.*

Listening

2 **Listen to two friends, Fred and Maryam, discussing what they are going to cook for Fred's birthday party. Which things from the list in Exercise 1 do they mention?**

3 **Listen to the conversation again. Copy and complete the table with the phrases that the friends use.**

Ask for suggestions	Give suggestions
Agree with ideas	Disagree with ideas

Speaking

4 **Imagine you are planning a family dinner. You have asked a classmate to help you. Work in pairs to complete these tasks.**

   a **Tell your partner who's coming to dinner and what some of them like or don't like to eat.**

   b **Discuss the three recipes on the next page and decide which one would be best and why.**

CHICKEN AND SQUASH TAGINE

Preparation time: 20 minutes

Cooking time: 2 hours

Total time: 2 hours 20 minutes

Serves: 6

Ingredients:

4 chicken thighs

4 chicken drumsticks

2 onions, sliced

4 garlic cloves, roughly chopped

2 tsp ground cumin

2 tsp ras el hanout

225 g jar of olives, drained

28 g pack of coriander, chopped

25 g pack of parsley, chopped

700 g squash, peeled and cut

1 x 26 g chicken stock cube

PASTA WITH TUNA

Preparation time: 10 minutes

Cooking time: 15 minutes

Total time: 25 minutes

Serves: 4

Ingredients:

2 tablespoons olive oil

6.5 oz can of tuna

1 onion chopped

3 garlic cloves minced

1 can of chopped tomatoes

2 tablespoons flat-leaf parsley chopped

salt and freshly ground pepper

½ cup pitted black olives

1 lb pasta

GREEN VEGETABLE CURRY

Preparation time: 10 minutes

Cooking time: 15 minutes

Total time: 25 minutes

Serves: 4

Ingredients:

1 tin of coconut milk

2 tbsp of Thai green curry paste

2 medium courgettes, sliced

1 large head of broccoli, divided into small florets

150 g mangetout, trimmed

150 g baby corn, cut in half

50 g unsalted cashew nuts

5   Work with another pair. Explain who is coming to dinner, what recipe you have chosen, and why. Then listen to the other pair and discuss whether you think they have chosen the best recipe, and why.

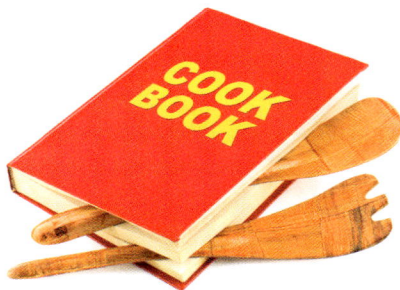

COMMUNICATION

Giving polite suggestions

When you want to suggest some changes to what someone else has proposed, you need to do it politely so that you don't upset anybody.
You should first comment on something positive and then suggest the change.

*I really like your suggestion, but **how about** using more vegetables instead?*

*That's quite an interesting idea, but **would it be possible to** make the dish vegetarian?*

Improve your writing: Report – survey results

1   Read the task and identify the main points that should be covered in the report.

> Your school runs a first-aid course as one of their after-school activities. The headteacher wants to introduce this course as part of the school main curriculum. You have been asked to interview students about the existing first-aid course and write a report about the results of your survey. In your report you should also suggest what can be improved in future.

2   Now read the report below and find the information that the task asks for. Which paragraph(s) did you find the information in? What helped you find the relevant information?

Including first aid as part of the main curriculum

1   **Introduction**

The main aim of this report is to evaluate the existing first-aid course. The final paragraph provides recommendations for what should be done next. For my report, I interviewed a number of students to find out their opinions, and my findings are outlined below.

2   **The existing first-aid course**

At the moment, our school offers a first-aid course as one of the after-school activity options. Most students said that attending this course has increased their confidence in general. The course has also helped a small minority of students with their future career choice. However, most importantly, one in four students who have attended this course have already put their first-aid knowledge into practice at school, while on holiday, or even at their own home. Almost all students felt that taking this course face to face is a better option than doing this type of course online. In addition, nearly three-quarters of students would like to have first-aid lessons at least once a week rather than the suggested once a month, as part of either their science or physical education lessons. A few interviewees also mentioned that sharing experiences with other students who have already helped somebody would be very beneficial.

3   **Recommendations**

As my own research has shown, the need for first aid is absolutely vital. This view was also supported by the students I have interviewed. In the light of all the information collected, I would therefore like to suggest the following:

- making first aid part of science or physical education lessons at least once a week

- including presentations and talks by students with experience of giving first aid

- giving awards to students who have helped others at the end-of-year school ceremony

4   In the meantime, I strongly suggest promoting the existing first-aid course and providing more first-aid information on the school website and on school noticeboards to raise awareness of first aid.

3 Read the report again and decide whether the following sentences are true or false. Check your answers in pairs and correct the false sentences.

   a The aim of all reports is to entertain the reader and to suggest something (for example, improvements).

   b Reports are usually written for someone in charge (for example, a boss) and should, therefore, use formal language.

   c Reports are divided into paragraphs with headings to make it easier for the reader to find the necessary information.

   d You shouldn't use lists and bullet points in your report.

   e You should express your opinion about the topic in the introduction.

   f The middle paragraphs contain factual information about the topic (for example, survey outcomes) or what other people think (for example, the advantages and disadvantages of something).

   g The final paragraph contains your opinion linked to the introduction. It also contains your suggestions, which are based on the information from the middle paragraphs.

4 Look through the first and last paragraphs. Are there any useful phrases or sentences that are often used in reports?

5 Look at some more useful phrases below. Work in pairs and decide which paragraph, introduction or recommendations, you could use them in.

   a I would therefore recommend… (+ -ing)

   b As requested, I have prepared a report on…(+ noun)

   c You may also wish to consider… (+ -ing)

   d Having considered all the options, I'd like to suggest (+ -ing)

   e In this report I will provide information about…

   f Taking all these points into consideration, I recommend that…

   g The purpose of this report is to…

USE OF ENGLISH

Reporting survey results: expressing statistics

When you carry out a survey, you can express the results in two ways:

- as approximate numbers and phrases

  almost a half of all students,

  almost 50% of the interviewees

  the vast majority of all students

  hardly anybody

- as exact numbers and phrases

  25% of students

  10 out of 15 students

  every other student.

6 Look at the sentences below, which all use exact numbers. Rewrite the sentences using approximate numbers and phrases.

   Example: **Nine out of 20 students** helped someone in an emergency. (exact)

   Almost half of the students helped someone in an emergency. (approximate)

   a 90% of the interviewees would like to learn more about first aid.

   b 10% of the students I talked to said they weren't happy with the online first-aid course.

   c 4 out of 10 interviewees were disappointed because the course was on late in the afternoon.

   d 75% of students would recommend this course to their friends.

   e 99% of my classmates think that being able to help others in an emergency is an important skill to have.

   f 55% of all students I interviewed suggested our school should offer more presentations and talks done by health professionals.

7 Write answers to these questions. Use exact numbers.

   a How many male/female students are there in your class today?

   b How many male/female teachers teach your class in total, in all the subjects that you study?

8   Work in small groups. Ask each other questions to find out how many students:

*   love science

*   like your science lab

*   are planning to study science at university

*   are planning to study at university abroad.

Then write sentences with your findings using exact or approximate numbers and phrases.

9   Work in pairs. Read the task and identify the main points. Then look at two examples of plans. Which one do you think is better, and why?

> Your school is planning to improve the science laboratory. The headteacher has asked you to interview other students in your class and find out their views about the lab. You should then write a report about your findings and make some recommendations. Write about 120–160 words.

Plan A

1. introduction

2. positive points

3. negative points

4. recommendations

Plan B

1. Interview students

Questions about: location / how often used / equipment

What students like / dislike

Ask students what improvements are needed

2. Write report

Paragraph 1 – introduction

Paragraph 2 – what students like

Paragraph 3 – what students dislike

Paragraph 4 – conclusion (suggest changes)

WRITING TIP

What to do before you start writing your answer

Read the task carefully and underline what the task asks you to do. Then plan your answer. Decide how many paragraphs you'll need and what points from the task you should include in each paragraph. Brainstorm concrete ideas for each paragraph. You should always do this before you start writing. If you start your written answer without planning first, your answer may not include all the necessary information. It may also be very chaotic and difficult for the reader to understand.

10   **Work in small groups. Plan what information you need to ask about in your survey and what the questions should be. Use plan B from Exercise 9 to help you think of the right questions. Then decide who is going to ask each question from your list.**

11   **Carry out your survey. Ask other students the question from Exercise 10. Take notes of the students' answers. Describe the results of your survey using expressions from the Use of English box. Listen to other students from your group and take notes of what they found out.**

12   **Now write your report using the information your group collected in Exercise 11. When you have finished writing your report, read it again to check that you have done everything that you should. Use the list below to help you.**

Have you…

✓   written a formal report?

✓   divided your report into paragraphs?

✓   labelled each paragraph with a heading?

✓   stated the purpose of your report and how you collected the information?

✓   included some positive points about the school lab?

✓   included some negative points about the school lab?

✓   suggested some improvements based on your findings from the survey?

✓   proofread your report and checked that you included the correct verb forms?

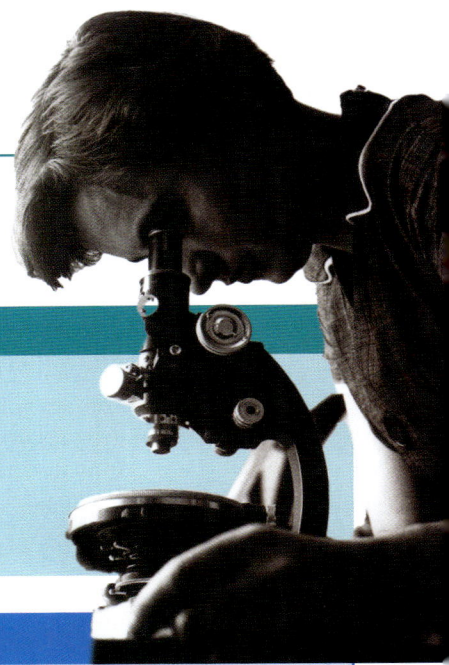

Project challenge

PROJECT LEARNING OBJECTIVES

In your project you will…

- carry out research and compare your findings with others

- extract information from a range of sources (e.g. a table, an interview)

- participate in a group discussion and express your opinion.

PROJECT OPTION 1

Research and carry out an interview

While some scientists are remembered for their discoveries, some names have been forgotten. You will research a scientist and carry out an imaginary interview with them.

Step 1: Look at the names of the four scientists. Do you know any of them and what their main research, invention or discovery was? Try to match the names with the discovery.

Jagadish Chandra Bose	**a**	DNA
Eunice Newton Foote	**b**	insulin
Rosalind Franklin	**c**	the greenhouse effect
Nicolae Paulescu	**d**	wireless telecommunication

Step 2: Work in four groups. Each group will research one of the scientists from step 1. First, look at the following list and find the information online. Make notes.

- Name
- Nationality
- Important information about their life
- What they worked on
- Reasons for not being recognised for their work

Step 3: Imagine you are going to do an interview with the scientist you researched in step 2. Work in the same group and prepare your questions. Use your notes to help you. For example: *Did you work on your discovery with anybody else?*

Decide who will take on the roles of the scientist and the interviewer. Practise your interview.

Step 4: Act out your interview in front of the class. Then watch the other groups' interviews.

SPEAKING TIP

Expressing a strong surprise

When you are surprised by something (either positive or negative), you can say:

I can't get over the fact that…

I'm really shocked by…

I'm absolutely speechless.

CRITICAL THINKING

Analysing and understanding links between events

To help you understand why things happened in the past, it is important to know things such as:

- what was allowed / not allowed
- what was appropriate / inappropriate behaviour
- what events affected people's lives, opinions, etc.

PROJECT OPTION 2

Plan a meal for your school canteen and make a poster

You are going to research and plan a healthy meal for your school canteen.

Step 1: Work in small groups. Look at the image and the phone conversation. What do you think the response 'Just eat a rainbow!' means? Compare your ideas in your group and write them down.

Step 2: Research the idea of 'eating the rainbow'. What does this theory suggest? Share your findings with your group. Say how similar or different your suggestions in step 1 were.

Step 3: Work in the same group to carry out more detailed research about different-coloured fruits and vegetables, what they contain and what some experts say this food may help us with. Decide which colour(s) fruits and vegetables each member of your group should focus on. Then do your research. Copy and complete the table with the information you find.

Step 4: Tell the others in your group what you found out about your colour. Then listen to the others and complete the table with their information.

Step 5: In your group you are going to plan a meal for your school canteen based on the rainbow theory. Using the information from steps 3 and 4, plan the meal. Discuss which ingredients you are going to use and what dish you want to make. Then make a poster with the recipe.

Step 6: Present your poster to the class and explain:

* why you chose the recipe
* what health benefits your dish could have, and why.

Then listen to the other groups and vote on the best dish.

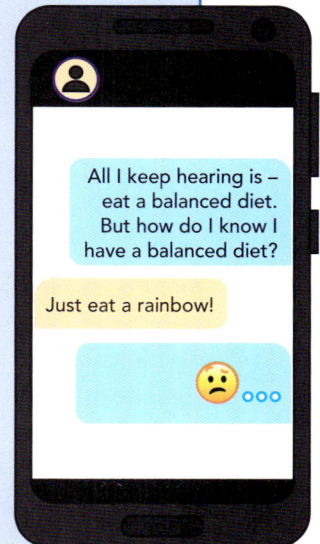

> All I keep hearing is – eat a balanced diet. But how do I know I have a balanced diet?
>
> Just eat a rainbow!
>
> 😕 ooo

Colour	Fruits / vegetables	Contains (vitamins and minerals)	Possible health benefits
Red			
Orange and yellow			
Green			
Blue and purple			
Dark red			
White and brown			

SELF AND PEER ASSESSMENT

Think about how well you, and your group, did in the project. Then complete the statements below.

a   Our group worked particularly well in the following activities:…

b   I really enjoyed working with… because he/she…

c   While doing this project, I learnt that I'm really good at… and I enjoy…

d   However, I need to practise… a bit more.

e   I learnt… and, in the future, this will help me…

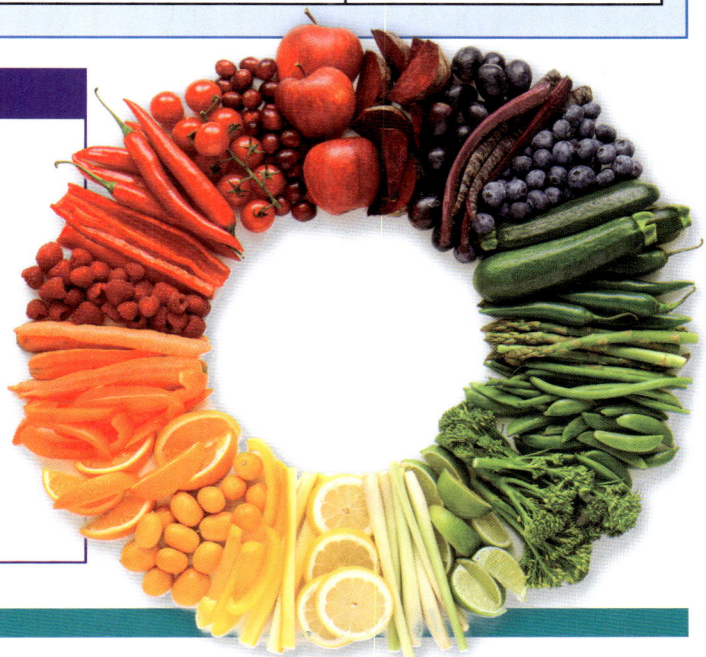

Practise and prepare

Reading

1   Read the following blogs written by students about their science lessons. Then answer questions (a–g).

Student A

When I read about the danger of bacteria becoming resistant to some antibiotics, I wanted to find out more. I researched the subject and discovered how teams of scientists have been racing against time to find new types of antibiotics, but there hasn't been a new type found since 1987. During my research, I came to admire some of these people, who dedicate their lives to discovering new life-saving medicines. So, it makes me a bit angry that antibiotics are still being prescribed when it's not necessary. People need to realise how serious the situation is and change their attitude to this medicine. At school we did some fascinating experiments and observed how the growth of certain bacteria can be affected by antibiotics, and it made me think that I'd like to do this for a living. I never realised before how interesting science can be.

Student B

Our science teacher has always been my hero. She knows a lot of stuff, but she also makes our lessons fun and interesting. We work on different experiments and always work in different groups, so I have got to know far more classmates than I normally would really well. The main focus of last week's lessons was the local environment. I already knew a lot about global warming etc., but I never fully realised how our choices can have widespread environmental consequences. For instance, buying polyester clothes means that microplastic fibres get released into the water when the clothes are washed. They then enter our food chain through the fish that we eat. It's shocking, and people should think twice about what they buy. I know I certainly do now. Sadly, not many people know this fact and that was one of the main reasons why I decided to put on a series of presentations to make others more environmentally conscious. My parents even think I should study environmental studies and make this my profession in life.

Student C

Our teacher tries very hard to make sure that all of us find science exciting. He's even inspired quite a few of my friends to choose science as their career. Last month we were all asked to bring potatoes into school and told that we'd be making a potato battery. He knows I love physics and am pretty good at it, so he put me in charge of our group. This was a bit out of my comfort zone, as I'm normally very shy. So it came a bit as a shock to me how much I actually enjoyed it. I never knew I had leadership skills. This personal discovery has since helped me in other subjects too, like English. However, not everything went very smoothly during our experiment and we almost ran out of time. But, thanks to my friends staying calm, we managed to complete everything within the given time, something one person alone would never have achieved by themselves. This was a useful observation for me. Science lessons aren't just about science, but also about looking more critically at the things we do every day.

Which student gives the following information? For each statement, choose the correct student, A, B or C.

a   It has taught me the importance of teamwork.

b   I have made a lot of new friends.

c   It has improved my confidence.

d   It has helped me decide on my future career.

e   It has inspired me to do something helpful.

f   I have changed my lifestyle as a result.

g   I have discovered new role models.

Writing

2   You school recently started a campaign for more young people to eat healthily. You did a survey among students and decided to write a report for the headteacher. In your report, say what eating habits most students have and suggest how the school canteen could help students make even more healthy choices. Write about 120–160 words.

Here are some comments from students at your school:

> I'm too busy to eat regularly.

> I follow blogs on healthy eating.

> I'm trying to eat less red meat.

> I never find what I like in the canteen.

The comments above may give you some ideas, but you should also use some ideas of your own.

Speaking

3   Work in pairs. Answer these questions as fully as possible.

a   Some people say science is the most important subject at school. Do you agree?

b   In some countries a lot of money is spent on scientific research. Do you think that's a good idea?

c   What do you think the main aim of science should be?

d   We have now discovered everything there is to discover. What's your opinion?

EXAM TIP

To answer exam questions fully, you can:

- provide examples
- give reasons for your opinions
- support your opinions with personal experience.

REFLECTION

1   Work in pairs. Look at the quotation by Carl Sagan and the question at the start of this unit. In your opinion, what does 'where' refer to? Does it refer to places that are far away and unknown, or near and familiar? Why do think so? Give examples of the places that 'where' could refer to and 'what' could be discovered or explored there.

2   Reflect on your progress as a learner while working on this unit. Discuss these questions with your partner.

a   In the Think about it lesson, what helped you match the questions to the correct answers from the interviews? Do you have similar opinions and experiences to the students from the interviews? What are they?

b   In the Science lesson, you learnt about different types of science. Which one do you find most exciting? Why? Would you like to choose one of these as your future career? Why or why not?

c   In the Talk about it lesson, you practised having a conversation. Do you think the tips on how to react to other people during conversations will help you in your conversations outside the classroom? How? Give examples.

d   In the Improve your writing lesson, you learnt how to write a report. Which aspect of report writing do you think you still need to improve, and how are you going to do that? Which of the three points below helped you most with your report writing, and why?

- seeing a model answer before writing your own report
- being given useful phrases before writing your own report
- using a checklist after writing your report to check you have remembered to include everything.

e   In the Project challenge lesson, you researched information on a given topic. What information from your research did you find most interesting, and why?

f   In the Practise and prepare lesson, you learnt about reading for specific information in reading texts. Did you find it easy to find the information you were asked to locate? Why or why not? What helped you to find it?

SUMMARY CHECKLIST

I can…

- [ ] follow short monologues and recognise what question is being answered.
- [ ] read an article and find specific details.
- [ ] participate in a discussion and solve a problem about what recipe to choose.
- [ ] express the results of a survey using either approximate or exact numbers.
- [ ] carry out research and write a report based on a survey.
- [ ] extract the necessary information from written as well as spoken sources.

4 The world of art

IN THIS UNIT YOU WILL...

- **listen** to interviews and a talk about different types of art
- **read** a blog and an article about music and its benefits
- **give** a talk about modern buildings and answer the audience's questions
- **write** a persuasive essay about street art that expresses a one-sided argument
- **practise** the passive used with modal verbs and passive infinitives
- **carry out** research and **evaluate** your findings and suggestions made by others.

GETTING STARTED

*"***Creativity takes courage.***"*
(Henri Matisse, French painter)

Does art unite us or divide us?

Watch this!

Think about it: Exploring different types of art

- What do you think of when you hear the word art?

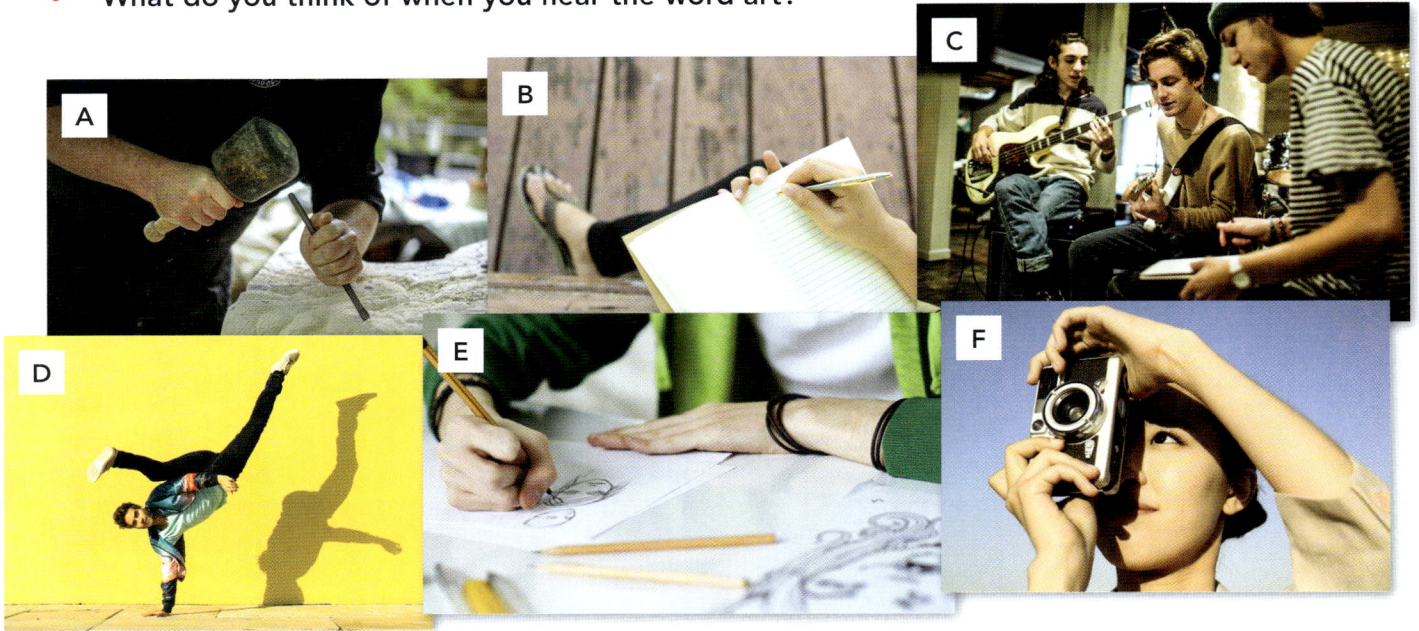

Vocabulary

1   Look at the vocabulary box and check the meaning of the words and phrases you don't know in a reliable dictionary.

abstract art	physically demanding
compose	publish a novel
conductor	redraft
dance moves	rhythm
form a band	sketch
in the spotlight	zoom in
live audience	
paints, colours and brushes	

2   In pairs, look at the photos. Can you name the types of art they show? Discuss what is happening in each photo. Try to use the vocabulary from Exercise 1.

3   Now discuss these questions.
   a   What is your favourite and least favourite type of art? Why?
   b   Why do you think people need art in their lives?

Listening

4   Listen to three people talking about what type of art they have taken up as their latest hobby. For each speaker, choose the correct photograph (A–F).

5   Read statements a–e. Then listen to the three speakers again and match the statements to the correct speaker. There are two extra statements that you do not need to use. Which phrase(s) from the recording helped you choose the correct answer?
   a   It has helped me become a more sociable person.
   b   I'm happy to be doing something for my neighbourhood.
   c   It has made my choice of future work much easier.
   d   The response to my new hobby has made me more motivated.
   e   I have found doing this really helps me relax.

USE OF ENGLISH

Using suffixes to make different word forms

We use suffixes (e.g. -ment, -al, -ly, -er) to change the form of a word and to make new nouns, adjectives, verbs or adverbs.

For example, the word 'art' is an abstract noun. The other forms we can make are:

• art**ist** (noun, person)

• artist**ic**/art**y** (adjective)

• artica**lly** (adverb)

If you know which suffixes make which forms, this will also help you with the meaning of the word. For example, the suffixes -er,-or and -ist tell you that the word relates to a person, such as singer, conductor, guitarist.

6 The words in the table have been taken from the recording. We can use these words to say how art makes us feel or what we think of it. In pairs, copy and complete the missing forms. Use the Use of English box and a reliable dictionary to help you. Then discuss how different types of art make you feel, and why.

Noun (abstract / person)	Adjective (feeling / situation)	Verb
	amused /	
		enjoy
	frustrated /	
	encouraging	
	happy	
interest	/	
enthusiasm /		
/		invent
passion		

Listening

7 You are going to listen to a talk about sand art. In pairs, look at the photo below. What do you think sand art is? Then listen to the introduction of the talk to check whether you were right.

8 Look at the five sentences below and guess what information is missing from each gap. Then listen to the rest of the talk, about a sand artist called Rahul Arya, and complete the gaps with one or two words, or a number.

a Sand was first used in film production in the year _____.

b Rahul used a _____ to draw his first pictures on.

c Rahul studied _____ at university.

d The speaker says that Rahul gave his most memorable performance at an _____.

e The speaker uses the word _____ to describe sand artists' creations during one show.

9 In the recording, the speaker mentions that many people experience success but also failure. In pairs, look at these quotations by Rahul Arya. What do you think they mean? Do you agree with the ideas?

> "Success is if you can make the world a better place before dying than how it was when you were born."

> "When your loss is big then your success will be bigger."

Music and psychology: The power of music

• **How can people benefit from music?**

Speaking

1 **Work in pairs to discuss the following questions.**

   a   How often, and when, do you listen to music?

   b   What music do you like listening to? Why do you like it?

   c   How does listening to different types of music make you feel?

2 **In pairs, discuss how you think people can benefit from music in the following areas:**

   • **Physical health**   • **Learning**
   • **Mood and mental well-being**   • **Relationships**

Reading

3 **Read the text about the benefits of music. Were your ideas in Exercise 2 similar to those in the text? Copy the list from Exercise 2 into your notebook and add examples from the text.**

1 Although we can't be sure exactly when human beings began making and listening to music, scientists do know something about why we do. Here's what research tells us about the power of music.

2 Some researchers think that one of the most important roles of music is to create a feeling of togetherness. For example, national anthems connect crowds at sporting events and lullabies sung by parents to their young children enable them to develop strong bonds.

3 It's also been suggested that music has a positive effect on the ability to memorise. Interestingly, music memory is one of the brain functions most resistant to dementia. That's why some carers use music to calm dementia patients and build up trust with them. There are also some interesting findings regarding how music influences our response to physical pain. While listening to music, people seem to manage pain better than with medication alone.

4 In one study, people were interviewed about why they listen to music. The study participants varied in terms of age, gender, and background, but they reported strikingly similar reasons. One reason given was that music helped them cope with their feelings better, for example helping them to feel calm in situations when they might become anxious. And it's listening to classical music, combined with jazz, in particular, that seems to have a positive effect on depression symptoms, even in situations when it has been resistant to medication. However, sad tunes can often have the opposite effect and increase symptoms of depression. So, it is very important to choose your music carefully.

5 The right kind of music can make people want to move, and the benefits of dancing are well-documented. Depending on the music's strength and speed, or 'tempo', it can change your breathing rate, heart rate and blood pressure. While slow music calms you down, fast tempos in music are very likely to improve your physical performance so that you can go on for longer or move faster during exercise.

6 Music has been proven to help motivation while studying. And if you choose your music carefully, it'll most certainly help you process new information more easily. So here are some tips to help you find the most suitable music for work and study.

   • **Avoid music with lyrics.** Any music that has lyrics in a language you understand will probably prove more distracting than helpful.

   • **Choose slow, instrumental music.** Existing research generally focuses on classical music, but if you don't enjoy this genre, you could also consider soft electronic or ambient music — the kind you might hear in a hotel lift or a shopping mall.

   • **Keep the volume low.** Study music should stay at a background volume level. If it's too loud, it could disrupt your thinking process.

   • **Stick to songs you don't have strong feelings about.** Listening to music you either love or hate can affect your ability to concentrate.

   • **Stream commercial-free music.** When you're listening to your chosen song online and a commercial suddenly cuts in, it will most likely break your concentration.

4   In pairs, look at the words and phrases in the Academic language box. Explain the meaning of these phrases using your own words. Use a reliable dictionary to help you.

ACADEMIC LANGUAGE

Music and psychology

ambient music	have a positive effect on
anthems	increase symptoms of
be resistant to something	instrumental music
	lullabies
breathing rate	lyrics
feeling of togetherness	response to pain

USE OF ENGLISH

Modal verbs and other phrases of probability

You learnt about modal verbs in earlier stages of this course. We often use them when we want to say how certain or uncertain we are about something happening in the future.

they **might** become anxious (modal verb – it is possible)

it **could** disrupt your thinking process (modal verb – it is possible)

sad tunes **can** often have the opposite effect (modal verb – it is quite possible)

fast tempos in music **are very likely to** improve your physical performance (phrase – it will probably happen)

it'll most certainly help you process (phrase – there is no doubt that something will happen)

Look back through the text about the benefits of music and find more examples of modal verbs and phrases of probability.

---

5   Reread paragraph 6 and complete these sentences with the correct ideas, using the Use of English box to help you. You can use your own words.

a   If you don't listen to _____, you are less likely to learn effectively.

b   Songs that have words in them are very likely to _____.

c   The kind of music that is good as background music is often heard in _____.

d   You are less likely to focus on your studies if _____ the songs you're playing.

e   It will be difficult for you to concentrate if you're listening to online music that _____.

6   In small groups, discuss whether you have benefited from music, and how.

7   Your school is thinking of introducing more music lessons. You have decided to write a short article for your school magazine on the same topic. In your article, discuss whether your school should or shouldn't include more music lessons, and why. Write about 120–160 words.

READING TIP

While you are reading a certain type of text (for example, an email, a blog, a magazine article), it is a good idea to notice how it is organised, whether the register is formal or informal and what vocabulary it uses. This will be useful for your own writing.

Talk about it: Wonders of modern architecture

- What is more important – how a building looks on the outside or how practical and comfortable it is on the inside?

Watch this!

Listening

1   Work in pairs to discuss these questions.

   a   What buildings do you see on your way to school? Give three examples.

   b   What do the buildings look like?

   c   Are they modern or old?

2   Look at photos A–C. Do you know any of the buildings? Listen to a student giving a short talk to his classmates about the three buildings. In which order does he mention the buildings?

A

B

C

3   In pairs, look at the vocabulary box and check the meanings of the words and phrases. Use a reliable dictionary to help you.

Art Nouveau	static
baroque	symbolise something
be at your peak	venues
performing arts	vibrant

4   Copy the table into your notebook. How much information about the buildings can you remember? Fill in as much information as you can, then listen to the talk again. Check your answers and complete the rest of the information. The speaker may not give all of the information for each category.

	Photo A	Photo B	Photo C
Name			
Location			
When built			
Size			
Used for			
Record(s) it holds			
Other interesting facts			

LANGUAGE TIP

Adding emphasis

To add emphasis to what we are saying means that we give it extra force for others to notice it. We can do this by adding extra words before adjectives and verbs, and by stressing these words when we say them.

*That's **absolutely** amazing.*

*It **does** look stunning.*

*Yes, they **certainly** have!*

However, be careful about which two words you use together. For example, you can say 'That's absolutely / so / really amazing', but you can't say 'That's very amazing.' This is because some words don't go together in English.

Speaking

5 **Work in small groups to discuss these questions. Remember to add emphasis to your ideas and opinions.**

    a Which of the three buildings would you like to visit? Why?

    b Do you like modern architecture? Why or why not?

SPEAKING TIP

Reacting to what others have said

When you like or agree with what someone else has said, you can say:

- *That's right.*

- *That's a very good question.*

- *You've just made a very good point!*

- *Oh, I love that.*

These phrases also show the other person that you are paying attention to what they're saying.

---

6 **During the talk, Himesh and Maya interrupt to ask Aidan questions. At the end of the talk, Aidan invites his classmates to ask questions before he ends the talk. Listen to the talk one more time. What phrases do the students use to do the following?**

    a interrupt politely to ask something (the audience)

    b invite listeners to ask questions at the end of a talk (the speaker)

    c end the talk (the speaker)

COMMUNICATION

Using your voice and body language when giving a talk

When giving a talk, it is important to make your listeners interested in what you have to say. It doesn't only depend on the content of your talk, but also how you say things. To make someone listen to you, try to do the following:

- vary how loudly you speak – raise your voice when you're saying something important

- sound passionate and speak confidently – this makes people listen to you more

- include pauses and don't rush – by speaking too fast, people get confused or tired and stop listening

- use shorter sentences – long, complicated sentences often confuse people.

Remember to smile and keep eye contact – this will help you to make a better connection with your audience.

---

7 **Choose one of the two topics below and prepare a two- to three-minute talk. Then give your talk to your class. Remember to invite them to ask questions at the end of your talk.**

    a An example of modern architecture in your city/country and what you think of it.

    b An example of an impressive historical building in the world and what makes it stand out.

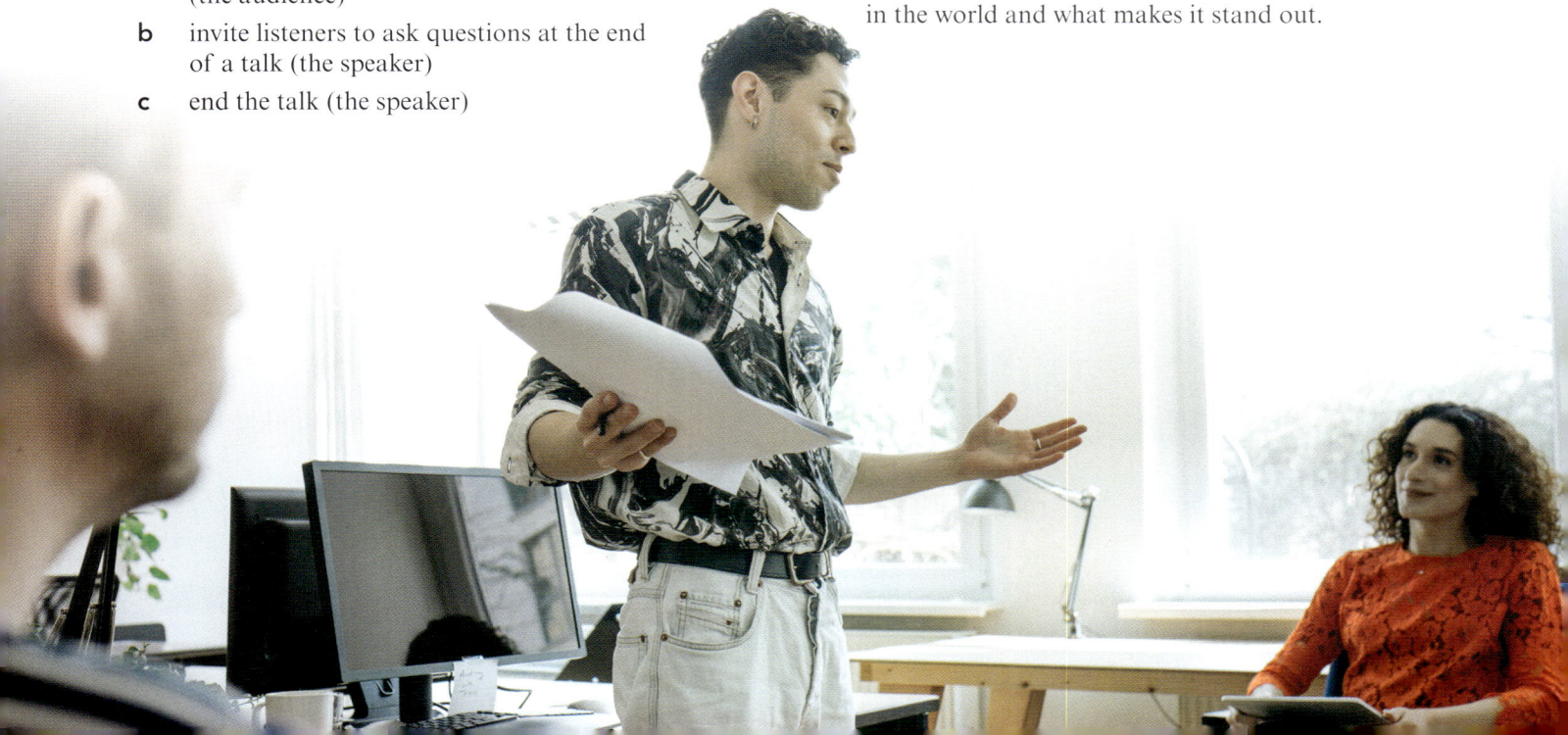

Improve your writing: An opinion essay

1   **What do you imagine when you hear the phrase 'street art'? Read some other opinions. Which one is the most similar to yours? Why?**

a   Paintings on walls make the run-down parts of the city more colourful.

b   I don't mind street art when it's done well, but some images are quite ugly and I don't want to be looking at them every time I go past.

c   Through street art, young artists can get noticed by the wider public.

d   I don't mind street art – it makes me happy, especially when it's done in cheerful bright colours.

e   The worry I have is that it is occasionally done on public spaces where it doesn't belong.

f   Thanks to street art, a lot of people have the opportunity to experience art without having to go to art galleries.

g   It's like having a conversation with the artist. They leave a message for us in the form of their art. I love looking at these and trying to work out what the art means. I find that very satisfying.

2   **Now read a model essay about street art. Is the writer for or against the idea of street art? Which of the opinions from Exercise 1 does the writer include in their essay?**

1   In some countries, it is sometimes claimed that street art should not be called art because the artists producing it disrespect the public spaces they use for their creations. This negative opinion needs to be challenged and people need to be shown how our cities can benefit from having street art.

2   To begin with, just like any other type of art, street art provides entertainment for people. In my view, street art is far more accessible to younger audiences than some of the more traditional types of art. Street art manages to capture people's attention, thanks to its diverse and vibrant images. Young people can relate to the topics shown in street art much better. In addition, some people find going to art galleries and museums intimidating. However, seeing images on public walls means they can enjoy art right on their doorstep, for free and, very often, without feeling they are being made to do something. They can decide for themselves whether they want to look at it or not.

3   Secondly, street art is invaluable for young artists who are just starting out. Not everyone can afford to buy the materials, like canvas, or to secure an exhibition in a venue that they might have to pay for. Street walls don't cost anything. By using public spaces for their art, these artists also ensure they get noticed by much wider audiences than they would if they had exhibited their art in a gallery.

4   Lastly, not all our cities are the most cheerful and brightest of places, especially areas such as industrial estates with concrete constructions or areas that are relatively neglected and run-down. I firmly believe that well-done street art using vibrant colours can make any of these spaces more exciting and bring a little bit more happiness to the passers-by. If local authorities are worried that some public spaces aren't suitable for street art, they can provide a list of places where artists are allowed and, in fact, encouraged to paint, as the local communities can also hugely benefit from the art.

5   To conclude, I am of the opinion that street art is vital to our lives. Many of the negative views about this art form come from the lack of information that people may have about what street art really is and how beneficial it is for urban communities.

3   **In pairs, look at the essay again and think about the style, register and organisation. Then complete the sentences below with the correct word or phrase.**

agree	middle
conclusion	persuade
disagree	register
formal (x2)	summarises
inform	teacher
introduces	think
introduction	

a   Essays are mostly written for a _____ and are supposed to _____ and/or _____ the reader about something.

b   In essays, students write what they _____ about a certain topic.

c   In opinion essays, students can either _____ or _____ with the main topic.

d   Essays tend to be more _____ in tone, so the _____ also needs to be _____.

e   The first paragraph in an essay is the _____, where the writer briefly _____ the topic.

f   The last paragraph in an essay is the _____, where the writer _____ their opinion about the topic. This is based on the ideas expressed in the _____ paragraphs.

WRITING TIP

Topic sentences in paragraphs

A topic sentence introduces the main idea presented in a paragraph. It is usually the first sentence. Other sentences provide further information that is linked to the topic sentence. Some paragraphs may not have any topic sentences.

Where appropriate, join your sentences within the paragraph with an appropriate linking word or phrase. Linked ideas and sentences are easier to read and follow.

4   **Read these questions. Then read the model essay again and answer the questions. When you finish, compare your answers with a partner.**

a   Does the writer clearly say what the essay is about and the reason for writing it?

b   How does each paragraph start? Why do you think this is?

c   Do the paragraphs 2–4 each have a topic sentence? Which one is it? What idea does it introduce?

d   What are the supporting ideas for each topic sentence?

e   Does the writer clearly express their overall opinion in the conclusion? How? What is the writer's opinion?

f   Does the writer link their conclusion back to the introduction? How?

USE OF ENGLISH

The passive

In Unit 2, you learnt about the passive and how to use it in different forms. Now look at some more examples of the passive. These passive structures are often used in essays as they make them sound more formal in tone.

This passive structure is often used to introduce an idea in essays:

***It is** sometimes **claimed** that…*

The infinitive passive structure is used after verbs that are followed by the infinitive verb form with *to*.

*People **need to be shown** how our cities can benefit from having street art.*

In the passive structure used after modal verbs, we don't use *to* with these structures like we do with the infinitive passive structures.

*…where local artists **could be encouraged** to paint their images…*

5   Read the following sentences. Can you find the mistakes in the passive forms and correct them? There is one mistake in each sentence.

a   The building should been completed next month.

b   Modern art can often be misunderstanding.

c   The meaning of the painting had to be explain to him by the artist.

d   Music can be often used in gyms to help people with their work-outs.

e   The navy-blue colour was the wrong shade, so the classroom will have be repainted with a more natural colour like white or beige.

f   The new school uniforms may to be designed by some of our students.

g   From next year onwards, dance is likely to be taught in our PE lessons.

6   Look at some more examples of the passive that can be used to introduce an idea about a topic in essays. Complete the sentences with your own ideas about the topics in the brackets. You can change the adverbs of frequency if you need to.

Example: It is often believed that _____. (classical music)

It is often believed that classical music is mostly appreciated by older generations.

a   It is often thought that _____. (theatres)

b   It is sometimes said that _____. (modern art)

c   It is frequently argued that _____. (singing)

d   It is sometimes expected that _____. (ballet)

7   You are now going to write an opinion essay. Choose one of the statements below for your essay.

• People shouldn't have to pay money to visit any galleries or museums.

• People don't need to study art at school to become an artist.

• Students should be allowed to design their own classrooms.

• Some people think art is boring because they don't understand it.

8   Before you write your opinion essay:

• decide if you agree or disagree with the statement you chose in Exercise 7

• think of some ideas you would like to include

• decide how many paragraphs you need

• decide which ideas to put in each paragraph.

9   Now write your opinion essay, using the scaffolding below and your plan from Exercise 8. Remember to use topic sentences where appropriate.

It is often said that…
To begin with,…
Secondly,…
Lastly,…
To conclude, I am of the opinion that…

WRITING TIP

Learn from your own mistakes

When your teacher corrects your writing, have a look at the mistakes you made. If you don't, you will just repeat the same mistakes in the future and your writing may not improve. It is a good idea to keep a list of your own mistakes in different areas (for example, tenses, word forms, prepositions, spelling) that you can review, to try to avoid them in the future.

10   **When you have finished writing your opinion essay, read it through to check that you have done everything that you should have. Use this checklist to help you.**

Have you…

- ✓   written an opinion essay either agreeing or disagreeing with the main statement?
- ✓   divided the essay into paragraphs?
- ✓   introduced the topic in the first paragraph?
- ✓   used linking words or phrases to start your paragraphs, where appropriate?
- ✓   used topic sentences in the middle paragraphs, where appropriate?
- ✓   provided supporting ideas for each topic sentence?
- ✓   linked ideas within your paragraphs using appropriate linking words and phrases?
- ✓   expressed your overall opinion on the topic in the last paragraph?

Project challenge

PROJECT LEARNING OBJECTIVES

In your project you will…

- take part in a group discussion
- evaluate suggestions
- make your own conclusion.

PROJECT OPTION 1

Suggest a new design for your classroom and organise an exhibition

Imagine your school is planning to redesign the classrooms. You are going to research and plan what design would be best.

DESIGN YOUR NEW CLASSROOM COMPETITION

We are planning to modernise our classrooms. As some of our students are interested in interior and graphic design, we are organising a competition for anyone who would like to take part in redesigning their classroom. You should put together a design or a model of what you think the new classroom should look like and submit it by the end of next month. We are looking forward to receiving your designs.

Step 1: Read the advert above. Prepare a questionnaire to interview other students. Ask what they like about their existing classroom and what they would like to change, and why.

Decide on one more area that each person from your group should focus on in their interview.

For example, Student A can ask about furniture. Other areas you can ask about are:

- colour
- equipment and technology
- artwork on walls
- seating arrangement
- boards (type, size, position)
- curtains/blinds on windows
- lighting (type, position)

Step 2: Interview other students and take notes of what they say. Then share the information with your group. Then decide together on the best idea for each area from the list in step 1.

Step 3: Using the ideas from step 2, create your design. This can be a collage of things (for example, photos of furniture stuck on A4 card, a piece of fabric, a piece of coloured paper, small models made with toothpicks, drawings).

Step 4: Organise a mini exhibition with all the designs. Then vote for the best design. Discuss what you like about the winning design.

COMMUNICATION

Reaching a conclusion

Before you decide what to do as a team, you should listen to the opinions of others in the group. After you have listened to all their suggestions, ask what the final decision should be. You can say:

- *So, from what we've heard, what do you think the best… would be?*
- *Based on what the others think, what… should we choose?*

COMMUNICATION

Expressing your views for and against

When you are agreeing or disagreeing with a statement or a theory, you can say:

• *I must say I agree with… because…* (for)

• *I can't really support this opinion / theory / view because…* (against).

You should always explain why you agree or disagree.

PROJECT OPTION 2

Evaluate a theory and write a short paragraph

You are going to research a theory called the Mozart effect. You will then relate it to your own experiences.

Step 1: In small groups, look at these two photos. What do you think the theory is about? Do some research to find out what it is about. Were your guesses correct? What do you think about the theory?

Step 2: You are going to do more research about the Mozart effect theory. Divide your group into two. The first group should focus on why some experts say this theory works. The other group should focus on why some experts disagree with this theory.

Step 3: The two groups come together and share their findings. Discuss whether you think this theory works or not, and why.

Step 4: You are going to do an experiment to see whether music affects how well you do things. For a week, do your everyday activities (such as exercise, cleaning your room, cycling, etc.), but listen to music while doing these activities. Keep a diary to see whether listening to music improves the way you do things.

At the end of your experiment, look at whether music helped you performed better or worse, or made no difference, and make a conclusion. Write a short paragraph about your experience.

Step 5: Share your experience and conclusion with your group. Discuss whether you have changed your opinion about the Mozart effect theory, and why.

SELF AND PEER ASSESSMENT

Think about how well you, and your group, did in the project. Then complete the statements below.

a Our group worked particularly well in the following activities:…

b I really enjoyed working with… because he/she…

c While doing this project, I learnt that I'm really good at… and I enjoy…

d However, I need to practise… a bit more.

e I learnt… and, in the future, this will help me…

Practise and prepare

Speaking

1   **In pairs, answer these questions as fully as possible.**
   a   What type of art do you enjoy? Why?
   b   When did you last do something that involved art, and what did you do?
   c   Do you think that people need art in their everyday lives? Why or why not?

Writing

2   At school you have been discussing the importance of art. Your teacher has asked you to write an essay about whether students should study more art at school. In your essay, discuss how important art is for students and whether schools need to include more art lessons. Write about 120–160 words.

Below are some comments from your classmates. They may give you some ideas, but you should also use some ideas of your own.

> Art makes me relaxed.

> We need to study more practical subjects like business or computer technology.

> In our art lessons we only focus on painting and drawing.

> At my friend's school, they organise exhibitions of students' artwork.

3   You will hear two conversations, one about weekend plans and one about a school art project. For each question, choose the correct answer A, B, or C.

a   What exhibition does Amira suggest seeing next?
- **A**   old coins
- **B**   modern sculptures
- **C**   theatre costumes

b   Sarah is unable to meet her cousin this weekend because of
- **A**   a lot of schoolwork.
- **B**   a visit from a relative.
- **C**   a friend's party.

c   What art did the boy choose for his last school project?
- **A**   photography
- **B**   pottery
- **C**   painting

d   The boy says he hesitated to enter the school art competition because
- **A**   he was worried about people's reactions to this art.
- **B**   he had never competed with his art before.
- **C**   he wanted more time to complete his art work.

Listening

EXAM TIP

Underlining key words in questions

It is very difficult to read and listen at the same time. So, before you listen to the recording in listening exams, read the questions carefully and underline the key words. This means that while you are listening to the recording you won't have to reread the questions. The important words from the question will also help you to make sure you select the correct answer, not the distracting detail.

REFLECTION

1   Work in pairs. At the start of this unit you were asked whether art unites us or divides us. Can you find examples in this unit where art might bring people together or cause disagreements? What do you think about art? Does it bring people together or divide them? Why?

2   With a partner, use these questions to help you reflect on your progress as a learner while working on this unit.

   a   In the Think about it lesson, you learnt how to increase your vocabulary. How do you think knowing different word forms will help you with your English? Do you have any other tips on how to learn new words in English? What are they?

   b   In the Music and psychology lesson, you read about the benefits of music. Do you think any of the information in the text might be useful for you in other lessons or in your everyday life? Give examples.

   c   In the Talk about it lesson, you practised giving a talk. What tip did you find most useful? Why? Did the advice in this lesson make you feel more confident about giving a talk in front of an audience? Explain why or why not.

   d   In the Improve your writing lesson, you were asked to write an essay. What exactly did you do before, during and after writing your essay? Was there anything that you learnt in this lesson that was particularly helpful for writing your essay?

   e   In the Project challenge lesson, you were asked to evaluate. Did you find evaluating easy or difficult? What helped you? What do you still need to work on?

   f   In the Practise and prepare lesson, did you underline the key words in the listening section? Did they help you to select the correct answer? What else helps you find the correct answer when doing listening tests?

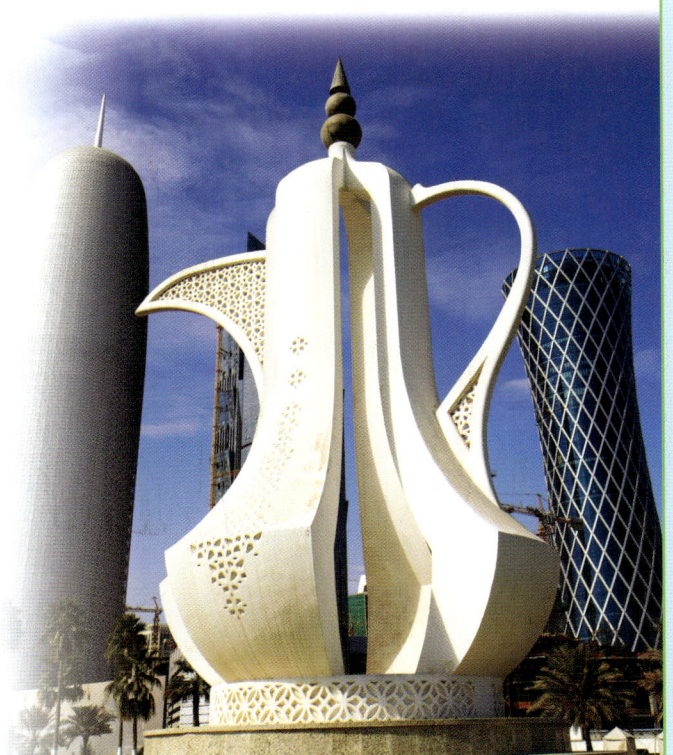

SUMMARY CHECKLIST

I can…

- [ ] follow interviews and talks and select the correct detail.
- [ ] read a blog about the benefits of music and summarise the ideas.
- [ ] give a talk and answer with the audience's questions.
- [ ] write a persuasive essay and express my views on the given topic.
- [ ] use passive forms in my writing to make it sound more formal.
- [ ] evaluate the findings from my own research and express my view(s) for or against.

5 Journeys

IN THIS UNIT YOU WILL...

- **listen** to a talk about animal migration
- **read** a text about a nomadic tribe and summarise it
- **interview** someone about their achievements and **respond** appropriately
- **describe** an unusual journey in a blog
- **practise** using the past simple, past continuous and past perfect when describing a past event
- **carry out** research about what other people think and **reach** a conclusion.

GETTING STARTED

"So much of who we are is where we have been."
(William Langewiesche, American journalist)

What can we discover through travelling?

Watch this!

Think about it: Amazing migrations

* **Why do people travel?**

Listening

1   Many wildlife species migrate by travelling from one place to another every year. Their migration journeys often cover long distances. In small groups, discuss why you think some animals migrate. Note down your ideas.

2   Listen to the first part of a talk about animal migration, given by a biology teacher. What reasons for the migration does she give? Did you have similar ideas?

3   Look at the vocabulary box and check the meaning of the words and phrases you do not know in a reliable dictionary.

beak	land mammals
calves	lay eggs
caterpillars	native species
coastal areas	retrace a route
fly the route in reverse	stopover
gain fat	toxic plants
grassy plains	wildebeest

4   In pairs, look at photos A–C. Can you match any of the words and phrases from the vocabulary box to the photos? Some words and phrases can go with more than one photo. Explain your choices.

For example: *A beak is a part of a bird's body. We can see it in photo C.*

5   Now listen to the rest of the talk given by the same teacher in Exercise 2. She is talking about three migration journeys made by the species shown in photos A–C. In which order does she mention them? Write the answers in your notebooks.

6   Reread the vocabulary box and listen to the talk again. Which words and phrases does the teacher use to talk about each migration journey? Write them next to the correct letter, A, B or C in your notebooks.

7   **What details can you remember from the talk? Copy and complete the table. Then listen to the talk one more time to add any missing information.**

Name	Starting point	Finishing point	Total distance	Total time	Interesting facts
Bar-tailed godwit					
Monarch butterfly					
Wildebeest					

8   **Working in pairs, use a map of the world to find the places mentioned in the recording. Can you trace the migration journey of each species on the map?**

USE OF ENGLISH

Superlative forms

When we are comparing three or more things in English, we use the adjectives in the superlative form. We can either use *the most* before the adjective or the suffix *-est* at the end of the adjective.

Words with one syllable use *the* + *-est* in the superlative form.

Their migration is **the longest** *nonstop flight of any known bird…* ('long' has one syllable)

Their incredible migration journey is probably **the greatest** *land mammal migration in the world.* ('great' has one syllable)

Words with three syllables use *the most* in the superlative form.

… they're one of **the most amazing** *butterflies I've ever seen.* ('amazing' has three syllables)

Now compare them with the superlative forms of adjectives with two syllables.

This butterfly is **the prettiest** *I've ever seen.*

The adjective *pretty* ends in *-y*, so we use *the* + *-est* in the superlative form.

When the birds reach their destination, that's when they feel **the most tired**.

The adjective *tired* doesn't end in *-y*, so we use *the most* in the superlative form.

Speaking

9   **Work in small groups. Use the information from the table in Exercise 7 and from the recording to discuss what you think about the three species and their migration journeys. Remember to use adjectives in the superlative form. Then write six sentences about what you have discussed.**

Example: *The bar-tailed godwit makes the longest migration journey of the three species. I found their journey the most fascinating one.*

10   **Still in your group, research other animal migration journeys and prepare a quiz for other students. For example, you can focus on the following:**

> **The migration record breakers**
> - the smallest migrant
> - the largest migrant
> - the longest mammal migration journey

Geography: Nomadic way of living

- How easy or difficult is it for nomadic tribes travelling from one place to another to keep their traditions in the 21st century?

Vocabulary

1 A nomad is someone from a group of people who move from one place to another, often with animals such as goats or camels. Discuss what the connection is between the photo below and the word 'nomad'. Compare your ideas with other pairs.

2 Look at the phrases in the Academic language box and the word list a–k. In pairs, find words or phrases from the Academic language box that match the meanings a–k. Use a reliable dictionary, if necessary.

ACADEMIC LANGUAGE

Human geography

global fish trade	shelter from something
herd reindeer	supplement your food with
intense heat	
make your living	sustain yourself by fishing
political unrest	
severe droughts	underwater vision
	unique design

a	very strong	g	to provide enough of
b	protests	h	to earn
c	extremely dry	i	to add something
d	worldwide	j	unusual
e	eyesight	k	to move a group
f	to protect		

3 Write complete definitions of the phrases in the Academic language box using the words from the word list in Exercise 2. Then compare your definitions with other pairs.

Reading

4 Copy the fact file below. Then read the text about three nomadic tribes. Choose one of the tribes and complete the fact file with the relevant information about them. Then check the information in pairs.

> **Fact file**
>
> Name: Way of life in the past:
> Location: Current situation:
> Population: Some interesting facts:

With a population of over 50,000, **the Himba people** lead a semi-nomadic life. They mostly live in the northern parts of Namibia. The tasks that women and men do are very different. The women undertake the
5 daily activities, such as taking care of the children or making clothing, while the men go hunting. Himba people like to wear a lot of jewellery. The necklaces and bracelets they wear can weigh up to 40 kilograms. The colour red is very important in Himba traditions as
10 it symbolises earth and blood, both of which represent life. Their red skin is one of the things that make the Himba unique. The red colour comes from paste produced by mixing animal fat and red ochre from the soil. They then apply this paste to their skin. It acts
15 as sunscreen against the intense heat in the desert. So far, the Himba people have managed to keep their culture and traditions free from
20 western influences, but they have had to deal with issues like severe droughts and political unrest in the area.

25 **The Bajau sea nomads** have lived at sea for more than a thousand years on long houseboats called lepa-lepa and also in huts built on long wooden stilts near the shore. It is difficult to say exactly what the Bajau population is, but it is estimated there are about

30 1,000,000 Bajau living in the waters in southeast Asia, between Indonesia, Malaysia and the Philippines. They still practise their traditional way of life at sea but come ashore to trade for supplies or to shelter from storms. The Bajau fish or collect their food by

35 free diving and can dive as deep as 70 metres with only goggles made of wood to protect their eyes. To hunt fish and octopuses, they use handmade spear guns. Some Bajau men can spend up to five hours under the water each day. Thanks to this lifestyle,

40 they have developed remarkable underwater vision. When they are at sea in their boats, they sometimes dust their faces with powder made from rice to keep themselves cool. Sadly, it is thought that the current generation could be

45 the last one to be able to sustain themselves just by fishing. The main reason for this has been the global

50 fish trade, which has disrupted the Bajau fishing traditions.

The Sami people live in northern Europe, in four countries: Norway, Sweden, Finland and Russia.

55 Their total population is about 80,000. The Sami culture is the oldest culture in northern Scandinavia. Even today, the Sami still wear traditional costumes during special occasions such as weddings. People can tell where the wearer comes from by the unique

60 design used on these costumes. In the past, the Sami people made their living from herding reindeer, and they organised their lives around the needs of their animals. They lived in tents because whole families migrated with the herds, supplementing

65 their food with fishing and hunting. Nowadays, a large proportion of the Sami people have moved into towns and found employment there. Their nomadic way of life has almost disappeared. However, in the second half of the 20th century, the Sami people put

70 a lot of effort into keeping their culture alive through the use of Sami languages in schools and the

75 protection of reindeer pastures. There are even Sami newspapers and radio programmes.

¹³ **ochre:** a type of red earth that is used to make paints for artists

5   Use the information from your fact file to prepare a short talk about the nomadic tribe.

STUDY TIP

Summarising a text

When you need to summarise a text as the basis for a talk, you should first skim-read the text very quickly to make yourself familiar with the information in it. Then read the text more slowly and highlight the most important information to include in your talk. Finally, think about how you're going to organise this information and how you can link the ideas together.

Speaking

6   Work together with two pairs who have prepared talks about the other two nomadic tribes. Give your talk about the tribe you each chose. As you listen to the other talks, complete fact files with the correct information about each tribe.

7   Using the information you have about the three tribes, answer these questions.
    Which tribe(s):
    a   has developed an unusually good sense thanks to their way of life? What sense is it and why did this happen?
    b   is famous for wearing accessories?
    c   still strictly divides their daily tasks between men and women? Why?
    d   need to protect their skin against the sun? What do they use to do this?
    e   has their own media? What are they and why do you think the tribe has them?
    f   lives in unusual houses? What kind of houses are they?
    g   has a tradition based around one colour? What is the belief?
    h   has been most influenced by the rest of the world? How has this affected their way of life?

Talk about it: The road to success

• **What qualities do people need to succeed in life?**

Watch this!

Listening

1 **Work in pairs. Look at the photo and discuss the questions below.**

   a What do you think the person in the photo has achieved?

   b What challenges do you think the person had to overcome to achieve this? Why?

2 **Listen to an interview with the person from the photo. Were your answers in Exercise 1 correct?**

3 **Work in small groups and discuss what you think of the person in the photo. Based on the information from the interview, what kind of person is she, and why?**

4 **When you were listening to the interview, how did the interviewer sound? How could you tell? Was she:**

   A impatient but friendly?

   B friendly and supportive?

   C confused and surprised?

5 **Listen to the interview again. Can you find example phrases for the following categories?**

   a short questions to show surprise

   b other phrases used to show surprise

   c phrases to show support and understanding

SPEAKING TIP

Rising and falling intonation to show interest

To show that you're interested in what other people are saying, you need to use rising and falling intonation. This means that you should go up and down with your voice when you're speaking. If your intonation is too flat, you may sound as if you're bored or not interested in the conversation.

6   Listen to two short conversations.
Which conversation sounds better? Why?

7   Now listen to the interviewer from Exercise 2 again.
Repeat what she says and copy the intonation.

USE OF ENGLISH

Short questions to show surprise in conversations

We can use short questions to show that we're surprised by something that other people have said.

A: **I came** first in a singing competition.

B: **Did you**?

A: **I could** speak three languages by the age of 6.

B: **Could you**?

A: **I'm** going to study abroad next year.

B: **Are you**?

You need to use negative questions to show surprise about responses that have negative verb forms.

A: **I've never** been on a plane before.

B: **Haven't you**?

A: **I won't** be taking part in the race tomorrow.

B: **Won't you**?

A: I **didn't** like the travel blog Peter recommended.

B: **Didn't you**?

8   Work in pairs. Have a conversation about one of the topics below. While you're talking, remember to show surprise and sound interested. To do that, use short questions from the Use of English box and rising and falling intonation.

- Your favourite hobby
- Your future dreams
- Something you're really proud of
- A time when you took part in a competition

9   You are going to interview another student about one of their achievements. First, think about the questions you can use to ask about the following:

- how it all started, and why
- the challenges they faced
- how they felt at different stages (for example, at the start and at the end)
- the outcomes / how they achieved their aim
- how they have benefitted from the process / experience
- what they're planning to do next.

10   Work in pairs and interview your partner. Remember to sound interested and to show surprise. Then exchange roles and give answers to your partner's questions.

SPEAKING TIP

Using appropriate language in different situations

It is important to choose the right phrases to fit the situation. For example, it would be wrong to say 'How amazing' when someone tells you something sad. Instead you should say 'How awful' or 'I'm so sorry to hear that'. By using the wrong phrases, you could make people feel uncomfortable or embarrassed. It is important to listen carefully to what other people say.

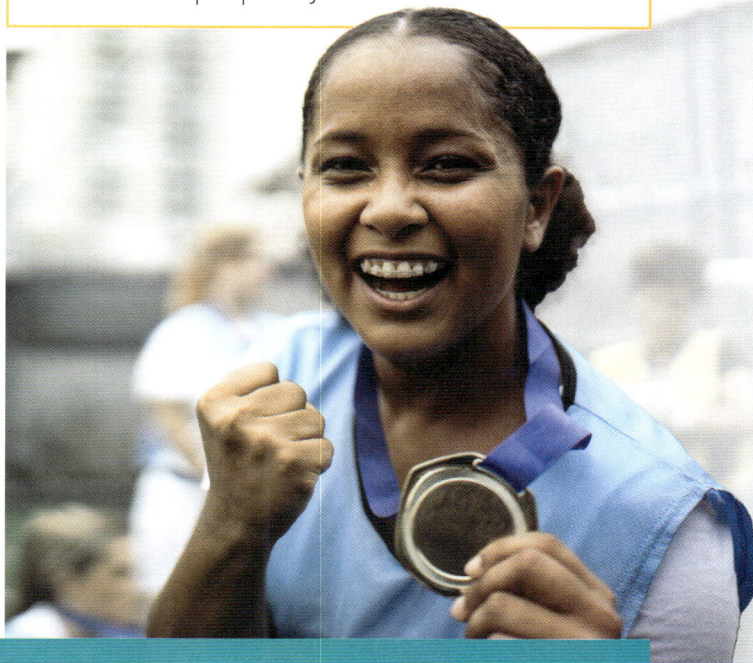

Improve your writing: Describe a journey in a blog

1   You are going to read short entries from a blog about a journey made on a skateboard. In pairs, look at the photo. Discuss what challenges the writer may have had on his journey.

2   Read the blog. What challenges does the writer mention? Were you right about them in Exercise 1?

3   Read the blog again. The entries are mixed up. Can you put them in the correct order? What helped you decide on the order?

4   Blogs are written for many different reasons. In pairs, look at Mateo's blog entries and answer the questions below.

   a   What do you think the main purpose of the blog is?

      A   entertain and inform the readers

      B   advise the readers where to go on holiday

      C   review the latest models of skateboards

      D   encourage the readers to become more adventurous

   b   Who do you think the intended audience is?

      A   geography students

      B   holiday makers

      C   the wider public

      D   business people

   c   What is the register of most travel blogs?

      A   very informal

      B   informal to semi-formal

      C   semi-formal

      D   very formal

   d   Why do you think this register is the most appropriate one for travel blogs?

   e   The choice of vocabulary and other language features need to match the register. What vocabulary and language features does Mateo use in his blog to match the register? Give examples.

   f   The blog entries that describe Mateo's experiences on his journey are similar to:

      A   a story

      B   a review

      C   an article

      D   a report

   g   Mateo also involves the readers. How does he do that?

1   Yesterday the annoying wind still hadn't stopped and it was blowing much harder. To make things worse, it was raining as well. Despite all my waterproof clothing, I was beginning to notice that the awful rain was starting to get through my clothes. I really needed to find shelter and dry off. The last thing I wanted was to get sick on the road. I kept on moving, even though my knee didn't feel quite right. 'I really need a break,' I thought to myself. Luckily, I was just passing through this picturesque village in Switzerland called Chexbres, just above Lake Geneva. The views were spectacular, even in the grim weather. I started thinking that all this effort going up the hill was really worth it. I just needed to find somewhere where I could put up my tent and get out of my soaking wet clothes. Suddenly, I heard a friendly voice saying something in French. I turned around and saw a kind face. In my broken French, I explained what I was doing there. I couldn't believe that this old guy invited me to his home. That night I had a warm dinner and slept in a comfortable bed. Just what I needed! I told Monsieur Chobaz I'd mention his name in my blog – so there you have it, Monsieur Chobaz – I've kept my promise! ☺ I just want to say a huge thank you for your unlimited generosity.

2   I came very close to breaking the world record set by Rob Thomson in 2007. I was 2160 kilometres short. Sadly, it wasn't meant to be this time, but there's always next time. Nevertheless, what I learnt on the way, the people I met, the stories I heard, the generosity I received and the personal victories I achieved will stay with me forever. So until the next time…

3   Hi, I'm Mateo and I'm crazy about skateboarding. In my native Costa Rica, I work as a civil engineer. But I work to live, I don't live to work – so any free time I get, I grab my skateboard and hit the road. I love the freedom it gives me. This year I've decided to take some time out and do something crazy – to break a world record by going on the longest skateboarding journey ever attempted. So here's my story.

4   The sun was beginning to rise and it was starting to feel noticeably warmer. Unfortunately, the roads on this stretch of the journey weren't very smooth. The rough surface wasn't doing the wheels any favours, not to mention my knees. I had already had to change the wheels twice. I was skating down the road when a water deer jumped out of nowhere, right in front of me. I swerved to the side, but lost my balance and landed in a ditch by the side of the road. Luckily, it was a soft landing thanks to all the grass and moss. But that wasn't the worst thing – as I picked up my board, I noticed one wheel had come off. I didn't feel like fixing the wheel, so I just sat down on a rock to enjoy the breathtaking landscape. I was near the end of my whole adventure, not far from Shanghai, and I started thinking about the journey I'd already completed and the journey still ahead of me. I could hear the bustling city only a few kilometres away. Then, out of the blue, I could hear kids' voices whispering. There was a group of five kids looking very curious. I couldn't speak any Mandarin, but I showed them the missing wheel and they immediately understood. They signalled to me that I should follow them, so I did. I couldn't believe it when they took me to their father's repair shop and he was able to fix my wheel. Once again, I was reminded of people's generosity and kindness.

5   It all started on the 8th June 2018. My journey was 12,000 kilometres long and it took me through three continents. I completed my journey in one year, two months and 26 days. It all started in the United States, California. I crossed the States, flew over to Europe and intended to carry on through some parts of Asia and finish back in the States.

Interested in following my story? Then click on the individual places in my journey to find out more.

WRITING TIP

Making writing more interesting

When you are writing about an experience that happened to you (such as in a story or a blog), try to make it interesting for the reader by:

- using adverbs and other phrases to increase the excitement (for example, *suddenly*) and link ideas

- avoiding adjectives such as *good* and *nice* and using more precise adjectives that help the reader imagine the situation better (for example, *breathtaking*)

- talking directly to the reader (for example, *Interested in my story?*)

- including your thoughts in the story (for example, '*I really need a break*', *I thought to myself*).

5 Read extract A again. Can you find examples of vocabulary for categories a–c? An example of each has been done for you.

a Adverbs and other phrases used to **add excitement** and to **link ideas**: *to make things worse…*

b Positive adjectives used instead of **nice** or **good**: *picturesque*

c Negative adjectives used instead of **bad**: *annoying*

6 Read this entry from a travel blog. Then discuss in pairs whether you enjoyed reading it. How could this text be improved? Rewrite the text using some of the words from Exercise 5.

> I was visiting Quebec, in the French part of Canada, for the first time. I was walking through the city centre. I realised I'd left my phone in the hotel room. The streets were nice, so I just carried on walking. I started to feel tired and hungry. I didn't know where I was. The weather was getting bad. I hurried inside a nearby restaurant. I sat down and ordered some food. It was very nice. I asked for the bill, but I couldn't find my wallet – I'd left it in the hotel room as well. One man was really nice and paid my bill. This is how I met Frederic. He became my best friend.

USE OF ENGLISH

Past simple, past continuous and past perfect simple used in storytelling

When you write about something that happened in the past, you should use a range of forms.

We use the **past continuous** to describe an action that lasted for a longer period of time and to set the scene of the story. It is often used in the opening paragraph.

*The sun **was beginning** to rise…* (was/were + -ing form)

We use the **past simple** to say what happened in the story. The actions are short and listed in the order they happen in the story.

*I just **sat** down on a rock to enjoy the breathtaking landscape.* (-ed form for regular verbs, past simple forms for irregular verbs)

We use the **past perfect** to show that one action happened or started before the events in the story. It is often used with the adverbs *already*, *never* and *just*.

*I **had** already **had** to change the wheels twice.* (had + past participle)

Read blog entry 4 and find more examples of all three forms. Think about why we need to use them.

7   **Complete these sentences with the past simple, past continuous or past perfect. Use the verbs in brackets.**

a   When I _____ (get) to the cinema, the film _____ (already start), so I _____ (miss) the beginning.

b   My sister _____ (turn up) just as the film _____ (end), so I _____ (feel) a bit annoyed with her about this.

c   My younger brother _____ (not want) to tell me what _____ (happen), but I _____ (can) tell that something was wrong.

d   The minute I _____ (close) the door, I _____ (know) my friends were up to something. When I _____ (walk) into the room, they _____ (start) singing happy birthday to me. They _____ (decorate) the room and _____ (even bake) a cake for me. I _____ (feel) very emotional.

8   **You are going to write a blog entry about a journey that you have made. Look at the outline below and write down some ideas.**

- Describe the scene at the start of the journey:
- Say what happened at the start of the journey:
- Add details – who with / where / when:
- How you felt:
- Explain why you think this happened:
- What happened next:
- What happened at the end:
- How you feel about the experience now:
- What you have learnt from the experience:

9   **Use your plan from Exercise 8 to write your blog entry. Then exchange it with another student. Proofread their work and check that they have included everything in the checklist below. Then give each other feedback.**

Have they included…
✓   adverbs?
✓   a range of adjectives to describe something?
✓   past continuous to set the scene?
✓   past simple to list the events?
✓   past perfect to say something happened before the main story?

10   **Rewrite your blog entry based on your partner's feedback.**

Project challenge

PROJECT LEARNING OBJECTIVES

In this project, you will…

- consider different views objectively

- discuss ideas and make suggestions

- evaluate arguments and reach a conclusion.

PROJECT OPTION 1

Research and write a report

Your school is trying to be more environmentally friendly. Your class has been asked to research how eco-friendly your last school trip was and how future trips could reduce the school's carbon footprint.

Step 1: In small groups, research what human activities increase the carbon footprint, and what people can do to reduce it. Then discuss which of these activities are likely to happen during school trips.

Step 2: Copy the table below. Think about your last school trip and fill in the information in the 'Last school trip' column. Then discuss whether the activities contributed to the rise of the carbon footprint, and how.

You can use online carbon footprint calculators to help you.

Step 3: In your group, brainstorm ideas about how your next school trip could be made eco-friendlier and reduce your school's carbon footprint. Add your ideas to the table in the 'Next school trip' column.

Step 4: Present your suggestions about how to make your next school trip eco-friendlier to the class. Listen to other groups' suggestions. Vote on the eco-friendliest trip.

Step 5: Using the information from your table, write a report for the headteacher. In your report, say how eco-friendly your last school trip was. Then suggest improvements for the next trip that could lower the school's carbon footprint. Write about 120–160 words.

	Last school trip	Next school trip
Travelled from… to…		
Distance travelled		
Means of transport		
School trip activities		
Food and drinks consumed		
Type of litter produced		

CRITICAL THINKING

Carrying out research on public opinion

When you are working on a project to help improve things for the public, it is a good idea to do a survey to find out what the public think first. You should then consider their opinions before you make your final decision.

SPEAKING TIP

Reporting results and expressing your opinion

You can use the following phrases:

- *Most students thought that…, which I find really surprising.*

- *Some students suggested…, which I think is a very good idea.*

PROJECT OPTION 2

Write a questionnaire and design a webpage

Your local authorities want to encourage more tourists of all ages to come and visit the area where you live. They have invited you to write a questionnaire about popular tourist sights and design a webpage to promote them.

Step 1: In small groups, prepare a questionnaire for other students, to find out what the interesting sights in your local area are and what tourists can do there. Decide what questions you want to ask about the sights and activities.

For example: *Is this activity suitable for all ages? How much time would the tourists need to see the old town?*

Step 2: Interview other students in your class using your questionnaire. Take notes of their answers.

Step 3: In your group, compare the outcomes of the questionnaire. What sights and activities did other students mention, and why? Discuss what you think about their suggestions. Then decide on the following:

- which sights and activities you want to include on your webpage

- what type of tourists you would like to target (for example, young families with children, young adults, pensioners)

- what other information should be included (for example, the admission fee).

Step 4: Before you design your webpage to promote your town to tourists, look at a few similar webpages promoting tourist destinations. Discuss what makes an interesting webpage.

Step 5: Decide in your group what you want to include on your webpage and who is going to be responsible for the different tasks (for example, the text, the photos). Then design your webpage.

Step 6: Present your webpage to the class. Then vote on the best one and explain why you like it.

SELF AND PEER ASSESSMENT

Think about how well you, and your group, did in the project. Then complete the statements below.

a   Our group worked particularly well in the following activities:…

b   I really enjoyed working with… because he/she…

c   While doing this project, I learnt that I'm really good at… and I enjoy…

d   However, I need to practise… a bit more.

e   I learnt… and, in the future, this will help me…

Practise and prepare

Speaking

1   **Work in pairs. Read the task below. Spend one minute preparing what you want to say. Then give your talk.**

> You have been planning your next summer holiday and what you would like to do. You are considering the following options:
>
> - helping your relative in the shop they own
>
> - visiting your cousin who lives abroad.
>
> Talk about the advantages and disadvantages of both options. Then say which one you would prefer, and why.

EXAM TIP

Plan before you write

It is very important that you plan your answer before you start writing. Brainstorm ideas and write them down. Then look at the ideas and plan which ideas can go together in the same paragraph. Finally, decide which order you want to put the paragraphs in. Also, check whether you've included everything that the question asks you for. Then you are ready to start writing your answer.

Writing

2   **You have just travelled to a place you have never been before. Write to a friend about it. Write about 120–160 words.**

In your email you should:

- describe the place you went to

- say what you enjoyed most about the trip

- explain what you have learnt from this trip.

Reading

3   Read the article below about Alyssa Carson, a girl who wants to live on Mars. Imagine you are going to give a talk about Alyssa to your classmates. Use words from the article to help you write some notes under these headings:

- Reasons for Alyssa's interest in space (give two details)

- Challenges before and during Alyssa's space training (give three details)

- Alyssa's plans before going to Mars. (give two details)

The girl who would like to live on Mars

As children, we are often asked the question "What do you want to do when you grow up?" and most often, we want to become sports professionals, princesses, adventurers or astronauts. As children, we believe that anything is possible but, regrettably, most of us give up on our dreams.

Not Alyssa Carson, though. At the age of three, she already dreamed of being involved in space exploration. "My father told me about the moon landings," she recalls. That got her curious about space and the possibility of going there. And after watching some videos about space exploration and reading books on the same topic, there was no stopping her. By the age of seven, she knew Mars was her destination and attended her first space camp in Alabama.

Space camps provide space programs, and training for children and adults alike. Some of the attendees who graduated from the space camps have become astronauts. Alyssa has attended six of these space camps, completing the training programs there, and is hoping she will become one of the lucky ones too. However, it hasn't always been easy to be taken seriously at such a young age in that industry. She explains that her older peers "have always been welcoming and nurtured my interest in space, but at the same time, I've always had the feeling I had to prove myself, and I had to show that I was just as skilled or could contribute just as well."

Alyssa loves space, so no matter what challenges she has to face, she is full of determination. However, she also thinks it's important not just to focus on her dreams of travelling to space; she definitely intends to take time out for fun and other activities too. This will help her keep the right balance in her life, something she has managed quite well so far, despite being busy.

As part of her training, Alyssa practised being in zero gravity, high up in the sky, and also deep under water. "The scariest experience was definitely my water survival training." Plus doing all the tasks in a space suit doesn't make things any less difficult, but Alyssa said it was also the one she learnt the most from. Once people learn to trust themselves and their abilities, any obstacle becomes manageable.

Right now, the mission to travel to Mars is set for the early 2030s. "This is great because I still have to finish school," she explains. Alyssa's practical nature keeps her relaxed about the upcoming mission and the role she will be playing, but she definitely intends to get some work experience before applying.

REFLECTION

1   Work in small groups and look at the image at the start of the lesson. What do you think it could symbolise? Then discuss what type of journeys and adventures are described in this unit. Are there all physical journeys? What can you learn from each type of journey/adventure?

2   With a partner, use these questions to help you reflect on your progress as a learner while working on this unit.

   a   In the Think about it lesson, you practised listening for general ideas and for specific detail. Which type of listening do you find easier? What can you listen to in order to practise the other type of listening? Give examples.

   b   In the Geography lesson, you practised summarising a text. Did you find this skill challenging? Why or why not? Will this skill be useful to have in other school subjects? Give examples.

   c   In the Talk about it lesson, you learnt how to respond appropriately and how to sound interested. After this lesson, have you changed anything you do when you're having a conversation in English? Give some examples. How will this skill help you in other subjects, or in the future?

   d   In the Improve your writing lesson, you practised using the past simple, past continuous and past perfect. Which form did you find easy to use and which one did you find difficult? What are you going to do to practise this form more and become more confident when using it?

   e   In the Project challenge lesson, you practised researching information. Do you enjoy doing research? Why or why not? Do you prefer getting information from a text online or from interviewing people face to face? Explain your preference.

   f   In the Practise and prepare lesson, did you follow the tip on planning before writing? Did the tip help you? How did you plan your answer in the writing exercise? In what other subjects can you apply this tip?

SUMMARY CHECKLIST

I can…

- [ ] follow a talk and select the correct specific details as well as ideas.
- [ ] read a text, select relevant information and summarise the text.
- [ ] respond appropriately and sound interested when I'm having a conversation with someone.
- [ ] write a blog describing a journey and make my writing interesting for the reader.
- [ ] use a range of grammatical structures in my writing to describe past events.
- [ ] reach a conclusion based on the opinions of other people.

6 Making a change

GETTING STARTED

"We're still in the first minutes of the first day of the internet revolution."
(Scott Cook, American businessman)

What do you, and other people you know, use the internet for?
Do you think you'll use the internet more or less in the near future? Why?

Watch this!

Think about it: Living with smart technology

● Is smart technology always a good thing?

Vocabulary

3 Look at the vocabulary box and check the meaning of the words and phrases you don't know. Use a reliable dictionary to help you.

avatar	screen time
crop a photo	smart technology
digital detox	social media account
digital equality	
freeze	store data in the cloud
have access to	touchscreen
reliable wi-fi connection	virtual reality

Listening

1 Look at the six photographs. Work in pairs and discuss these questions.

a Can you name the digital devices in each photo?

b What activities have these devices made easier for people?

c Have these devices created new problems? What do you think they are?

2 Listen to three podcasts on the topic of living with smart technology. Which digital devices from photos A–F does each speaker mention? Which device is the main topic of each podcast?

LISTENING TIP

Understanding implied attitudes

When speakers talk about their attitudes to something, for example their feelings or opinions, this information is often implied. This means that the speaker doesn't say directly what they think about something. Instead, you have to listen to what the speaker suggests. For example, if the speaker says 'my friends tell me I'm always looking at a screen', the speaker implies that they spend too much time online.

Listening

4   Listen to the three podcasts again. Answer the questions below. Then compare your answers in pairs and discuss which of the three attitudes is most similar to your attitude, and how.

   a   Does each speaker have a very positive, quite negative or mixed attitude to technology? Explain your opinion.

   b   Has their life become easier or more difficult as a result of modern technology? Give examples.

5   The speakers in the podcasts mentioned some issues that modern technology has created. In small groups, look at the issues and discuss what they are about. Then discuss the questions.

- FOMO (fear of missing out)
- digital inequality
- peer pressure
- the amount of screen time
- becoming addicted to smart devices
- the need for digital detox
- difficulty switching off
- living in virtual reality

   a   How serious are the issues, and why?

   b   Are there any other issues caused by modern technology?

USE OF ENGLISH

Multi-word verbs

In Unit 1, you learnt some multi-word verbs. These are verbs that consist of one common verb, such as *go*, *turn*, *look*, and two or three particles, such as *on*, *off*, *over*. Sometimes the meaning of the multi-word verb is easy to guess as it has the same or very similar meaning to the common verb used in it. However, sometimes the meaning is quite different. Compare these two examples:

I **printed out** too many pages.

Print out has the same meaning as *print* on its own.

I always **back up** all my files.

The meaning of *back up* is very different from the meaning of *back*. *Back up* means to copy your files so that you have another copy in case something goes wrong.

---

6   The speakers in the podcasts use some multi-word verbs. Listen to them again and write down the multi-word verbs that you hear. Then compare your answers in pairs.

7   Look at the definitions below. Can you match the multi-word verbs from Exercise 6 to their correct definitions below? If necessary, use a reliable dictionary to help you.

   a   when you put numbers together and calculate the total

   b   to be looking for something in particular

   c   to think of ideas or to find solutions to something

   d   to organise something (such as a celebration)

   e   to find the time to do something

   f   to get interrupted, usually because of a bad connection

   g   to start or create something

   h   to continue to use or practise something

   i   to stop thinking about something and start relaxing your mind

Speaking

8   Use the multi-word verbs from Exercise 6 to make sentences about yourself and smart technology. Then work in pairs and use these sentences as a dialogue opener to have a discussion with your partner.

For example:

   A: 'I spend quite a lot of time online. It can add up to about eight hours a day.'

   B: 'Wow, that's quite a lot, isn't it? Do you have enough time to do anything else, like meeting your friends?'

Technology: Robots are the future

- **Does our society need robots?**

Reading

1   In small groups, think of three jobs where robots are already used to help people and discuss how essential the robots are in these jobs. Then compare your ideas with other groups.

> **READING TIP**
>
> **Dealing with unknown vocabulary**
>
> When we read texts for pleasure or to understand the general idea of the whole text, we don't always have to understand all the words to be able to follow the text. That is why you shouldn't stop reading every time you get to a word you don't understand.

2   Read the article about the use of robots in six different jobs and areas of life. What are the six examples? Are any of these examples the same as yours from Exercise 1?

³⁰ **sewage pipes:** the pipes that carry used water and other waste away from people's houses

1   Do you think robots have already helped you in your life? If your answer is no, then think again. The number of robots around the world is increasing rapidly. And it's said that automation will threaten more than 800 million jobs worldwide by 2030.

2   ⁵ If you eat rice, the chances are that every grain you consume is sorted by a robotic machine with a lightning-fast vision system. These machines are an incredible example of automation and most people have no idea they exist. All the grains of rice you buy in a bag at the supermarket look the ¹⁰ same colour because every grain of rice passes through a robotic machine that uses very high-speed cameras, lights and a computer where it is graded. Jets of air are turned on and off to move each grain into the correct bin. This happens hundreds of times per second. In fact, rice is not the only food ¹⁵ that is sorted by robots; robotic machines also sort wheat, seeds and pulses such as beans, lentils and peas.

3   When we go to see a healthcare professional, they're definitely human, but did you know that many nurses, paramedics and doctors now train on robot patients? These ²⁰ robots can simulate various conditions and give medical students the opportunity to practise treating patients. Some of these robots are life-sized and look like a real person, but some represent an arm, for example.

4   Some medications that people have to take to prevent ²⁵ malaria, for example, may use scorpion venom as one of the ingredients. The extraction of venom from scorpions is quite dangerous for people but a completely safe job for a robot.

5   We don't often think about our sewers, but when they go wrong, it is not pleasant. Fatbergs, which are large masses ³⁰ of fat collected in sewage pipes over a period of time, have become a major problem in many cities around the world. Sewer checks and maintenance are more important than ever before, and inspection workers now have robots to help them.

6   Jobs in education also benefit from robots, and some schools ³⁵ may well look to robots as an alternative to human tutors very soon. Robots are expected to improve teaching by providing services such as greater individualised learning. Yuki, the first robot lecturer, was introduced in Germany in 2019. Yuki has already started delivering lectures to university students at ⁴⁰ one German university. The robot also acts as a teaching assistant during lectures. It evaluates how students are doing academically, and what kind of support they need. Some students have found Yuki useful – despite the fact that it still requires some significant improvements to be fully functional.

7   ⁴⁵ So that's just five ways that robots may have helped you recently, or will do so in the near future. Of course, there are many more examples of how robots help us. The point is that the so-called 'robot revolution' that is often talked about in the media is already happening, but not many of us have ⁵⁰ noticed yet.

ACADEMIC LANGUAGE

Technology and robotics

automation	high-speed cameras
extraction	life-sized robots
fully functional	maintenance
grade something	simulate a situation
grow / increase rapidly	threaten jobs

3   Look at your answers from Exercise 2. What related vocabulary helped you decide on the jobs and areas where robots are used? Make a mind map for each job and area with the related vocabulary.

4   Read the text again and answer these questions.

   a   In paragraph 1, why do you think the author mentions how many jobs done by people may be lost because of robots?

   b   What is the author's opinion of the robots used to sort out food, like rice grains? Give an example from the text.

   c   The author talks about medical students training on robots instead of real patients. What do you think the benefits of this are? Explain your opinion.

   d   What global issue do robots help with in a lot of urban areas?

   e   What two examples does the author give to show the benefits of using robots in schools?

   f   What do you think was the author's main purpose for writing this article?

Speaking

5   In small groups, discuss why you think robots, rather than people, need to be used in the jobs and areas mentioned in the article. Was there anything in the article that surprised you? Why?

USE OF ENGLISH

Expressing probability and certainty

In Unit 4, you studied modal verbs used to express probability and certainty. Now look at some other phrases and verb forms you can use to do the same.

Probability

*…**the chances are** that every grain you consume is sorted by a robotic machine…*

*…some schools **may well** look to robots as an alternative to human tutors very soon.*

Certainty

*…and it's said that automation **will** threaten more than 800 million jobs worldwide by 2030.*

6   In pairs, discuss how you think robots can be used in the places listed below. Are there any tasks that can't be done by robots? Would you be happy to be helped by robots? Why or why not? Use the phrases from the Use of English box.

- in hospitals
- in classrooms
- in hotels
- in restaurants
- in laboratories
- in space
- in people's homes
- in factories
- in laboratories

Writing

7   Write a short article for your school magazine discussing whether you think robots will do all human jobs in the future. Use the information and language you learnt in this lesson. Write about 120–160 words.

Talk about it: Living online

- **Do you think family members spend enough time together?**

Watch this!

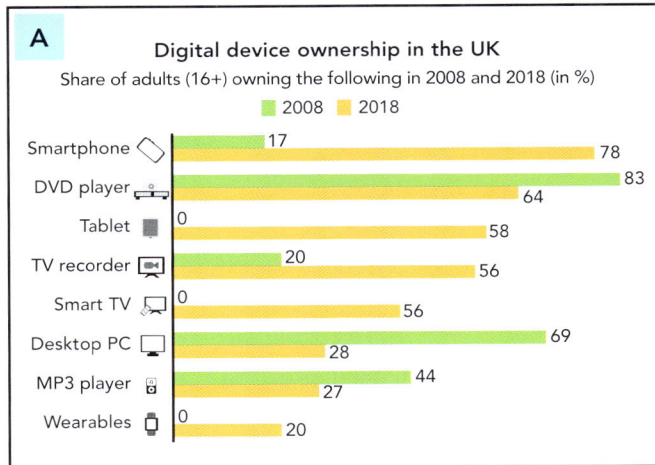

A

Digital device ownership in the UK

Share of adults (16+) owning the following in 2008 and 2018 (in %)

2008 | 2018

Device	2008	2018
Smartphone	17	78
DVD player	83	64
Tablet	0	58
TV recorder	20	56
Smart TV	0	56
Desktop PC	69	28
MP3 player	44	27
Wearables	0	20

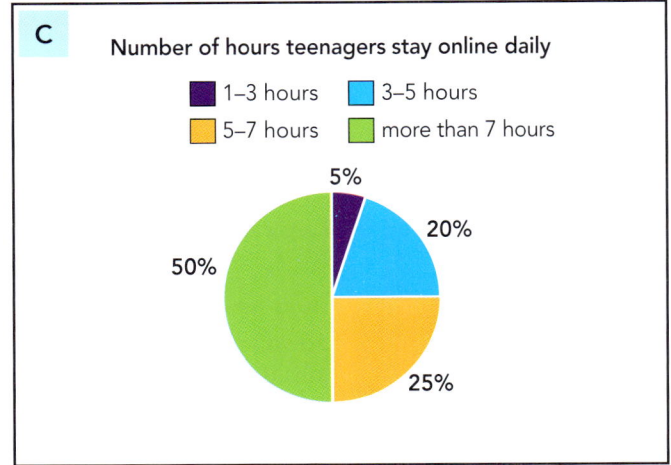

C

Number of hours teenagers stay online daily

1–3 hours | 3–5 hours
5–7 hours | more than 7 hours

5% | 20% | 25% | 50%

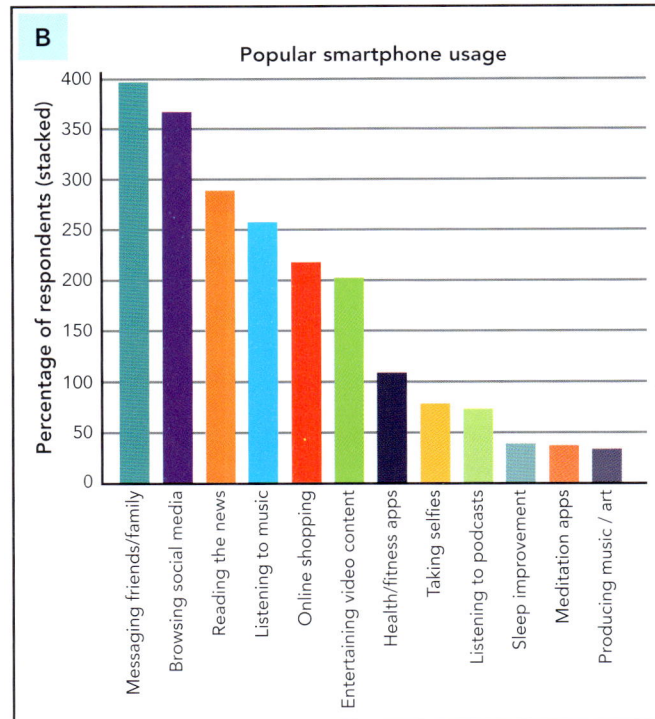

B

Popular smartphone usage

Percentage of respondents (stacked)

- Messaging friends/family
- Browsing social media
- Reading the news
- Listening to music
- Online shopping
- Entertaining video content
- Health/fitness apps
- Taking selfies
- Listening to podcasts
- Sleep improvement
- Meditation apps
- Producing music / art

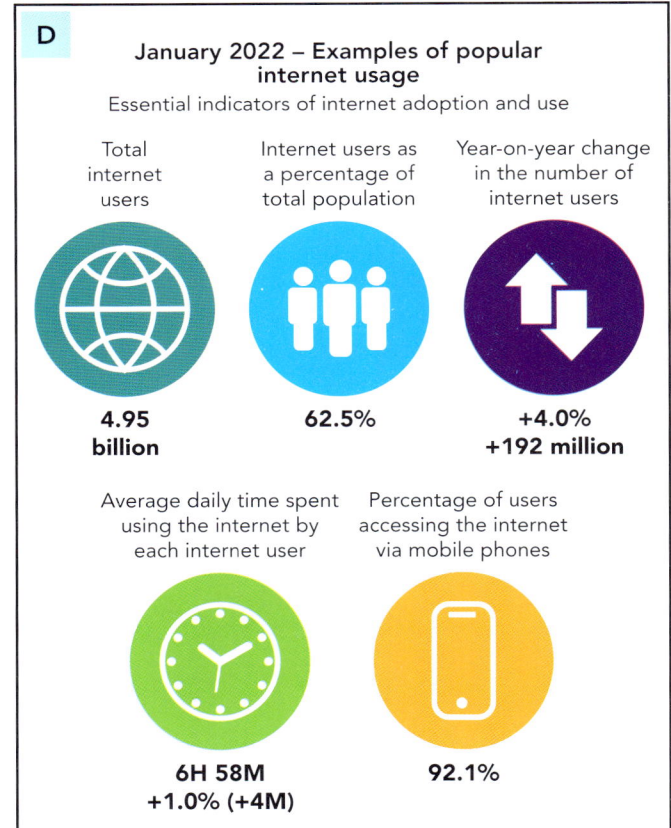

D

January 2022 – Examples of popular internet usage

Essential indicators of internet adoption and use

Total internet users
4.95 billion

Internet users as a percentage of total population
62.5%

Year-on-year change in the number of internet users
+4.0%
+192 million

Average daily time spent using the internet by each internet user
6H 58M
+1.0% (+4M)

Percentage of users accessing the internet via mobile phones
92.1%

Speaking

> **STUDY TIP**
>
> **Using different diagrams**
>
> There are many different types of diagrams, but the most common are pie charts (see diagram C in Exercise 1) and bar charts (see diagram B). Pie charts are often used to show percentages and amounts of the same category, while bar charts can be used to show percentages and amounts for different aspects of one particular topic. Remember to choose the type of diagram that shows the information you want in the clearest possible way.

1 **Look at diagrams A–D. Then work in pairs to answer these questions.**

- a What information do the diagrams show?
- b Is there anything that surprises you about the data that they show? Why or why not?
- c Is the information in the diagrams very similar or different to what you do? Give examples.

Listening

34

2 **Listen to a student giving a presentation about the use of the internet and other digital devices. In which order does she mention diagrams A–D? What helped you decide on the order of the diagrams?**

3 **Work in five groups. Each group will focus on one of the categories below. First copy your category into your notebook. Then listen to the presentation again and write down examples of phrases for your category.**

- a telling the listener which diagram to look at/moving on to the next diagram
- b introducing what information the diagram shows
- c explaining what the data or results mean
- d saying that some facts are interesting or unusual
- e making a final conclusion

4 **Work in a new group with students who listened to different phrases to you. Share all the phrases together and write them in your notebook in the correct category. Continue to work with new groups until you have all of the phrases.**

5 **Choose one of diagrams A–D. Copy these sentence starters and complete them with the information from your chosen diagram.**

- This diagram shows…
- From this diagram we can also see…
- The data seems to suggest that…
- The results indicate that…
- You may find this fact surprising, but…
- Looking at the diagram, we can conclude that…

6 **You are going to interview other classmates about similar topics to diagrams A–D for a survey. Work in groups and choose one of the topics below. Write down the question(s) you want to ask other students about your topic. Then carry out your survey.**

- popular digital devices
- uses of smartphones
- screen time

7 **Use the results from your survey to make a suitable diagram. Then prepare a short presentation about your findings. Deliver your presentation to the class, remembering to use the phrases from Exercises 3 and 4. How similar were your findings to the information in diagrams A–D?**

> **CRITICAL THINKING**
>
> **What can impact your survey results**
>
> It is important to remember that certain circumstances can affect what the results of a survey might be, for example the participants' age, gender, background, previous experience of the topic, etc. This means the results can be very different from one specific group to another. If you want your results to be as objective and as wide-ranging as possible, it is important to do a survey among a very mixed group of people.

Improve your writing: A discursive essay

1 **In small groups, discuss these questions.**
  a What are the benefits and drawbacks of spending time online or watching television?
  b How many hours a day do you think is a good amount of screen time, and why?
  c Do you think other people, like your parents and teachers, would agree with this? Why or why not?

2 **Read the model essay and find examples of the advantages and disadvantages of screen time for children and young people.**

3 **Compare your ideas in pairs and discuss whether you agree or disagree with these ideas, and explain why.**

4 **In pairs, look at the model essay again. What ideas does each paragraph provide? Match the ideas below to the correct paragraph. Then find examples of phrases that are used to introduce the ideas in paragraphs 1 and 4.**
  a personal opinion with a short explanation
  b arguments against with examples
  c conclusion
  d arguments for with examples
  e introduction to the topic
  f general view(s)

USE OF ENGLISH

Linking words and phrases (contrast and addition)

To link two opposing ideas, use linking words and phrases of contrast. Study the examples below.

These phrases are followed by a complete sentence:

On one hand, I really wanted to stay at home and play the new computer game.

On the other hand, I knew Mark would be upset if I cancelled our meeting.

Although there are so many ads, I love the new music app.

CONTINUED

Even though is used in the same way.

These linking words are quite formal and are followed by a complete sentence:

The internet enables people to see places they could never go to see in real life. **However**, *people enjoy a new experience more when it's shared with **other people.***

Nevertheless is used in the same way.

These linking words are followed by a noun or a noun phrase:

Despite parents being worried, children benefit from spending time online.

In spite of is used in the same way

To link two similar ideas, use linking words and phrases of addition. Look at the examples below.

These linking words are followed by a noun or a noun phrase:

As well as playing computer games, she loves playing basketball with her friends in the local park.

In addition to... is used in the same way, but is more formal

These linking words are used between two complete sentences:

Children can learn a lot of interesting facts from the internet. **Moreover**, *they become more aware of global issues.*

Furthermore, *what is more* and *additionally* are used in the same way, and all three are quite formal.

Look at all the examples again and notice how we use the linking words and phrases.

5 **Read the model essay again and find examples of the linking words and phrases from the Use of English box. Notice how they are used.**

1. It is often said that children spend too much time online or using other digital devices these days. Many parents worry that screen time is harmful for their children and try to limit it to only a few hours a week, which can cause tension between the two generations.

2. On the one hand, the internet is a great source of information. Children can use educational sites to practise what they have been studying at school, or simply to research information for projects and other school work. Being able to go online also means that children can stay in touch with relatives who don't live near them or with friends who have moved away. Keeping up to date with our loved ones is very important for our well-being and would be much harder without the internet and digital devices. The digital world also brings the outside world closer to people. Nowadays, people don't have to travel far away and spend a lot of money to see famous tourist sites or art exhibitions in galleries around the world. University students can follow their lectures even if they're unwell and have to stay at home. Without any access to screen time, none of this would be possible.

3. On the other hand, it is important to be aware of how easy it is to become addicted to digital devices. This could have a negative impact on people's well-being, as everybody needs to spend some time outdoors and with other human beings. Despite the fact that digital devices can provide entertainment, they should never replace real friends and family. Also, too much screen time can create a feeling of anxiety in some people. They become scared of missing out on something that may be important to them if they go offline. In addition, spending a long time looking at a screen or sitting in the same position can cause harm to our physical health. Some experts also warn about relying too much on various applications that do things for us, for example reminding us what to buy. This may lead to people losing the ability to remember things.

4. On balance, I am of the opinion that in our highly digitalised world, it is absolutely impossible to avoid using digital devices and, therefore, spending time looking at a screen. Nevertheless, people should be aware of how much time they spend online or looking at their digital devices. That's why I feel that parents need to ensure that their children are given an amount of screen time that not only suits their needs, but is also appropriate for their age.

6   Work in groups of three. Each of you chooses one of texts A, B or C. Read what
    the writer says about screen time and modern technology. Then tell the others
    in your group what you found out and discuss whether you agree or disagree
    with the ideas.

A We need to look at the research as a whole. The impact of screen time on children and young adults is still being debated. More and more experts are starting to suggest that we should focus on what our children are doing online and not so much on how long they spend there. We can't ignore the fact that interacting with computers improves hand–eye coordination and students are likely to perform better academically. Technology also takes away physical barriers, promotes greater respect and celebrates differences. But there are some downsides too. For example, people born after 2000 are more forgetful than people who grew up before the internet era. When people know they'll be able to find information easily online, they're less likely to memorise it.

B My mum often asks me where I learnt some of the interesting facts I know. She is surprised when I tell her I read them online. I think she's pleased that I know so much thanks to the internet and she doesn't limit my screen time, but I know she worries about me. That's why I always reassure her that we have so many lessons at school about how to stay safe online. My friends and I look out for each other. I think, thanks to the internet, our generation is big on respecting others and I'm proud of that.

C When people say my children would be better off reading a book than spending time online, I say there are just as many bad books out there as there are inspiring things online. Just because something's online doesn't mean it's bad. I think the internet is great for kids, but we have to watch out for online bullying and other dangers that the internet has presented. But that's what parents do – they make sure their children are safe, just like our parents had to in the past. The difference then was that it didn't happen online. I feel we, as parents, have to set rules and make sure our children stick to them.

7 Use the ideas from texts A–C to make sentences. To link the ideas together, use the most appropriate linking words or phrases from the Use of English box.

8 You are going to write a discursive essay about a topic related to technology. Choose one of the topics below.

> learning online
> computer games
> social media
> artificial intelligence
> smartphone applications
> communication between people
> digital technology and different generations

9 Follow the plan below to help you prepare for your essay. Copy the boxes and write down some notes with your ideas. You can also use some of the ideas from Exercise 6.

Introduction
- What is the general view about this topic?

↓

Main body of the essay 1
- What are the arguments for?
- What are the benefits/advantages?
- Why do people enjoy this?
- What do people find easy about this?

↓

Main body of the essay 2
- What are the arguments against?
- What are the drawbacks/disadvantages?
- Why do people criticise this?
- What do people find difficult about this?

↓

Conclusion
- What is your personal opinion about the topic?
- Which arguments do you agree more with, the arguments for or against?
Briefly explain your reasons for your view(s).

WRITING TIP

Brainstorming ideas for discursive essays

Sometimes it is difficult to think of ideas for your essay. To help you, try to think what other people may say about the issue (for example, your parents, your best friend, your cousin, someone older and someone younger). Doing this will help you to have a range of ideas for and against to choose from for your essay.

10 Using your notes from Exercise 9, write your essay. Remember to use some of the useful phrases and linking words you have learnt in this lesson.

11 Exchange essays with another student. Read their essay and complete the checklist.

> The essay...
> ✓ is clearly organised in paragraphs and is easy to read
> ✓ has a clear introduction expressing a general view
> ✓ is balanced and contains ideas for as well as against
> ✓ has a clear conclusion expressing a personal view that includes an explanation
> ✓ uses appropriate linking words to join ideas together.

12 Give feedback to your partner using the bulleted list from Exercise 11. Then listen to the feedback your partner gives you. Rewrite your essay based on their feedback.

Project challenge

PROJECT LEARNING OBJECTIVES

In your project you will...

- gather information from other people's opinions
- select the best idea and explain your reasons
- evaluate something you have produced.

PROJECT OPTION 1

Prepare a guide, trial it and respond to feedback

Your school is organising a digital awareness week. The two major areas this year are online safety and digital well-being. Your class has decided to prepare a guide to help people with one of these areas.

Step 1: In small groups, discuss why online safety and digital well-being are important.

Step 2: Decide which area from step 1 you want to focus on. In your group, research what can negatively affect this area and what people should do to prevent this from happening. Take notes of the ideas you find.

Step 3: Now you are going to prepare a guide to raise awareness of the issues you have researched and provide advice on what people should or shouldn't do when they are online.

Together, decide on:

- the age group that would benefit most from your guide
- how many tips you want to include
- how you want to present the information (for example, diagrams, pictures)
- who will be responsible for individual tasks (for example, typing up the tips, preparing diagrams).

Then prepare your guide.

Step 4: Present your guide to the target group (for example, other classmates, your grandparents, younger siblings). Ask them how useful they have found it, how easy it was to follow the information, and why. Take notes of what they say.

Step 5: In groups, analyse the feedback. Decide whether you need to change anything. Produce the final draft of your guide. Then check that it is error-free.

Step 6: Share your guide with the rest of the class. Vote for the best guide and then discuss why the guide deserves to win.

COMMUNICATION

Giving written instructions

It is important to use simple language when writing instructions – don't make your sentences too long. Also, remember that using visual aids such as diagrams helps people understand the instructions much better than only using text. You may also consider recording your instructions for people who cannot see very well and need to listen to instructions rather than read them.

CREATIVITY

Designing slides for a presentation

To make your slides enjoyable, you should consider the following:

- the font(s) used
- a clear layout
- the colour scheme
- other features (for example, audio recordings, sound effects, web links, images)
- how much written text should go on each slide.

You should also consider your target audience (for example, their age, interests) and what they are likely to find attractive.

PROJECT OPTION 2

Prepare a digital presentation using different media

Your school wants to add a webpage to the school website to tell new students what is great about the school. They want their existing students to make a presentation about the school using different media. The best team will be asked to help design the new webpage.

Step 1: In small groups, discuss what is good about your school and why you like studying there. Ask one student to take notes of the ideas.

Step 2: Look at the notes from step 1 and decide which information you want to include in your presentation, for example the location of the school, an interview with a student, a popular event like a sports day, the school library resources. Then decide which information would be best shown as:

- text
- photographs
- audio clips
- video clips

Step 3: Discuss how many slides your presentation should have and what information to include in each slide. Then split your group into smaller teams and decide who will be responsible for each slide.

Step 4: Carry out your task from step 3 and design the slide with the necessary information.

Step 5: Get together with the rest of the group. Compare your slides and put the presentation together.

Step 6: Decide what you are going to say about each slide. As a team, practise giving your presentation with the commentary.

Step 7: Deliver your presentation. Then watch other teams' presentations and decide which presentation represents your school the best.

SELF AND PEER ASSESSMENT

Think about how well you, and your group, did in the project. Then complete the statements below.

a   Our group worked particularly well in the following activities:…

b   I really enjoyed working with… because he/she…

c   While doing this project, I learnt that I'm really good at… and I enjoy…

d   However, I need to practise… a bit more.

e   I learnt… and, in the future, this will help me…

Practise and prepare

Speaking

1   **In pairs, answer these questions as fully as possible.**

   a   Do you think that, in the future, all lessons will be online? Why or why not?

   b   Some people say that computers and other digital devices waste a lot of people's time. What is your opinion?

   c   In some countries, there is an age limit on when children can start using social media. Do you think it's a good idea?

   d   'Parents should decide how much time their children spend online or playing video games.' Do you agree with this idea?

Writing

> **EXAM TIP**
>
> **Answering a question fully in your written answers**
>
> To make sure that you have included all the information the question asks you for in written exams, you should do the following:
>
> •   Before you start writing, read the question carefully and underline all the information you need to include in your answer.
>
> •   After you finish writing, look at the information that you underlined at the start to check one more time that you have included everything.

2   **You did an experiment at school that involved students not using any digital devices for a day. Write an email to your friend about the experiment. Write about 120–160 words.**

   In your email you should:

   •   **describe what you found hard to cope with**

   •   **explain what you have learnt from the experience**

   •   **say whether you will change anything in your life, and why.**

Listening

3   **You will hear a student called Matt give a talk about video games and electronic sports, also known as e-sports. For each question choose the correct answer, A, B or C. Your teacher will play the recording twice.**

a   Matt was surprised when he found out how many video game players…

   A   are from the USA.

   B   are women.

   C   are over 30 years old.

b   Matt claims that thanks to _____ available at the moment, the gaming industry is particularly successful.

   A   the range of digital devices

   B   the reliable internet connections

   C   the affordable video games

c   The video game called _____ was the one that was played at the first official e-sports tournament.

   A   *Street Fighter*

   B   *Space Invaders*

   C   *Donkey Kong*

d   Matt believes that e-sports should be played at the Olympic Games because they…

   A   would attract more audiences.

   B   are as demanding as other sports.

   C   have been played for a long time.

REFLECTION

1   Look at the opening quotation again. Work in pairs and discuss why you think it compares the internet to a revolution. In this unit, you have also learnt about some of the issues that using digital devices can cause. Which ones surprised you the most, and why? What can people do to prevent these issues?

2   Talk to a partner and use these questions to help you reflect on your progress as a learner while working on this unit.

a   In the Think about it lesson, you practised listening to implied attitudes. Did you find it easy or difficult to recognise each speaker's attitude to modern technology? What helped you decide what the attitude was? What else can you do to practise this listening skill?

b   In the Technology lesson, you read an article about robots and how they are used to help people. How did you deal with the new vocabulary in this article while you were reading the text for the first time? Did any of the tips in this lesson help you?

c   In the Talk about it lesson, you practised giving a presentation. Do you think your presentation skills are improving? What do you think you still need to improve?

d   In the Improve your writing lesson, you practised planning your essay and brainstorming ideas before writing your first draft. Did you find the planning stage useful? Why or why not? What helped you think of some ideas for your chosen topic?

e   In the Project challenge lesson, you designed something using digital devices. What would be difficult about the project if you couldn't use the devices? Do you think digital devices help you learn? Why or why not?

f   In the Practise and prepare lesson, you learnt two exam tips. Did you follow these tips? How useful did you find them? Do you think you performed better in the practice questions in this lesson as a result of these two tips? Why or why not?

SUMMARY CHECKLIST

I can…

- [ ] follow a podcast and understand people's attitudes.
- [ ] read a longer text containing unfamiliar vocabulary and understand the main ideas.
- [ ] make a diagram and present the data from the diagram in a presentation.
- [ ] write a discursive essay that includes arguments for and against.
- [ ] join two ideas together to make a longer sentence and use an appropriate linking word or phrase.
- [ ] participate in a discussion about technology and evaluate ideas.

7 Our planet, our home

IN THIS UNIT YOU WILL...

- **listen** to young environmentalists who have helped the environment
- **read** an article about plastic and plastic pollution
- **take part** in a three-way discussion about environmental issues and **take turns** to express your opinion
- **write** a formal email and **make** suggestions
- **practise** using different verb forms
- **evaluate** other people's work and **make** suggestions.

GETTING STARTED

"I made a decision to protect the only place I call home: Earth.
And so I joined other young people all over the globe to protect our future."
(Hilda Flavia Nakabuye, Ugandan environmental activist)

What do you think the main threat to our planet is? What do you think we have to do to make sure our planet is safe?

Watch this!

Think about it: Every little change helps

• **What can individual people do to help to save the planet?**

Vocabulary

1 **Look at the vocabulary box and check any words and phrases you don't know in a reliable dictionary.**

campaign	initiative
die out	non-profit organisation
dump something in landfills	plastic pollution
energy-efficient	sea currents
environmentally friendly	sign petitions
	single-use plastic

2 **In pairs, look at the photo and discuss what you think is happening. Try to use words and phrases from the vocabulary box as well as words you already know.**

Listening

> **LISTENING TIP**
>
> **What to do before you listen to a recording**
>
> It is important to read the questions or statements carefully and identify the key detail from each question/statement before you listen to the recording. This will help you to locate the necessary information in the recording more easily.

3 **Listen to a recording about five young people who have done something to help the environment. What environmental issues did the young people focus on?**

4 **Divide into five groups. Each group should focus on one of the young people from the recording. Copy the table below, listen to the recording and complete the missing information about your person. Share the information with the whole class and complete the rest of the table.**

	Wijsen sisters	Boyan Slat	Ryan Hickman	Mikaila Ulmer	Ann Makosinski
Where they come from					
What they invented/ started					
Name of their company/ campaign					
How we know they've been successful					

5   **Now look at all the information in the table from Exercise 4. In groups, discuss these questions.**

   a   Who do you think has helped the environment the most, and why?

   b   If you could campaign for the environment, what you would focus on, and why?

6   **Read the information below. Then listen to the recording about the five young people again and match the information to the correct recording. There are two extra pieces of information that you don't need to use.**

   a   has had a lot of help from their family

   b   has also helped poorer people from their local area

   c   got their idea from a similar project abroad

   d   has set up their own TV channel to inspire others

   e   got inspired during a tour of a local facility

   f   took part in a contest after finding out about a local environmental issue

   g   relies on their company funds to make a difference

USE OF ENGLISH

Compound nouns and adjectives

In English you can put two words together to make a new noun or adjective. We call the new words compound nouns and compound adjectives.

Compound nouns: *land + fill =* **landfill**, *flash + light =* **flashlight**

Compound adjectives: *world + wide =* **worldwide**, *single + use =* **single-use**, *locally + made =* **locally made**

Compound words are sometimes written as one word (for example, *greenhouse*), with a hyphen (for example, *eco-friendly*) and sometimes as two words (for example, *climate change*). If you are not sure how to write compound words, or which two words can go together, check this in a reliable English dictionary.

---

7   **Work in pairs and look at the nouns and adjectives in the box below. Using other words that you know, how many compound nouns and adjectives can you make? Use a reliable dictionary to help you.**

   For example: *rainwater, acid rain*

plastic	rain	light
air	waste	land
traffic	friendly	
home	hand	

8   **Work in pairs. Choose six compound words from Exercise 7 and write sentences using these words.**

9   **Work in the same pairs. Use your sentences from Exercise 8 as opening statements for a discussion.**

   For example: *Our city has a problem with traffic jams.*

   A: This is very true. I think people shouldn't drive everywhere; they should use the public transport instead.

   B: **Absolutely. For example, I've started cycling to school on some days of the week. I feel good because I feel fitter and I know I'm not contributing to air pollution.**

10   **Work in small groups. Discuss what environmental issues you have learnt about in this lesson, which ones you would like to help with and what you can do to improve them.**

Environmental science: Plastic pollution

• **Do you think people can live without plastic? Why or why not?**

Vocabulary

1   **In pairs, look at the Academic language box. Check the meaning of any unknown words and phrases in a reliable dictionary.**

ACADEMIC LANGUAGE	
Plastic and the environment	
corrode	natural fibres
decompose	plastic debris
degrade	polyethylene
disposable cups	reusable
generate waste	toxic to the
heat-sealed	environment
implants	water- / heat-resistant

2   **In small groups, look at the picture below and discuss the questions. Use the words and phrases from the Academic language box.**

  a   What environmental issue does it show?

  b   What do you already know about this issue?

  c   Is your country is affected by this issue?

Reading

3   **Read the article on the next page about plastic. Does the article give a one-sided view or a balanced argument? Give examples to support your opinion.**

4   **Read the article and find the details below in the text. What do they refer to? Then work in pairs and explain your ideas to your partner using your own words.**

10%	2050
1000	food shortages
meats and cheese	160,000
medical implants	hormones
the 1950s	90%
aluminium cans	natural fibres

5   **Read the article again and answer these questions.**

  a   In paragraph 1, why does the author use the ellipsis (three dots)?

  b   In paragraph 2, how does the author show that the issue of plastic is very serious?

  c   In paragraph 3, why does the author compare plastic to a loaf of bread?

  d   In paragraph 5, why does author use the verb 'corrode'?

  e   What do the author's examples in paragraphs 5 and 6 tell us about going plastic-free?

  f   In the paragraph 7, what does the adjective 'precious' tell us about the author's attitude?

6   **In small groups, discuss these questions.**

  a   What do you think people should do about the issue of plastic?

  b   Do you think that plastic pollution will get better or worse in the future? Why?

USE OF ENGLISH
First and second conditional structures
We use the first conditional to talk about real possibilities that can happen now or in the future.
If plastic production **continues** *at its current rate, there* **will be** *more plastic pollution in our seas than fish by 2050.*
We use the second conditional to talk about unreal situations that cannot happen or are extremely unlikely to happen now or in the future.
If we **could** *gather it all in one place, this plastic mountain* **would be** *bigger than Mount Everest.*
If we **eliminated** *plastic from our lives, we* **would save** *hundreds of marine species.*

What if plastic had never been invented?

1 Once a revolutionary invention, it's now filling up our oceans and killing thousands of whales, birds, turtles… Just how much plastic do we have around us? Would our life be less comfortable without it?

2 Since the 1950s we've created 6.3 billion tons of plastic. Only 9% of it has been recycled and another 12% has been burned. That leaves us with 4.9 billion tonnes of plastic waste. Plastic makes up about 10% of the total waste we generate. If we could gather it all in one place, this plastic mountain would be bigger than Mount Everest. Plastic makes up approximately 90% of all the rubbish that exists on the ocean's surface, with about 46,000 pieces of plastic per square mile. Around 160,000 plastic bags are used around the world every second and five trillion plastic bags are created every year. If plastic production continues at its current rate, there will be more plastic pollution in our seas than fish by 2050.

3 Plastic won't decompose the way a loaf of bread will, for example. It will only start degrading after 700 years and will fully degrade in 1000 years, meaning that all plastic produced by humans has yet to start degrading. Another issue is the production of plastic. It's toxic to the environment because of the chemicals that are used and then released into our seas, not to mention the plastic waste itself that ends up in the sea, killing marine animals who mistake some plastic product for food. If we removed all plastic from our lives, we'd save hundreds of marine species. Plastic can also negatively impact our health – some of the chemicals present in plastic have been found to affect hormones and lead to other potentially serious health risks.

4 But what would our life be like without plastic? Even if you avoided using plastic containers to bring your lunch to school or work, or packed your groceries into reusable shopping bags, you'd still be nowhere near plastic-free. Plastic is everywhere and the extent to which we depend on it grows every year.

5 Aluminium cans are lined with a type of plastic substance. Without it, your fizzy drink would corrode and break down the can within three days. No plastic would also mean no tea bags, since many are heat-sealed with a type of plastic called polyethylene. Without plastic, grocery shopping would look very different. Our liquids would come in reusable glass bottles and our meats and cheese would be wrapped in paper. One of the main benefits of plastic packaging is that it keeps food fresh for longer. Without this basic method of preserving food, a lot of our food would need to be grown and produced locally, and much of it would only be available seasonally. This is not a bad thing, but with an increasing population this might mean food shortages.

6 With no plastic, our clothing would be limited to natural fibres, like cotton. Heat- and water-resistant safety clothing wouldn't exist either. We also use plastics to produce our technology, furniture, and other important items. Plastic is a major part of most cooking utensils. It is also an important part of our medical technologies and is used to create glasses, different medical implants, and other devices that keep us alive and in good condition. Without the invention of plastic, we wouldn't have been able to produce the inexpensive wires needed in our phones or computers.

7 If we gave up all plastic products, our lives would become much harder, but we wouldn't be polluting our precious planet with disposable coffee cups, water bottles, toothbrushes and other plastic debris.

7 **Look through the article and find examples of situations that are unlikely to happen. Then use these situations to make sentences using the second conditional structure.**

8 **In pairs, discuss what challenges you would face if you decided to go plastic-free and whether it would be possible for you. Take notes of your ideas.**

Writing

9 **Use your ideas from Exercise 8 to help you write an article for your school magazine on the topic of going plastic-free. Write about 120–160 words.**

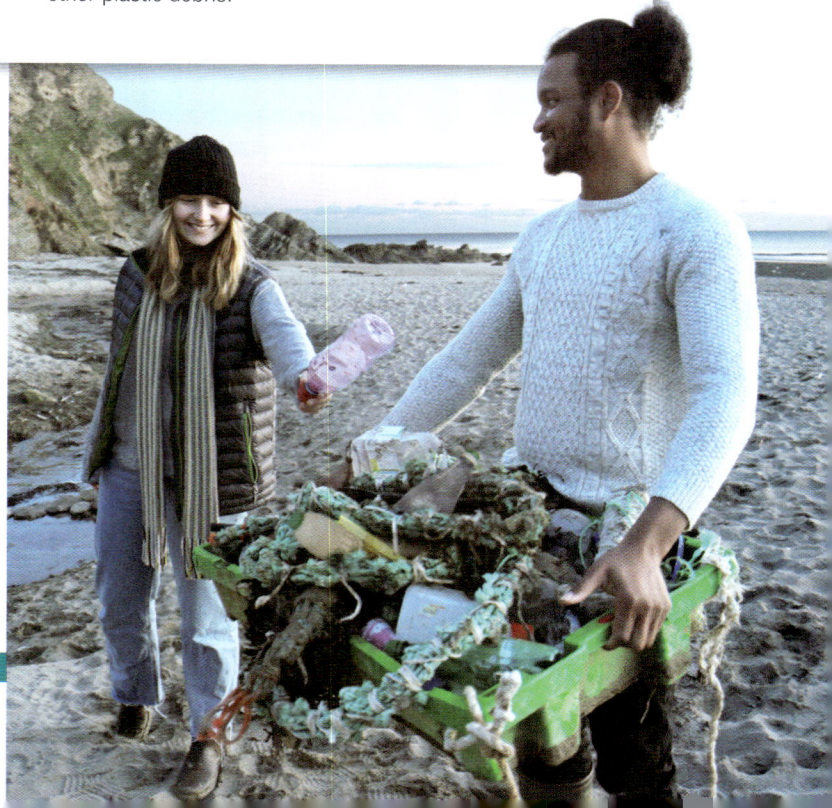

Talk about it: Environmental success stories

● What can you do in your everyday life to help the environment?

Watch this!

Listening

1 In small groups, look at the five photos. What environmental issue do you think each photo shows? Discuss how much you know about these issues.

2 Listen to three students discussing four environmental issues. Which issues from photos A–E do they mention? In which order do they mention them?

3 In the same groups, discuss which of the issues from Exercise 2 you think is the most serious one, and why.

4 Listen to the discussion again. Which projects does each student mention? Where is the project based and what is it about?

COMMUNICATION

Taking turns during discussions

Turn-taking is an essential skill during discussions (and conversations). A discussion shouldn't feel like long monologues delivered by each speaker, but shorter exchanges between the speakers. In order to participate effectively in discussions, it is important to know when to listen to others and when to speak. It is also important to know how to link what you say to what others have said (for example, expressing your opinion about it) and how to invite other people to speak (for example, by asking a question).

5 Compare your answers in groups and discuss which project you found the most interesting, and why.

6 Below are some techniques you can use to take turns in discussions and examples of these techniques. Match each example (i–v) to the correct technique (a–e).

a inviting others to speak by asking them a question

b asking a question to find out more information

c saying what you think about something that someone else has said

d adding more information to what someone else has said

e agreeing (or disagreeing) with something that someone else has said

i Speaking of plastic, I have one example for you, which…

ii That's exactly what I was thinking.

iii Wouldn't you agree?

iv That's right. And I believe that…

v What's it about exactly?

7 Listen to the three students again and write down one more example for each technique.

8 Think of one environmental issue that you know about. In small groups, discuss the issue together. In your discussion, talk about how serious the issue is and whether anything has been done to improve it. Remember to take turns and use some of the turn-taking language from Exercise 6.

9 Look at some possible future environmental solutions in the picture below. In pairs, discuss the questions. Remember to take turns and use some of the turn-taking language from Exercise 6.

a What solutions does the picture show?

b What environmental issues do you think these solutions can help with?

c Do you think our society can achieve these solutions in five years' time? Why or why not?

d Which of the solutions do you like best? Why?

SOCIAL RESPONSIBILITY

Understanding a global issue and its effects

Understanding a global issue often helps us explain what is happening in local communities and their environment. We call the impact the 'knock-on effect'. This also applies to the issue of global warming. It is a global issue, but it affects different parts of the world in so many different ways.

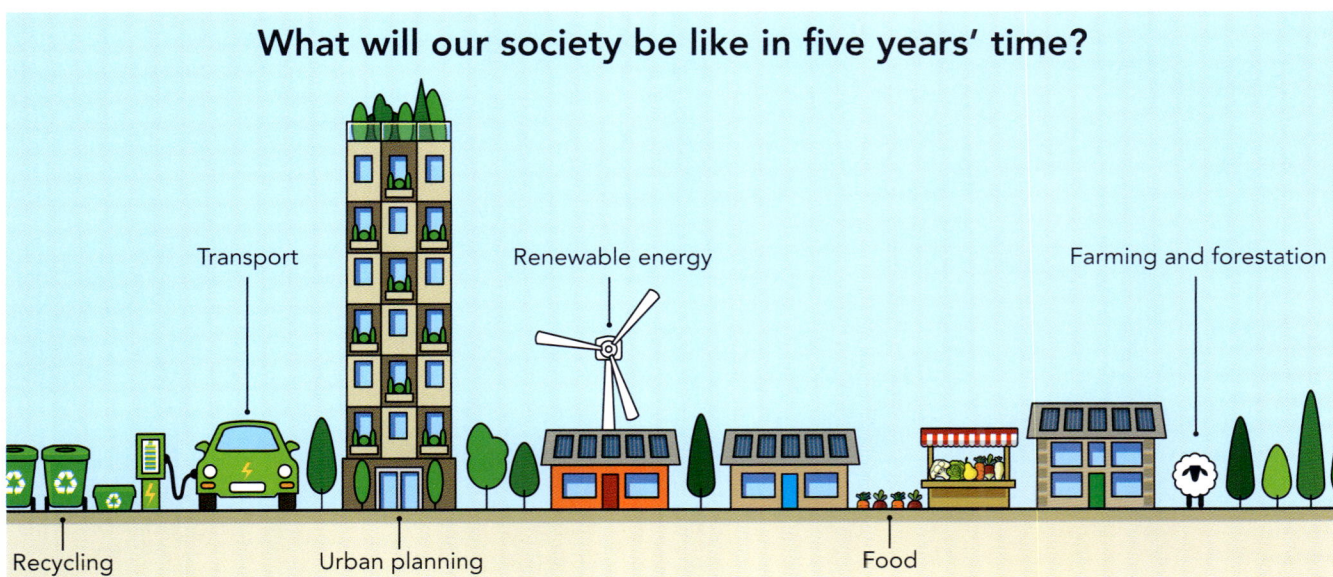

What will our society be like in five years' time?

Transport · Renewable energy · Farming and forestation · Recycling · Urban planning · Food

Improve your writing: Making suggestions in formal emails

1 Read the writing task below and identify the main points. Then read the model email and find the answers.

> There are plans to make your school eco-friendlier. Your headteacher has asked students for ideas about what changes they would like to see and what eco-projects the school should organise. Write an email to the headteacher with your suggestions.

WRITING TIP

Choosing the correct register (formality)

Before you start writing, think who you are writing to. This information will help you decide whether you need to write in an informal, formal or semi-formal register. For example, if you are writing to someone you don't know or someone who is in charge (for example, the headteacher or an online company), you should write in a formal register. If you choose the wrong register for the wrong situation, you may offend or upset somebody, or the person may think you are being rude to them. In written exams, you are often tested on the use of the correct register.

From: k.leipzig@starlingcollege.ac.uk
To: m.zhang@starling college.ac.uk

Dear Mr Zhang,

I am writing on behalf of my whole class. My classmates and I were excited to hear about the initiative to make our school eco-friendlier. Our class is very passionate about the environment and has been discussing what could be done. Please see our suggestions below.

First of all, we feel that our priority should be to reduce plastic. We already have some recycling facilities, but I believe we shouldn't just be recycling, we should also encourage our students to use fewer plastic products and find ways of using other materials instead. I therefore suggest organising 'Say NO to plastic' days. We could choose one day a week when our students would try to use less plastic. Also, it might be a good idea to organise talks with experts to provide information about alternatives to plastic. We would like to share other students' ideas too. Would it be at all possible to have some space on our school website to start a forum where students could share ideas on this topic?

Another area that needs our attention is food waste. Even though we try to avoid throwing food away in the school canteen, there is still some left at the end of each day. One possible solution to this could be to contact local charities and organise a food collection at the end of each day. The charities could then distribute the food where it is needed. I recently read about a similar initiative in one country where food collections were arranged from restaurants at the end of each day for a week. It proved very successful and helped reduce food waste to almost zero.

Our last suggestion doesn't concern our school directly, but the nearby beach. We have noticed that the amount of plastic pollution washed up on the beach hasn't improved – quite the opposite, in fact. As many of our students and their families enjoy spending their weekends by the sea, we should consider organising a beach clean-up. In our lessons, we have been studying plastic pollution and what it does to marine wildlife, and this is something that we are all very concerned about and would like to help with. It would be very useful if our school could organise an event to address this issue.

We hope you find our suggestions useful and together we can make our school eco-friendlier. Please do not hesitate to contact us if you have any more questions or need any clarification. Thank you.

We look forward to hearing from you.

Yours sincerely,

Karin Leipzig

(on behalf of class 8B)

In formal emails, use Mr (for a man) or Ms (for a woman) plus the surname of the person you are writing to.

Paragraph 1: State the reason why you are writing. Keep this paragraph short.

Paragraph 2: Introduce your first idea. Use an appropriate linking word to start the paragraph. Provide details in this paragraph.

Paragraph 3: Introduce your next idea. Use an appropriate linking word to start your paragraph. Provide details in this paragraph.

Paragraph 4: Introduce your last idea. Use an appropriate linking word to start your paragraph. Provide details in this paragraph.

Paragraph 5: Say what action you would like the other person to take. Keep this paragraph short.

End your email with a generic formal phrase.

Sign off formal emails with 'Yours sincerely' if you know the name of the person you are writing to. If you don't know their name, use 'Yours faithfully'.

Use your full name in formal emails.

Use the phrase 'on behalf of' if you are writing your email for someone else (e.g. a group of other students).

2   Work in pairs and study the model email.
    Decide whether the features in the table below
    are appropriate for the formal register or not,
    and try to find examples of them in the email.

Features	Formal?	Examples
Paragraphs		
Leaving out some words in sentences		
The passive voice		
Shortened words		
Short forms (contractions)		
Directly addressing the person you are writing to in the main body of the email		
Using longer structures before making suggestions or requests, in order to sound less direct and more polite		
Using mainly standard verbs rather than multi-word verbs		
Multi-word verbs and idioms		

3   Scan the model email and find the phrases that
    Karin uses to make suggestions. Compare your
    answers in pairs.

4   Work in the same pairs. Read these situations and
    write a suggestion for each one. Use phrases from
    Exercise 3.
    a   how to reduce plastic waste
    b   how to reduce light pollution
    c   how to reduce traffic jams in cities
    d   how to encourage people to use less plastic
    e   what people can do to keep their use of
        electricity low
    f   how to reduce food waste in restaurants

USE OF ENGLISH

Verb forms

When two verbs are used together in English,
the second verb can take on three different forms:
the infinitive form, the bare infinitive (the infinitive
without *to*) or the *-ing* form.

Some verbs are followed by the infinitive form
to and another verb. For example, we encourage
somebody *to do* something.

*…we should also **encourage** our students **to use**
fewer plastic products…*

Some verbs are followed by the *-ing* form.
For example, we suggest *doing* something.

*…I therefore suggest **organising** a series of
'Say NO to plastic' days.*

A few verbs are followed by the bare infinitive,
for example modal verbs. For example, we could
do something.

*We could **choose** one day every week for
this initiative…*

5   Look through the model email and find more
    examples of verbs that are followed by the three
    verb forms from the Use of English box.

6   Copy the table on the next page. Look at the verbs in
    the box and decide which verb form they are followed
    by and complete the table. Use a reliable dictionary
    to check your answers. The first verb has been done
    for you as an example.

avoid	mention
can	miss
claim	must
consider	offer
encourage somebody	postpone
hesitate	practise
learn	recommend
let somebody	refuse
make somebody	seem
manage	should
	suggest

Infinitive with *to*	Bare infinitive	*-ing* form
		avoid doing

7   Complete these sentences with your own ideas. Use the correct verb form to complete each sentence. Then work in pairs. Read out your sentences and check them together.

a   Nowadays people really miss…

b   I try to encourage my friends…

c   My parents always let me…

d   When I go on holiday, I always avoid…

e   To improve the state of our environment, we should all…

f   I've never considered… before, but I think it's such a good idea.

g   When I was younger, I managed…

h   When I'm older, I'm going to learn…

8   Work in small groups. Imagine your headteacher has asked the students at your school to suggest what could be done to make your school eco-friendlier.

Before you write an email to the headteacher:

*   brainstorm some suggestions

*   group the ideas into paragraphs

*   decide what useful language from the model email you could use in your own email.

9   In the same group, write your email.

Give each member of your group a different role:

*   the person who types the email

*   the spelling checker

*   the grammar checker

*   the appropriate formal vocabulary checker

*   the paragraph checker

*   the linking word checker.

10   When you finish writing your email, read it again and check that it is well-organised into paragraphs. Also check how formal it sounds and whether it uses appropriate formal vocabulary.

Project challenge

PROJECT LEARNING OBJECTIVES

In your project you will…

- make suggestions
- participate in a problem-solving task
- evaluate what someone else has done.

PROJECT OPTION 1

Make a public speech

You are going to give a speech to encourage others to join an environmental project.

Step 1: Your teacher will show you videos of speeches by two young environmentalists. Then discuss these questions.

a   What was the main message each speaker tried to communicate to the audience?

b   Which speech was more memorable, and why?

Step 2: In groups, watch one of the speeches again and evaluate the speech and the speaker.

Consider the following:

- body language (for example, gestures)
- dramatic pauses
- the speaker's tone of voice
- how the speaker opened the speech
- how the speaker ended the speech
- inclusion of shocking statistics, personal anecdotes and examples.

Step 3: Watch the speech again and focus on the language the speaker uses to make the speech more interesting. Take notes of the language they use to do this. Compare your notes in your group.

Step 4: Read this advert about Earth Day and projects students can do to help the environment.

What is Earth Day?

Earth Day has been celebrated in many countries on 22 April since 1970. The aim is to raise awareness of the environmental issues that all of us are facing. Every year, many schools organise events to teach students about conservation and how to help our planet. So, this year, why not get involved in one of these projects?

- Create a school garden
- Make a bird feeder
- Organise a zero-waste lunch day

Step 5: To encourage other students to get involved in the project, your group has decided to give a speech. Plan and practise your speech. In your speech, you should:

- explain what Earth Day is
- introduce the project you want to organise and why students should join you
- inform students about when and where the project will start and whether they need anything.

Step 6: Deliver your speech to your class. Listen to the other groups' speeches. Then evaluate them and choose the most memorable one.

COMMUNICATION

Being a good public speaker

To make the audience interested in what you are saying, try to speak enthusiastically about the topic. Also try to:

- use rising and falling intonation

- emphasise important words
- include pauses
- look at the audience, not just at your notes
- use gestures and facial expressions to emphasise what you are saying.

PROJECT OPTION 2

Prepare an exhibition and write a social media post

Kinga Raclawska

2 March

I'm on a mission to help our planet, so I've decided to do something about plastic. Plastic is everywhere. So here's my challenge for all of us – let's use less of it! Look for products that aren't made of plastic. Or if you can't replace it, at least use plastic products for longer. Or even better – upcycle it to give it a new life as something else. Go on – I know you can do it! Let me know how you get on! ☺

Read Kinga Raclawska's socai media post. Imagine you decide to take up her challenge.

Step 1: In small groups, discuss what items you need to do the activities below. How many of these items are made of plastic? For the next lesson, bring some of the items with you (for example, a toothbrush, a cleaning sponge, a pen, plastic food container, a tennis ball).

- studying
- cooking
- eating and drinking
- shopping
- washing
- cleaning
- doing your hobbies

Step 2: In small groups, compare the plastic items. Choose 10 items and group them into three categories: A can't be replaced; B can be replaced with other materials; C can be upcycled.

Step 3: Look at the items in category C and suggest what they could be upcycled as (for example, old toothbrushes as cleaning brushes for keyboards).

Step 4: You are going to organise an exhibition of upcycled plastic items. Choose the best suggestions from step 3 and exhibit your upcycled items. Write a short description of what the item can be used as to go with each item.

Step 5: Look at the other groups' exhibited items. Discuss which idea you think is the best, and why.

Step 6: In the same groups, write a reply to Kinga about your project and how successful you have been with her challenge.

SELF AND PEER ASSESSMENT

Think about how well you, and your group, did in the project. Then complete the statements below.

a Our group worked particularly well in the following activities:…

b I really enjoyed working with… because he/she…

c While doing this project, I learnt that I'm really good at… and I enjoy…

d However, I need to practise… a bit more.

e I learnt… and, in the future, this will help me…

Practise and prepare

Speaking

1   **In pairs, answer these questions as fully as possible.**

   a What plastic products do you use every day and what for?

   b Can you tell me something about a time you did something to help the environment?

   c Do you think that younger people are more interested in environmental issues than older people? Why or why not?

Writing

2   **You recently took part in an environmental project organised by your school on Earth Day. Write an email to your friend about the event. Write about 120–160 words.**

   In your email you should:

- **describe what the project was about**
- **say what you did on the day**
- **explain what you enjoyed most, and why.**

Reading

> **EXAM TIP**
>
> **Identifying what words refer to in texts**
>
> In some reading exams, you are tested on understanding referencing words (for example, *this*, *those*, *them*, *it*). These words are used to avoid repeating the same word or phrase and refer to words or ideas mentioned earlier in the text. To decide which word or idea the referencing word replaces, you need to read the sentence that comes before it.

3   **Read the blog written by a student about fast fashion and then answer the questions.**

   a Angela used to spend her weekends shopping for clothes because

      A she wanted to do what everyone else did.

      B it was one of her favourite hobbies.

      C there was nothing else to do in her local area.

   b In paragraph 2, what does Angela suggest had the biggest impact on her?

      A the amount of brand-new clothes that are thrown away

      B online videos about the fashion industry and the environment

      C finding out how much damage fast fashion has caused

   c In line 36, what does *these* refer to?

      A shops selling used clothes

      B people who sell their clothes

      C clothes that are sustainable

   d What was Angela's main reason for writing her blog?

      A to highlight the negative effects of the fast fashion industry

      B to provide personal examples of how to live more sustainably

      C to encourage others to think more carefully about their shopping habits

Fast fashion and me

by Angela Mao

Whenever we had a free weekend, my friends and I would always find ourselves at the local shopping mall. It was the perfect place for a bunch of teenagers to hang out: it had food and shopping (our favourite things). Cheap, accessible options
5   combined with my love of shopping meant that I bought a lot of clothes, all the time. Most of it was from popular, trendy stores that everyone around me bought clothes from. I didn't give a second thought to the consequences of my shopping and the larger problem that it contributed to.

10   I had always been passionate about environmental issues – climate change, pollution, and a variety of other topics, so I started watching a YouTuber who speaks in support of sustainable fashion and how the environment and fast fashion don't go together. When I found out that fast fashion
15   creates 1.2 billion tons of CO2 per year, more than air travel and shipping combined, I was appalled. The statistics were impossible to ignore. For example, fast fashion produces 20% of global wastewater and 60% of clothes are made of synthetic materials. Additionally, 97% of fast fashion is produced in
20   countries with poor labour laws, where workers frequently face terrible conditions and don't even earn enough money to pay for their basic needs. Another issue that not many people are aware of is how many unsold clothes end up in landfill because of our constant demand for new trends in clothes.

25   Knowing this, I decided to make several changes to make my lifestyle more sustainable. First, I reduced the amount of clothing I bought. I decided to avoid fast-fashion brands and instead buy from companies that were sustainable. However, I realised that there are a lot of obstacles for young people
30   when it comes to switching their lifestyle. One obvious issue is that sustainable brands can be very expensive, especially for students, who can rarely afford them. Of course, there is an alternative solution – people can buy second-hand clothes from thrift shops or online platforms that arrange
35   for people to sell their unwanted clothes to someone else. Sadly, *these* are often associated with economic hardship and that is why some of us tend to avoid them.

So, what is the best way to persuade more young people to switch to a more sustainable lifestyle? For one, it is important
40   that people are made aware of the environmental impact of fashion on our planet. It is also essential to avoid criticising someone if their lifestyle isn't particularly sustainable. Nobody is perfect and no one is expected to be 100% sustainable overnight. However, we should all acknowledge the negative
45   impact of our shopping habits and, at the very least, reflect on them.

REFLECTION

1   Work in small groups to discuss the following questions.

- What do you think the opening photograph of the Earth symbolises?

- Why do you think the young environmentalist used the phrase 'to protect our future' in the opening quotation?

- Did you learn about any threats to our planet in this lesson that you didn't know about before? Give examples.

- Do you think it's important to learn about environmental issues at school? Why or why not?

2   With a partner, use these questions to help you reflect on your progress as a learner while working on this unit.

a   In the Think about it lesson, you practised two different listening skills: listening for specific detail (for example, a country) and listening for more complex ideas (for example, reasons). Which of these skills did you find more difficult? What do you think you can do to practise this skill?

b   In the Science lesson, you practised the second conditional to talk about unreal situations that are unlikely to happen. What helps you learn grammatical structures like these? Do you prefer practising new structures as writing or speaking activities? Why?

c   In the Talk about it lesson, you also learnt how important it is to take turns in discussions. Which technique did you like most, and why? Do you find it easier to have pair or group discussions? Why do you think this is?

d   In the Improve your writing lesson, you learnt some tips about how to write a formal email. Have you used any of these tips? How useful did you find them?

e   In the Project challenge lesson, you compared what you did with what other groups produced. How useful did you find seeing what other groups produced? How did this help you improve your own work? Give examples.

f   In the Practise and prepare lesson, you practised writing an email to a friend. Did you use any of the ideas you learnt in this unit? Give examples. What helped you most with writing your informal email, and why?

SUMMARY CHECKLIST

I can…

☐ follow a short recording and understand expressed ideas.

☐ follow a longer piece of text and understand specific details as well as the author's intentions.

☐ take turns in a group discussion about environmental issues and express my opinion.

☐ write a formal email using appropriate vocabulary.

☐ use the correct verb forms confidently with a range of verbs.

☐ make suggestions to help solve a problem.

8 Old and new

IN THIS UNIT YOU WILL...

- **listen** to a talk and monologues about grandparents
- **read** an article about an old Viking settlement
- **discuss** what you think of ideas from an article about food waste
- **write** an informal email using appropriate grammar and vocabulary
- **revise** a range of verb forms and **practise** using them to express different ideas
- **carry out** research and **give** a speech.

GETTING STARTED

"If you want to understand today you have to search yesterday."
(Pearl S. Buck, American novelist (1892–1973)

How have some past inventions and discoveries improved our modern lives?

📹 **Watch this!**

Think about it: Bridging the generation gap

- What advice can grandparents give to their grandchildren?

Speaking

1   Work in pairs. Look at the vocabulary. Check any unknown words and phrases in a reliable dictionary. Then, discuss which of the words and phrases you connect with grandparents. Why?

comfort	mature
encouragement	mentally active
experienced	physically active
family history	quality time
generation gap	role models
good manners	rules
life lessons	trust

2   Now discuss why it is important for children to spend time with their grandparents. Write down your ideas.

Listening

3   Listen to a talk given by a psychologist about how grandchildren and grandparents can benefit from spending time together. Does the psychologist mention any of your ideas from Exercise 2?

4   These sentences are taken from the talk. Can you match the correct halves together?

a   It's a **win-win**…

b   if we want our children to be less…

c   Spending time with grandparents means that children have the chance to **pick up**…

d   grandparents can often give the perfect advice to **set**…

e   Grandchildren can **light**…

f   our grandparents are **a wealth**…

g   Spending time together doesn't just **create a sense**…

h   Grandparents can help children **see** their parents **in**…

i   …these useful **skills**.

ii   …**of purpose** but it also helps keep grandparents active, both physically and mentally.

iii   …**ageist,** and more accepting of the older generation

iv   …**up** the **lives** of their grandparents.

v   …**situation** for the grandparents as well as the grandchildren.

vi   …**of knowledge**

vii   …a **different light** through anecdotes and stories.

viii   …their grandchildren **on the right path** in life.

5   Work in pairs and look at the words and phrases in bold in Exercise 4. Can you match each phrase with the correct definition?

a   to make someone happy and cheerful

b   to give someone a strong reason for doing something

c   the time when everybody gains something positive

d   to help someone see what is right and what they should be doing

e   to learn a range of things that are important in life or in a particular job

f   to change your opinion about someone, usually for the better

g   to treat people unfairly because of their age

h   to know a lot of useful things

6 Copy the headings 'Benefits for grandparents' and 'Benefits for grandchildren' into your notebook. Then listen to the talk again and take notes of the benefits the psychologist mentions and write them under the correct heading.

Speaking

7 Work in small groups to discuss these questions.

a Which benefits from the talk surprised you? Why?

b Have you experienced any of the benefits mentioned in the talk? Give examples.

c In your opinion, what would be a good way of celebrating Grandparents' Day?

d What do you think grandchildren and grandparents can learn from each other?

8 Listen to three speakers talking about spending time with their grandparents. Write down how each speaker benefited from being with their grandparents and how their grandparents benefited. Then compare your answers in pairs.

Reading

9 Work in small groups. Each group should look at one of the word boxes A–C. The phrases are taken from the listening activity in Exercise 8. Try to work out the meaning of each phrase from the context, from a dictionary and by looking online. Write your definitions on strips of paper. Then exchange your strips with another group's. Can you match the definitions to the correct words and phrases?

A

> to get up to something
>
> something's on my mind
>
> ongoing

B

> to come over
>
> to be into something
>
> to come clean

C

> invaluable experiences
>
> vital for something
>
> to broaden your horizons

10 Think of a time when you learnt something from someone older than you or when you taught something to someone older than you. Make short notes of your ideas. Then use your notes to tell your partner about it. Try to use some of the vocabulary from the word boxes in Exercise 9.

Think about these questions when you write your ideas:

- Who and what was it?

- What was it like? What did you do exactly?

- How did you feel, and why?

History and science: Uncovering the past

- How do you think modern technology can help us discover new things about history?

Reading

1   Read the words in the Academic language box. They are taken from the article on the next page. Look up any words that you don't know in a reliable dictionary.

> **ACADEMIC LANGUAGE**
>
> **History and science**
>
> | | |
> |---|---|
> | absorb | fragment |
> | archives | indigenous people |
> | artefacts | radiocarbon dating |
> | date something | settlement |
> | debate a theory | the evidence proves |
> | extract something | |

2   In pairs, look at the word box below. Check the meaning of any words and phrases you do not know in a reliable dictionary. Then look at the photos A–C. Which words and phrases from the box go with each photo, and why?

> | | |
> |---|---|
> | a cosmic event | longships |
> | a solar storm | timber |
> | atmosphere | to cross the Atlantic |
> | a tree trunk | tree rings |
> | bark | |

3   In pairs, discuss how you think the photos A–C are linked to the article. Take notes of your ideas, then read the article to check.

4   Five sentences have been removed from the article. First read sentences a–e and then the text. Choose the sentence that best fits each gap (1–5). Then listen to the article to check your answers. What helped you decide?

a   The 'scars' left by iron blades on these pieces of wood can still be seen after more than 1000 years.

b   Scientists used three rough pieces of wood left behind by Vikings.

c   For reasons that are still unclear, the Vikings never settled in North America for a very long time.

d   Many questions may never be answered, but researchers now have an extremely accurate date for when the Vikings were present in North America.

e   The tree grows a new ring every year and that's how it can be dated to the exact year it was formed.

> **READING TIP**
>
> **Understanding cohesion**
>
> Cohesion is how a text is 'glued' together. This could be within a sentence, a paragraph or a longer piece of text. When you are asked to insert missing sentences back into the text, knowing cohesion will help you. For example, look for referencing words (*this*, *them*), linking words (*that's why*), the definite article (*the*) or related vocabulary. When you decide which sentence should go in the gap, read the sentence before and after to check that your sentence really fits in.

Vikings were definitely present in North America in 1021 CE

A new study of wooden artefacts found at Newfoundland's historical site shows that Vikings lived in North America in the year 1021 CE. The evidence proves that Vikings successfully completed the earliest known crossing of the Atlantic from Europe to the Americas. [1] So how was such incredibly precise dating even possible?

[2] Timber was critical for the Vikings in Newfoundland; wood provided fuel for heat and cooking as well as material to build their famous longships. Hundreds of fragments of wood from the workshops at the Newfoundland settlement have been found. The scientists selected three wooden artefacts that were produced by Vikings, not only because they were found at the site but also because they were clearly cut and shaped with metal tools, which weren't used by the area's Indigenous people. [3]

The scientific method used to date the pieces of wood is called dendrochronology. This method involves counting the rings inside a tree after extracting a sample from the tree trunk. [4] But this is not all. Dendrochronological and radio carbon dating archives from around the world, in Germany, Ireland, Arizona and Japan, provided evidence that in 993 CE a cosmic radiation event, probably an enormous solar storm, caused a huge increase in the carbon levels in our atmosphere. Such events can clearly be measured in tree rings. This is because solar storms create a sudden increase of radiocarbon that gets absorbed by tree rings, which makes a visible change to the pattern of these rings.

After identifying this unusual change in the tree rings of each wooden artefact, the scientists simply had to count the remaining rings all the way to the bark layer. The team discovered that each of the three different trees used to produce the wooden artefacts was cut down exactly 28 years after the major cosmic event.

According to old Viking stories, the Vikings established several settlements in Newfoundland and even explored areas further south, but just how far south we may never know. [5] One theory that has been debated is that it might have been to do with their relations with Native Americans, which were not exactly very friendly.

The Vikings were amazing sailors and undoubtedly knew their way around their part of the world. They sailed west from Scandinavia to the British Isles, settled in Iceland by 874 and continued exploring Greenland until they eventually became the first to cross the Atlantic.

5 You are going to test other classmates to see how much information they can remember from the article. Read the text again and, in pairs, prepare true or false statements about the information in the article. Read them out to another pair and see whether they can remember if the statements are true or false.

For example: A: *Vikings most likely travelled as far as Japan.*

   B: *That's false.*

USE OF ENGLISH

The third conditional

We use the third conditional structure to speculate about a past event.

The Vikings wouldn't have been able to travel so far if they hadn't had such great navigation skills.

This is a hypothetical situation that didn't happen in real life. In reality, the Vikings *had* good navigation skills and that is why they *were* able to travel so far.

We use the past perfect after the *if* part of the structure and we use *would* (or other modal verbs) + *have* + past participle in the other part of the conditional structure.

*If the Vikings **had had** better relations with the native people in North America, they **might have stayed** there permanently.*

6 In pairs, look through the article about Vikings and try to make more third conditional sentences. Use the examples in the Use of English box as a model.

7 In small groups, discuss what information from the article you found most surprising, and why. Try to use the vocabulary and grammar you have learnt in this lesson.

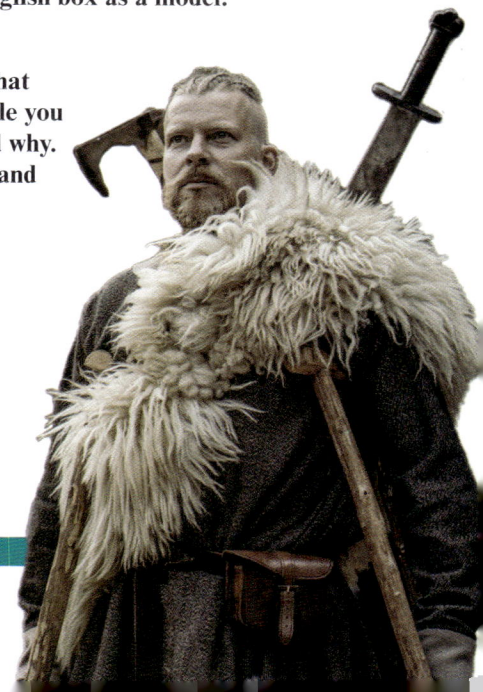

Talk about it: New ways of solving old problems

• What global issues do you think we are currently facing?

Watch this!

Listening

1   Look at the photo. In small groups, discuss which issue you think the photo shows, and why you think so. Choose from one of the three options below.

   A   surviving in space for a long period of time

   B   space pollution called space junk

   C   the challenges of developing new technology for space exploration

2   Listen to two students discussing the same issue as in the photo. What issue is it? Were you right?

3   In the conversation, the students are discussing what they think of the ideas from an article they read. Listen again and write down the phrases they use to express a negative or positive reaction to these ideas.

4   Listen to the positive and negative reactions from the conversation. Highlight which word or part of the word the speaker stresses in each phrase. Listen for a final time, repeat the phrases and copy the stress.

5   Use some of the phrases from Exercise 3 and complete them with your own ideas. Write down your sentences.

For example: *I find it absolutely unacceptable that some people drop litter on public transport.*

6   In pairs, read your sentences out to each other. Use the sentences as opening statements to start a discussion. Pay attention to the words you stress.

A fresh take on expired food

A supermarket in Copenhagen selling food that has passed its sell-by date has proved to be so popular it recently opened a second store.

5 'It's awesome that instead of throwing things away they are selling it for less. You support a good cause,' said one local student, after picking up a bottle of an expensive brand of olive oil for only 20 Danish kroner.

'Isn't it great?' pensioner Olga Fruerlund said, holding up a jar of sweets that she planned to give to her 10 grandchildren. 'The sweets can last for a hundred years because there is sugar in them,' she added.

Selling expired food is legal in Denmark as long as it is clearly advertised and it is safe to consume. 'We look, we smell, we feel the product and see if it's still 15 consumable,' project leader Bassel Hmeidan said.

All products are donated by producers, import and export companies and major food stores, and are collected by supermarket's staff, all of whom are volunteers. The store's profits go to charity. Prices 20 are around half of what they would be elsewhere and the products available depend on what is available from donors, resulting in a mix that changes from one day to another.

Food waste has become an increasingly hot topic in 25 recent years, with initiatives including a global network of cafés serving dishes made from food that would have been otherwise thrown away. A similar project based in Britain, called The Real Junk Food Project, has opened the country's first food waste supermarket in a 30 warehouse near Leeds and it focuses mainly on feeding the poor. The British project urges customers to simply 'pay as much as they feel'.

A United Nations' panel said earlier this month that supermarkets' preference for perfect-looking fruit and 35 vegetables and the use of unreasonable 'best before' labels causes massive food waste. In fact, all this wasted food could feed the world's hungry. Nearly 1.3 billion tonnes of food are wasted every year, more than enough to help feed the one billion people suffering 40 from hunger globally, the United Nations' Food and Agriculture Organization (FAO) said.

> [2] **sell-by date:** a date printed on food products to show the products shouldn't be sold after the date because they might not be safe to eat
>
> [24] **hot topic:** a topic that a lot of people like to discuss

Reading

7   Look at the heading of this article. In pairs, discuss what issues the article might be about. Then read and listen to the text to check.

8   What solutions are mentioned in the text? Read the article again and note them down.

9   In pairs, discuss the issues and solutions from the article and how you feel about these ideas. Use the phrases from Exercise 3.

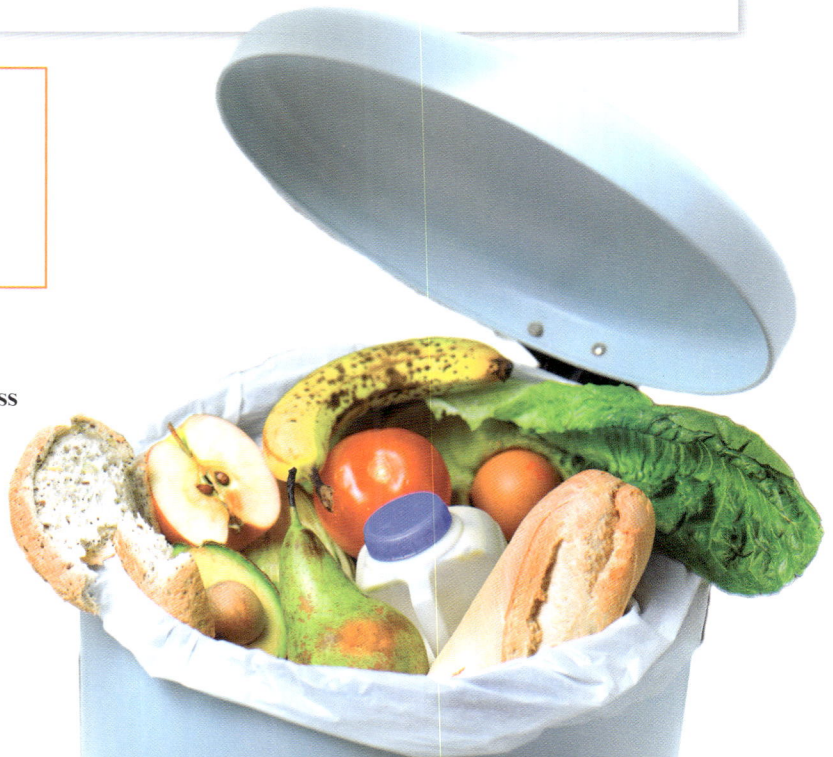

Improve your writing: Informal emails

1   **Work in small groups to discuss these questions.**

a   How do you keep in touch with different members of your family/your friends/other classmates?

b   How important is it to keep in touch with other people in our lives?

c   How often do you write to other people, and why?

d   Do you think writing to people is sometimes better than talking to people face to face? What are the advantages/disadvantages of writing to people?

2   **Read the tasks A and B. Identify who you are writing to and what the main points of each task are.**

Task A

Your family have moved to a new city and you have started a new school. Write an email to your grandparents telling them about your new life. Say what your new school is like and explain what you like best about the new city where you now live.

Task B

Your family have moved to a new city and you have decided to write an email about your new life to your best friend, whom you have known for a long time. Invite your friend to stay with you for the weekend and suggest what you can do together.

3 Read these two emails and match each email to the correct task, A or B.
Then read the emails again and find the answers to the main points from
each task that you identified in Exercise 2.

a

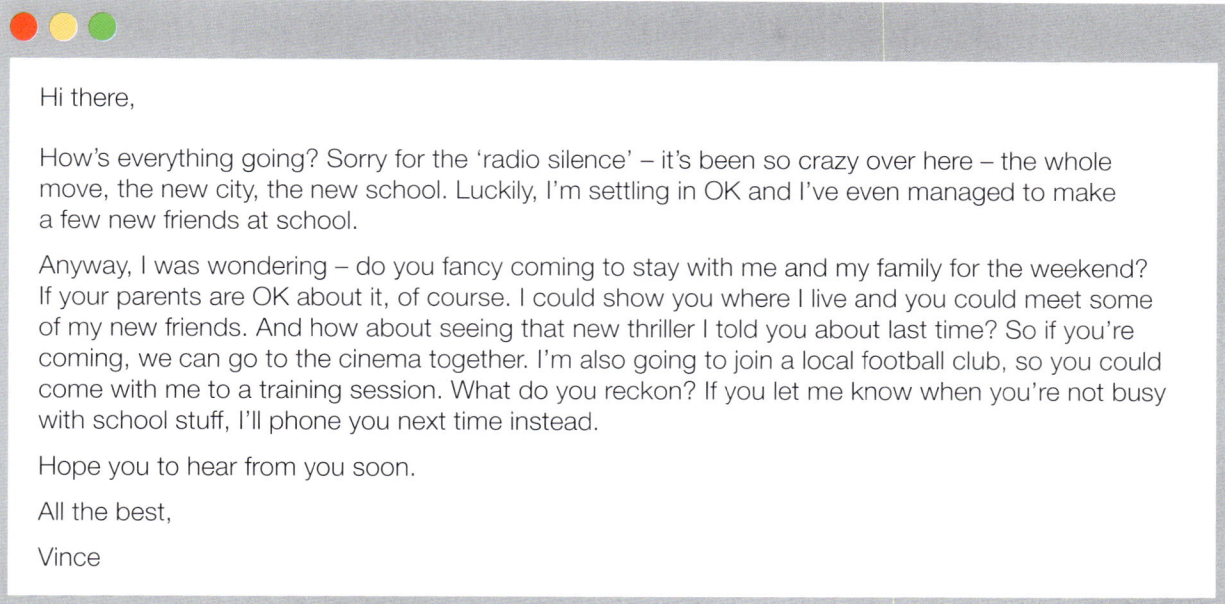

Hi there,

How's everything going? Sorry for the 'radio silence' – it's been so crazy over here – the whole
move, the new city, the new school. Luckily, I'm settling in OK and I've even managed to make
a few new friends at school.

Anyway, I was wondering – do you fancy coming to stay with me and my family for the weekend?
If your parents are OK about it, of course. I could show you where I live and you could meet some
of my new friends. And how about seeing that new thriller I told you about last time? So if you're
coming, we can go to the cinema together. I'm also going to join a local football club, so you could
come with me to a training session. What do you reckon? If you let me know when you're not busy
with school stuff, I'll phone you next time instead.

Hope you to hear from you soon.

All the best,

Vince

b

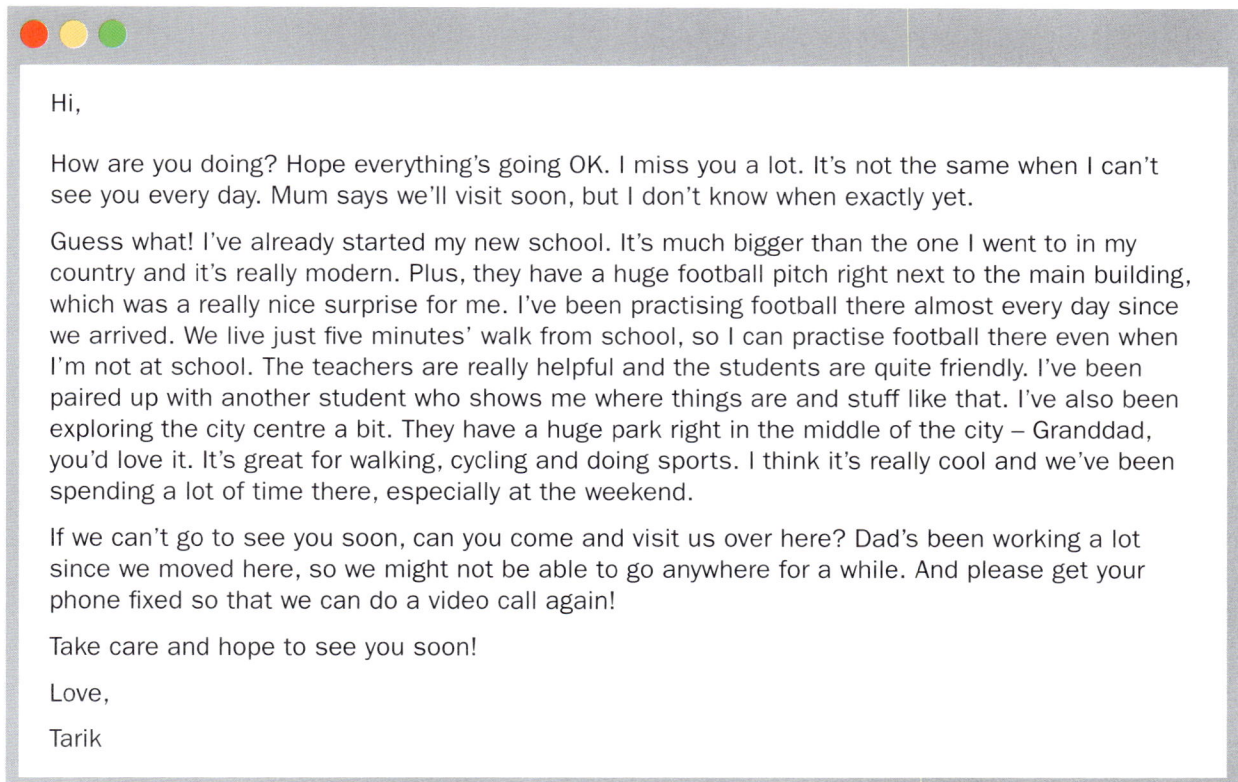

Hi,

How are you doing? Hope everything's going OK. I miss you a lot. It's not the same when I can't
see you every day. Mum says we'll visit soon, but I don't know when exactly yet.

Guess what! I've already started my new school. It's much bigger than the one I went to in my
country and it's really modern. Plus, they have a huge football pitch right next to the main building,
which was a really nice surprise for me. I've been practising football there almost every day since
we arrived. We live just five minutes' walk from school, so I can practise football there even when
I'm not at school. The teachers are really helpful and the students are quite friendly. I've been
paired up with another student who shows me where things are and stuff like that. I've also been
exploring the city centre a bit. They have a huge park right in the middle of the city – Granddad,
you'd love it. It's great for walking, cycling and doing sports. I think it's really cool and we've been
spending a lot of time there, especially at the weekend.

If we can't go to see you soon, can you come and visit us over here? Dad's been working a lot
since we moved here, so we might not be able to go anywhere for a while. And please get your
phone fixed so that we can do a video call again!

Take care and hope to see you soon!

Love,

Tarik

4   Look at the emails again. Copy the table and complete it with examples of useful language for each type of email.

Type of email	Invitation	Giving news
Useful language		

5   Look at the sentences below with some more useful language. Can you match the correct halves together? Then decide which type of email from Exercise 4 this language is suitable for.

a   It'd be…

b   This may…

c   I was…

d   You'll never…

e   I'm thinking…

f   I've got…

i   wondering if you'd like to go to the shopping mall tomorrow.

ii   great if you could come to the cinema with me.

iii   of organising a surprise party for Hamza. Could you come?

iv   surprise you, but I've recently moved house.

v   something exciting to tell you – my brother's getting married next month.

vi   believe this, but I've won the school spelling competition.

6   Work in pairs and read the tasks below. Choose one and decide who takes on each role. Then do a role-play for each situation. When you finish, exchange roles and do the same for the other task. Use the photos to help you think of what to say in your role-plays. Remember to use the useful language from Exercises 4 and 5.

Task A

Imagine you have moved house and would like to invite your best friend to spend the weekend at your home. Suggest what activities you could do that weekend and what your friend needs to bring with them.

Task B

Imagine you've just started a new school and you are telling your best friend about it. Say what the school and teachers are like and what you enjoy most about your lessons.

USE OF ENGLISH

Verb forms to talk about past events, recent news, future plans and decisions

Present perfect

We use the present perfect simple to express an action that is complete and happened at some time between the past and now, but we don't know exactly when.

*We've just **moved** to a new house.*

We use the present perfect continuous to express an action that started in the past and is still happening now.

*We've **been walking** to school for the past week because somebody stole my bike.*

Future

We use *will* to express an instant decision made at the time of speaking.

*I think I'll **invite** all the students from my class to the party.*

We use the present continuous with future meaning to express a fixed arrangement.

*We're **having** an extended family get-together tomorrow at 3 p.m.*

We use *going to* to express a future plan that we've been thinking about for some time.

*I'm **going to be** the DJ at my sister's wedding party.*

7   Look at the verb forms in the Use of English box. Then read the model emails from Exercise 3 and find more examples of these forms. Which of the forms are appropriate for each type of email?

8   Look at these sentences. They have some words missing (for example, prepositions, articles *a* and *the*, pronouns). Can you rewrite them as complete sentences? Make sure you use the verbs in the correct form from the Use of English box. Check your answers in pairs.

   a   My parents / drive us / town centre sometime next week.

   b   Next Monday, we / have / big family meal / all my cousins, so I / introduce them / you.

   c   Our school organises / lot / competitions and I / just win first prize / story-writing competition.

   d   When you come to visit, I / show you / new school.

   e   I / study / new school / six months now and I / already make / lot / new friends.

   f   Next Saturday I / visit / grandparents, so I / not able / see you then.

9   Choose one of the tasks from Exercise 6 and write an email to your friend. Use the ideas from your role-play as the basis for your email.

10   Proofread your email and check your verbs. Did you use the appropriate verb forms for that type of email? Did you use them correctly?

11   Swap your email with another student's email. Read it and decide which task the email answers. Then copy the checklist below and tick which things have been done well. Give feedback to the other student.

Did the email…

   ✓   answer all the points from the task?

   ✓   use the correct greeting and signing off phrase?

   ✓   use some of the useful language from this lesson appropriately?

   ✓   use appropriate grammatical forms for the task?

   ✓   use grammatical forms correctly?

Project challenge

PROJECT LEARNING OBJECTIVES

In your project you will…

- evaluate ideas
- select relevant information
- give a speech.

PROJECT OPTION 1

An interview and an exhibition

Your school wants to organise an exhibition of what life was like for teenagers in a different decade.

Step 1: In small groups, decide on which decade you want to target (for example, 1960s, 1980s, 2000s). Then decide who each person from your group will interview about that decade (for example, a teacher, a neighbour, an older cousin, a grandparent, etc.). Also, decide what type of interview you want to do, face-to-face or virtual.

Step 2: Brainstorm what information each person from your group should ask about in their interview, for example popular music, a typical school day, fashion, popular free-time activities.

Step 3: Carry out your interview and take notes of what the interviewee says.

Step 4: Share your findings with the rest of the group. Then:

- discuss what you think was typical for the decade (for example, the clothes young people wore, the music they listened to, the games children played)

- compare life then with the present decade

- say what aspects of life were better then and which are better now, and why.

Step 5: Write a short speech introducing the decade that you chose. Use the information from step 4.

Step 6: Research on the internet to find examples of typical things from the decade you chose. For example, you could find photos of fashionable clothes and print some out.

Step 7: Organise an exhibition of the decade you chose. Display the items you collected in your classroom or other suitable area and write a short note to explain what each item is.

Step 8: At the opening of your exhibition, read out your speech to introduce the decade.

COMMUNICATION

Improving your speaking fluency

Sometimes you may not know the exact word in English when, for example, you are giving a talk or having a conversation. To make sure your communication doesn't break down, you can use a synonym, a word or phrase with the same or similar meaning, or describe the word.

PROJECT OPTION 2

Make a poster and give a speech

World Heritage Sites are cultural or natural places in the world which are very important for humanity and, therefore, need to be protected. They are selected by UNESCO, an international organisation that is part of the United Nations. In your class, you have been talking about important sites from around the world that are protected by UNESCO World Heritage. You have decided to select one site from your country.

Step 1: Research what the requirements are before a site can be considered for a World Heritage Site. There are six requirements for cultural sites and four for natural sites. List the information under the two headings below.

- Cultural sites
- Natural sites

Step 2: Discuss interesting sites in your country, both cultural and natural places that are not currently on the UNESCO World Heritage list. List three for each category. Then decide together which site you think should be protected by UNESCO World Heritage, and why.

Step 3: Research the site you selected in step 2. Copy the table below and complete the information.

Location	
Type of site (cultural or natural)	
A short description	
Interesting facts	
Reasons why it should be listed as a World Heritage Site	
Personal reasons for choosing this site	

Step 4: Work in two groups. One group will work on a poster to introduce the site you chose. The other group will prepare a speech to explain why the site should be accepted as a World Heritage Site. Decide which students should work in each group based on their strengths (for example, good communication skills or graphic skills). Both groups should also use the information from step 4 to complete their task.

Step 5: Come together as one group again and review what each group prepared. Practise giving the speech with your whole group, using the poster to support your ideas from the presentation.

Step 6: Present the poster to the class and give your speech. Then listen to other groups presenting their sites. Decide which site from your country should be selected as one of the World Heritage Sites, and why.

SELF AND PEER ASSESSMENT

Think about how well you, and your group, did in the project. Then complete the statements below.

a Our group worked particularly well in the following activities:…

b I really enjoyed working with… because he/she…

c While doing this project, I learnt that I'm really good at… and I enjoy…

d However, I need to practise… a bit more.

e I learnt… and, in the future, this will help me…

Practise and prepare

Speaking

1   **Work in pairs. Read the task below. Spend one minute preparing what you want to say. Then give your talk.**

> You family is planning next summer's holiday and deciding where to go. You are considering the following options:
>
> - a seaside resort that your family goes to every summer
> - a visit to a city abroad that your family have never been to before.
>
> Talk about the advantages and disadvantages of each option. Say which option you would prefer, and why.

Writing

WRITING TIP

Generating your own ideas for writing

In some written exams, you are given prompts to help you with ideas for your writing. However, you should also try to include your own ideas. To think of things to say, first try to think what your personal experience is and what your friends say. Also, try to read a wide range of articles and other texts to learn about interesting facts and other people's opinions.

2 In class, you have been discussing how important it is to learn about the past. Your teacher has asked you to write an article for a school magazine. In your article you should say why it is important to study history at school and what could be done to make more young people interested in this subject. Here are some comments from other students in your class. These may give you some ideas, and you should also use some ideas of your own. Write about 120–160 words.

> I'd love to see the places we study about in our history lessons.

> There are just too many dates to learn.

> We can learn from our ancestors and avoid the mistakes that they made.

> Science is more exciting because we do experiments.

Listening

3 You will hear four people talking about trying a new hobby. For each questions 1–4, choose from the list (A–F) which idea they express. Use each letter only once. There are two extra letters that you do not need to use.

A   It has improved my fitness.

B   I almost gave up at the start.

C   I can recommend this activity to everybody.

D   It has given me more confidence.

E   My family didn't share my enthusiasm.

F   I had to save up some money first.

Speaker 1   1

Speaker 2   2

Speaker 3   3

Speaker 4   4

REFLECTION

1   Work in a small group. Look at the photo in the unit opener and read the quotation under it. In pairs, discuss how the photo reflects the idea(s) expressed in the quotation.

2   With a partner, use these questions to help you reflect on your progress as a learner while working on this unit.

   a   In the Think about it lesson, you practised listening to a longer talk and shorter monologues. Which one did you find easier to follow? Why? What can you listen to in order to improve your listening to the other task type?

   b   In the History and science lesson, you practised grouping vocabulary into similar vocabulary sets and matching them to photos. Did this technique help you remember the new words? What other techniques do you like when learning new vocabulary? Why?

   c   In the Talk about it lesson, you practised word stress in longer phrases. Did you find it easy to hear the stressed words? Did you enjoy practising pronunciation? Why or why not?

   d   In the Improve your writing lesson, you practised using a range of grammatical forms. Which forms did you find easy to use? Which forms did you find challenging to use? What can you do to further practise these forms?

   e   In the Project challenge lesson, your group practised giving a speech. What was your role in the task? Did you enjoy this role? What role would you like to try next time? Why?

   f   In the Practise and prepare lesson, you learnt about different ways you can generate ideas for your written answers. Were these tips helpful? How did you generate your ideas? Are you going to try any of the other ways suggested? Why or why not?

SUMMARY CHECKLIST

I can…

- [ ] identify the main ideas in a longer talk as well as in shorter monologues.
- [ ] read a longer text and understand the links between ideas.
- [ ] take part in a conversation and react negatively as well as positively to different ideas.
- [ ] write an informal email and use appropriate vocabulary.
- [ ] use the correct grammatical forms for the given situation.

9 Tales and stories

IN THIS UNIT YOU WILL...

- **listen** to a short story and a radio programme about the benefits of reading
- **read** three texts about literacy, **extract** relevant ideas and **understand** the connections between them
- **lead** a group discussion and **move** the discussion forward
- **write** a short story and **use** some techniques to create an effect on the reader
- **practise** using narrative tenses in simple and continuous forms
- **obtain** relevant information from a range of different texts.

GETTING STARTED

"A reader lives a thousand lives before he dies... The man who never reads lives only one."
(George R.R. Martin, American novelist)

Do you think people will continue reading paper books in the future? Why or why not?

Watch this!

Think about it:
The joy of reading

- How often do you read, and why?

Speaking

1   Work in small groups and discuss what you think of when you hear the word *reading* (for example, feelings, types of books, places to read), and why. Then compare your ideas with the whole class. What were the most common answers?

2   Look at the word cloud below, which contains words that people often use to describe their reading habits and their reasons for reading. The bigger the word, the more common the answer is. In your groups discuss these questions.

   a   What do you think the words in the word cloud say about people's reading habits ?

   b   How similar were your answers from Exercise 1 to the answers in the word cloud?

Listening

3   Look at statements a–e, which express some of the benefits of reading. Then listen to the radio programme about the benefits of reading and put the benefits in the order the speaker mentions them.

   a   Reading helps you remember.

   b   Reading means you are never alone.

   c   Reading allows you to experience more than one reality.

   d   Reading helps you forget.

   e   Reading challenges your way of thinking.

interesting escape enjoyable pleasure
information
relaxing really find book entertaining mind books imagination time enjoy work
away people quiet gain
gives to read go relax always reality world learning
just reading takes going enjoyment getting love stories guess way life educational
helps histories know fiction education art escape learn place
Knowledge everything take different new
reading things entertainment read
something

4   Copy the table. Then listen to some of the key words from the radio programme and write them in the correct column. A word in each column has been done for you as an example. Now complete the table with the missing word forms. Then listen to check your answers. Which suffixes are often used to make nouns and adjectives?

Abstract nouns	Adjectives
1	satisfied
2 responsibilities	
3	
4	
5	
6	
7	
8	
9	
10	
11	
12	
13	
14	

5   Listen to the words from the completed table again and mark the syllable stress for each word. Is the stress on the same syllable for the noun and adjective, or does it change? Then read the pair of words out loud, stressing the correct syllable.

6   Work in small groups. Discuss your experience of reading and how you have benefited from it. In your answers, try to use some of the words from Exercise 4.

STUDY TIP

Reading in English for pleasure

When you start reading longer texts in English, start with something easier to build your confidence. If you're reading something you understand, you're more likely to enjoy reading it. Try reading children's books – they use easier language. Manga or comic books are also good as they use pictures to help you understand what you're reading about and will help you guess unknown vocabulary.

Vocabulary

7   In pairs, look at the vocabulary box and put the words and phrases into two groups: types of books and vocabulary used to talk about a book. Use a reliable dictionary to help you. Then compare your vocabulary groups with another pair.

audiobook	moral
autobiography	narrator
comic strip	novel based on a true
dialogue	story
fiction book	plot
folk tale	setting
main hero	suspense

8   Think of a book or story you have read and tell other students about it. Use the words and phrases from the vocabulary box.

Listening

9   Listen to a story from Somalia called 'The Well'. Who do you think this story is for? Why?

10   Listen to the story again. Copy and complete the fact file below. Then check your answers in pairs.

> Name:
>
> Genre:
>
> Main characters:
>
> Main plot:
>
> Ending:

11   Work in small groups to discuss these questions.

a   What do you think the moral of this story is?

b   Did you enjoy the story? Why or why not?

c   Do you think you have benefited from hearing this story? Why or why not?

d   What type of books and stories do you enjoy reading, and why?

e   Can reading stories help you learn English? Give examples.

Sociology and education: The right to learn how to read and write

• **In what aspects of everyday life do we use reading or writing?**

Reading

1 Work in small groups. Tell each other what you can remember about the time when you were learning to read and write. What did you enjoy about it? What or who helped you learn?

2 In pairs, look at the words and phrases in the Academic language box. Do you know the meanings of any of them? Look up any words you don't know in a reliable dictionary.

ACADEMIC LANGUAGE

Sociology and education

access education	lack basic skills
communities	launch a literacy programme
compulsory education	literacy issues persist
empower somebody	preschool children
from birth	promote literacy skills
illiteracy	the inability to read
individuals	
inspire somebody	

3 Read the two texts about literacy, which is the ability to read and write. Answer these questions in pairs.

a What type of source are you likely to find each text in? What helped you decide?

 A an encyclopaedia B a magazine

b Which image, A or B, would go best with each text? Explain your choice.

Text 1: World Literacy Day

The idea for a World Literacy Day was first discussed during the World Conference of Ministers of Education in 1965. On 26 October 1966, UNESCO decided that 8 September would become the World Literacy Day, to address global illiteracy.

5 The first World Literacy Day was held in 1967, and since then it has become an annual event.

World Literacy Day is held to educate the public about the value of literacy and to promote literacy skills. The main aim is to empower individuals and their communities to help people across
10 the world to access education, find work and improve their lives.

While UNESCO has recorded positive developments in children's literacy levels, partly due to compulsory education, the same cannot be said about adults. Unfortunately, literacy issues persist, with approximately 773 million individuals lacking
15 basic literacy skills, globally.

[3] **UNESCO:** the United Nations Educational, Scientific and Cultural Organization is an international organisation that promotes world peace, security and cooperation in education, science, arts and culture

Text 2: Bright Sparks Club

Conni Reinhar, an English teacher in a local primary school, never expected that her project for young children and their parents would bring her fame. She started small with one club that met at the local primary school once a week. It soon
5 became very popular and other primary schools became interested in the same idea. And before Conni knew it, the project had spread nationwide.

When asked what gave her the idea for the project, she said that it was mainly her own childhood experience when her
10 grandfather would read her bedtime stories. She still vividly remembers how much she enjoyed imagining she was the main character in a story where anything was possible. She wanted all young children to have the same experience. And when she later read about a famous American singer launching a literacy
15 programme for preschool children and how beneficial it was for the children as well as their local communities, she knew she wanted to do something similar. And that's when the idea of the Bright Sparks Club was born.

'How it works is that I ask young local families to donate books
20 their children no longer read because they've grown too "old" for them. Then I give these books to parents from our Bright Sparks Club to read to their children. When we all meet at the next club, we encourage children to talk about the books and what they liked about them. Other children then choose their
25 next book to read based on what they've heard,' Conni explains.

Conni believes that reading can give children the freedom to dream about what they can achieve and who they can become. To inspire children, they need to feel a love for reading first. 'Reading shouldn't feel like a chore or something they have
30 to do too. That's why, at the club, we also introduce other activities connected with the books children read, like quizzes or illustrate-your-favourite-story challenges,' Conni adds.

Conni has also noticed one interesting fact in her own classroom; young pupils, who were read stories as very
35 small children at bedtime, usually learn to read more quickly themselves. She believes that this is down to their desire to continue reading by themselves and exploring the wonderful world of books. 'I really think that like this we can end illiteracy in individuals and in whole communities.'

4 Now answer these questions. Read the texts again to check your answers.

a Where and when was the idea of celebrating literacy mentioned for the first time?

b How do we know that the project has been successful? Give two examples.

c Who inspired the teacher to set up a reading club for children?

d What are the main aims of World Literacy Day? Give at least two details.

e According to the text, why is it important that reading should be fun? Give two reasons.

f According to the text, what can reading at bedtime help children with later in life?

5 Read these sentences and then choose one word or phrase from the Academic language box to complete each gap. Make sure the word form you use fits the gap grammatically.

a His charity to encourage young kids to read more was _____ last year.

b We need to _____ more interest in our after-school book reading club.

c The issue of _____ still remains a global problem despite all the efforts.

d People shouldn't be expected to pay money to be able to _____ university education.

e He claims that he was _____ by his grandfather, who was also a writer.

f The basic level of literacy skills in some remote _____ is the result of limited education opportunities.

g Our school wants to _____ all our students to believe they can achieve their dreams.

6 Work in small groups to discuss the questions below. In your answers, try to use words and phrases from the Academic language box.

a Why do you think there are more literacy issues among adults than children nowadays?

b Do you think that books are one of the most important things in children's lives? Why or why not?

c Some people say that success in life doesn't depend on what education people have. Do you agree?

7 In groups, prepare a talk for other students about the importance of World Literacy Day. First, plan your talk – include some ideas from the texts and your own discussions. Then deliver your talk. Try to use the vocabulary you learnt in this lesson.

Talk about it: Every life tells a story

- Do you think it's easy to achieve success in life? Why or why not?

Watch this!

Reading

1 Work in pairs to discuss these questions.

   a   Do you know who the two people in the photos are?

   b   What do you think they have in common?

2 Skim-read the two accounts and check your answers to Exercise 1. Then discuss what you think about each person's quotation about success. Do you agree with them? Why or why not?

Albert Einstein (1879–1955)

The word 'Einstein' is associated with intelligence and people associate it with genius. Yet, the scientist behind the theory of relativity, Albert Einstein, could not speak fluently until the age of nine. He was asked to leave school because of his poor behaviour, and he was refused entry to university.

His earlier failures did not stop him from winning the Nobel Prize in Physics in 1921. After all, he believed that: 'Success is failure in progress.'

To this day, his research has influenced various aspects of life including culture, religion and art.

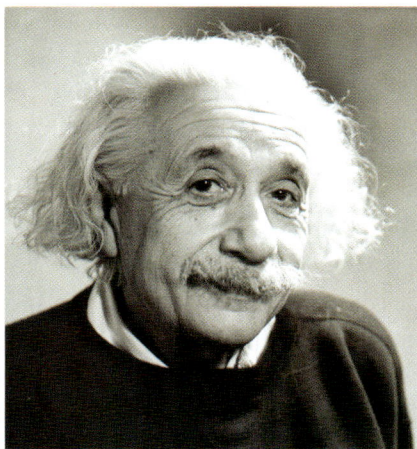

Michael Jordan (1963–)

'I've missed more than 9000 shots in my career. I've lost almost 300 games. Twenty-six times, I've been trusted to take the game's winning shot and missed. I've failed over and over and over again in my life. And that is why I succeed.'

This quote by retired basketball legend Michael Jordan speaks for itself. It would be wrong to think that Jordan's basketball skills revolve around natural talent. In fact, in his younger years, basketball coaches had trouble looking past the fact that Jordan didn't yet reach the minimum height. It was years of effort, practice, and failure that made him the star we know today.

Michael Jordan's success all came down to his motivation and determination, two of the most important characteristics that drive people to succeed.

Listening

3 Listen to a group of students discussing the two people from Exercise 2. Work in pairs to answer these questions.

    a Which person do they choose for their presentation about inspirational life stories?

    b What are their reasons for choosing this person?

    c What other facts do they want to include in their presentation?

4 Listen to the discussion again. What phrases do all three students use to agree, disagree politely or suggest an idea? Try to get at least one phrase for each category.

Agree	
Disagree politely	
Suggest an idea	

5 In pairs, discuss what type of celebrity makes a good role model for young people, and why. Try to use the phrases from Exercise 4.

6 Listen to the discussion one more time. One student is leading the discussion. Look at the categories and complete the table with at least one phrase for each one.

Ask for other people's opinions	
Move the conversation forward	
Deal with other people who disagree	

7 Work in small groups. Discuss what life lessons young people can learn from their role models and how these can help them in their own lives. Take it in turns to lead the discussion. Try to use the phrases from Exercise 6.

Speaking

COMMUNICATION

Contributing effectively to a group discussion and reaching a conclusion

During a group discussion, take turns with others to express your opinions on the given topic. It is completely normal that people may have different opinions to yours. Remember, the aim of the discussion isn't to persuade everyone that your opinion is the only correct opinion – it is to express your view and listen to others to find out what they think. To reach a conclusion at the end of a discussion, you should consider all the opinions and go with what the majority of people think.

8 Work in small groups. You are going to prepare a presentation about an inspirational person and what young people can learn from the person's life. During your discussion, remember to use the phrases from Exercises 4 and 6. Prepare your presentation and then deliver it to the class.

First decide who is going to lead your discussion. Then agree on the following:

- which of the three famous women suggested below you want to choose (you can also choose a role model you like):
  - Lady Gaga (a singer)
  - Vera Wang (a fashion designer)
  - Lidia Thorpe (a politician)
- reasons for your choice
- what facts about the person's life you want to include
- what young people can learn from the famous person's life story.

Improve your writing: A short story

1   Work in pairs. You are going to read a story written by a student for a writing competition. First look at the photos and say what you can see. Using the photos, try to guess what happens in the story. Compare your ideas with other students. Whose story was the most exciting?

2   Now read the story and check what really happens. Put the photos in the correct order based on the events in the story.

1   It was a beautiful, sunny autumn day. My friend and I had decided to spend the day hiking in the nearby woods. The days were getting shorter and the sun wasn't as strong as a couple of months ago,
5   but it was still warm enough. I closed my eyes and was soaking up the sun while I was waiting for my friend Ollie to get ready. He'd already parked his sixties campervan in a tiny car park on the edge of the woods and was checking he had everything
10 he needed. I wasn't paying much attention to the world around me so Ollie made me jump when, out of the blue, he shouted, 'Janosh, let's go!'

2   I opened my eyes, feeling a bit annoyed about the sudden interruption, but, at the same time, I was
15 excited about the prospect of a satisfying hike through my favourite woods.

3   Ollie insisted he knew the route and we didn't need a map. But I'd packed one anyway. Getting lost because my phone has died on me was not
20 something I fancied in the middle of nowhere!

4   The hike started gently, following the winding creek before rising sharply into the woods. We followed a narrow path. I was enjoying the sun and the autumnal colours; yellow, red, brown and orange.
25 The woodland floor was already covered with fallen leaves and dotted with mushrooms, acorns and conkers. We'd been walking for a couple of hours when my stomach announced it was lunchtime. We decided to have a picnic on top of the hill we'd
30 just climbed. The views were breathtaking – I was totally enchanted by the beauty around me.

5   'Which way do we go now, Ollie?' I asked, expecting a confident answer from my friend. No answer. 'Ollie, which way do we need to go now?' I repeated
35 my question and sharply turned around to where Ollie was standing. I got this very unpleasant feeling in my stomach. Something wasn't quite right. Ollie glanced at me and then stared back at the three different paths, scratching his head. This could only
40 mean one thing – we were lost!

6   'Ollie?' I called to my friend with a shaking voice, 'Please tell me it's not what I'm thinking!'

'Janosh, I'm really sorry, but do you think I could borrow your map? You see this blue line on

45 the map, right here? That's the trail we've been following.' Ollie explained.

'So?'

'There are three paths here, but only one on the map.'

'Hmm. I see, well… shall we take the middle one?'
50 I suggested with a shaky voice.

7   And to my surprise, Ollie nodded and off we went. We'd been walking for some time and I was becoming more and more anxious. The sun was starting to set and, suddenly, the woods didn't feel
55 as magical in the evening light; quite the opposite.

8   Then I heard a very loud noise. A very scary noise. I turned to Ollie, hoping to hear that everything was fine, but he looked at me in horror and I knew instantly what to do – run! That was the only
60 thing I could hear in my head – run! Judging by Ollie's reaction, his survival instinct must have told him to do the same. He started sprinting and I followed him. Sprinting through long grass and low branches, I was so terrified I didn't feel all the
65 tiny cuts. Up, down, up, down – I could hear my heart pumping. It felt like we'd been running for hours when we got to a creek, which was narrow enough to jump over. So I did. But I slipped on a wet rock. I lost my balance and fell flat on my
70 face into mud. I don't know what happened, but, suddenly, I remembered there was a creek next to the car park where we'd left the car.

9   'Are you alright, Janosh?' I heard Ollie say in a worried voice.

75 'Ollie, this must be the same creek we saw this morning!'

Ollie's eyes lit up with excitement. 'Janosh, you're a star!'

10 And that's how a creek saved our lives. We got to
80 the car park to find Ollie's campervan still there. Exhausted, but over the moon, we got in the van and drove home. We certainly won't forget the hike any time soon.

11 Oh, and that noise? Later that week, we found
85 out the local deer are particularly loud at this time of year!

WRITING TIP

Using personification in story writing

To make a story more interesting, you can use personification. This means you can talk about things as if they were a person. For example, the story says: '…my stomach announced it was lunchtime'. It is more interesting that just saying 'I was hungry.'

3   **Work in small groups. Look at the opening paragraph of the model story and answer these questions.**

   a   How does the writer set the scene at the start of the story?

      A   by describing the main characters

      B   by describing what's happening

      C   by describing the landscape

   b   What verb forms does the writer use at the start of the story to set the scene?

4   **Work in small groups and write an alternative opening paragraph to the model story. Imagine Ollie is the narrator this time and write the opening paragraph from his point of view. Change details like the weather, the landscape and what Ollie says about Janosh.**

5   **Now look at the description of the woods in paragraph 4. The writer makes the reader feel as if they were also in the woods. Find examples of how the writer achieves this.**

6   **Think of the woods in a different season, different weather or a different part of the day. Imagine what you might see, hear and smell or the emotions you might feel if you were there at that time. Write an alternative description of the woods. You can use the pictures below to help you.**

7   **How does the writer finish the story? Read the ending of the model story and choose from the two phrases below. What effect do you think this type of ending has on the reader?**

•   short and sudden

•   long and descriptive

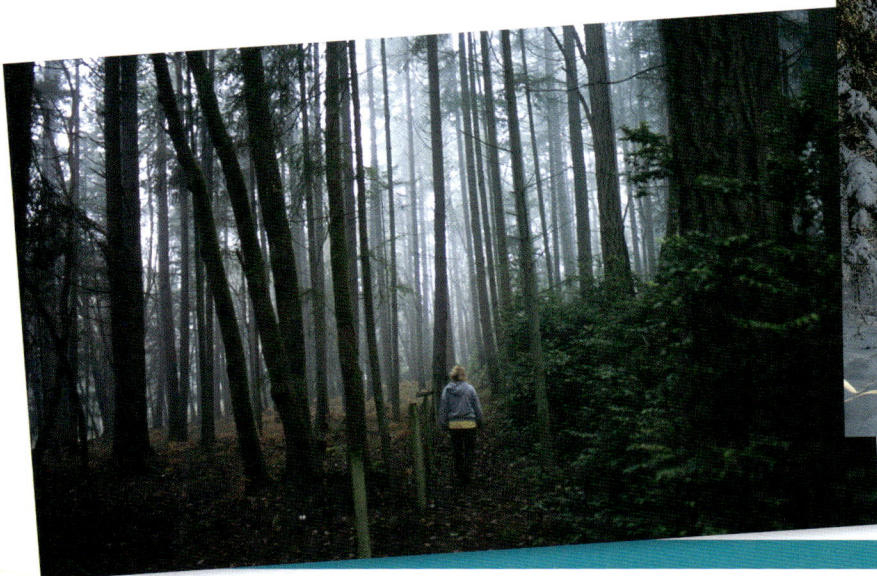

8   **Work in small groups and imagine a different ending to the story. Write the ending.**

USE OF ENGLISH

Narrative verb forms – past simple, past perfect and past continuous

In Unit 5, you studied these verb forms in storytelling. They come either in simple or continuous forms.

We use the past simple form to express ideas or activities that are complete, are only done once or happen for a short moment.

Past simple

*I **opened** my eyes.* (done once)

*We **followed** a narrow path.* (completed)

Past perfect simple

*My friend and I had **decided** to spend the day hiking in the nearby woods.* (happened for a short time)

*He'd already **parked** his sixties campervan in a tiny car park on the edge of the woods.* (completed)

We use the past continuous forms to express ideas or activities that are still in progress, incomplete or interrupted by another action.

Past continuous

*I **was soaking** up the sun.* (still in progress)

*I **was becoming** more and more anxious.* (incomplete)

Past perfect continuous

*We'**d been walking** for some time.* (still in progress)

*We'**d been running** for hours when we got to a creek.* (interrupted)

Find more examples in the model story.

---

9   **Complete these sentences with the verb in the correct past form.**

a   When I _____ (see) him in town the other day, I _____ (know) I _____ (meet) him somewhere before.

b   As we _____ (come) out of the woods, we _____ (see) a huge deer that _____ (look) straight at us.

c   I _____ (walk) for hours in the hot sun, when I _____ (realise) I _____ (not put) any sunblock on. My skin _____ (already start) to turn red.

d   Peter _____ (think) about his plans for the next day, so he _____ (not notice) the huge rock in front him and _____ (walk) straight into it.

e   I _____ (do) my homework when my sister _____ (ring) me from outside the house to tell me that she _____ (lose) her house keys and if I _____ (can) let her in.

10   **Work in small groups and look at the alternative paragraphs and descriptions you have written so far. Put them in the correct order and write some more text in between to make the sections fit together. Use some of the forms from the Use of English box. Make sure you use the correct past forms.**

11   **Proofread your story. Then read it to the rest of the class. Listen to other groups' stories and discuss what you liked about them and how they made you feel.**

Project challenge

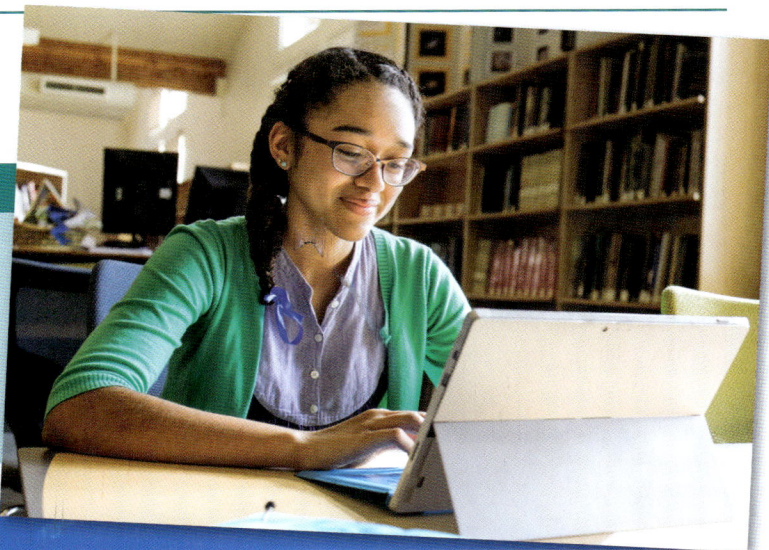

PROJECT LEARNING OBJECTIVES

In your project you will…

- obtain information from a written text

- organise an event and respond creatively

- produce a written text to persuade others to do something.

PROJECT OPTION 1

Organise an event and make a poster

Imagine that you recently discovered your local library is closing down. You have decided to organise an event to raise awareness of the importance of libraries for local communities.

Step 1: Do online research into what services libraries provide and why they're important for local communities. Also research comments on forums about how libraries have changed people's lives.

Step 2: In groups, compare your findings. Decide on the five most important services that libraries provide. Also select one forum comment to support the importance of libraries.

Step 3: Prepare a short presentation on the topic of 'Libraries change lives'. In your presentation include:

- the reasons you agreed on in step 2 why libraries are important for local communities

- a strong message to encourage other people to support using local libraries more

- a role-play between a reporter and a person whose life has been changed because of a library. (Use the information from step 1.)

Step 4: In the same group, discuss the event you want to organise to save your local library.

Decide on the following:

- the date and time

- duration (from/to)

- the venue

- the order of the activities you want to present (for example, a role-play, a talk/presentation)

- whether you want to include guest speakers/ who to invite

- which student from your group is going to lead or present the event.

Step 5: Design a poster to promote your event and persuade people to save your local library. Decide what information you need to include on the poster.

Step 6: Present your poster to the class. Deliver your presentation and act out the role-play.

Step 7: Discuss which group delivered the strongest message, and why.

SPEAKING TIP

Making your message more powerful

When you want to persuade other people that something is important, you can say:

You would be really helping us out if you could…

We urgently need your help with…

COMMUNICATION

Brainstorming and trying out new ideas

Before you start working on something new, write down a lot of ideas (for example, from your own research, what others think/say about the topic). Then look at the ideas and select the best ones. Don't be afraid of trying out new ideas and experimenting with them. Remember, it is important to enjoy the process and learn which ideas work and which don't. It is also useful to have someone else look at your final work. Think of their feedback as something positive that will help you improve next time – don't just think of feedback as criticism.

PROJECT OPTION 2

Take part in a group discussion and produce a written text

Imagine you are a member of a book club that meets regularly to discuss books all the members have read. You are going to discuss a story and then produce a piece of writing related to it.

Step 1: In small groups, choose one short story that you all want to read. Decide how long you need to read the story.

Step 2: Read the short story. Then make notes with facts and your opinions about the story.

Use this list to help you:

- Title
- Genre
- Main characters
- Your favourite character and why
- Your favourite scene/event and why
- What you thought of the ending and whether you would change it
- What you learnt

- Whether you would recommend the book and why.

Step 3: In small groups, discuss the story you have read. Use the information from your notes as a basis for your discussion. Express your own opinions and react to other people's.

Step 4: In your book club you have also decided to produce your own writing based on the story you have all read. Choose from this list what type of writing you would like to produce:

- a book review
- a magazine article about an event from the story
- a contemporary short story based on the original story
- a report about an event from the story
- a written interview with one of the characters
- an alternative ending for the story.

Step 5: Write your new text. At the end, proofread it and make changes and corrections.

Step 6: Read your text to the rest of your group. Can they guess which task from step 4 you chose?

SELF AND PEER ASSESSMENT

Think about how well you, and your group, did in the project. Then complete the statements below.

a   Our group worked particularly well in the following activities:…

b   I really enjoyed working with… because he/she…

c   While doing this project, I learnt that I'm really good at… and I enjoy…

d   However, I need to practise… a bit more.

e   I learnt… and, in the future, this will help me…

Practise and prepare

Speaking

1   **Work in pairs. Answer these questions as fully as possible.**

   a   Some people say that there is no need to keep libraries open in the future. What's your opinion?

   b   Do you think it's still important to teach children to write at school? Why or why not?

   c   There is an opinion that students should choose what books they should read in their literature lessons themselves. Do you agree?

   d   A story is better told in a film rather than written down in a book. What do you think?

Writing

> **EXAM TIP**
>
> **Writing at the appropriate length**
>
> In writing exams, you are always given the word limit. You shouldn't write too little, as this may mean that you do not cover all the necessary details and you could lose marks as a result. But you shouldn't write too much, as this will take too much time and you may run out of time to complete the whole paper. You don't have to count every single word in your answer – just count the words on one line. Like this, you can guess approximately how many lines you will need to write. Also, it is a good idea to time yourself when you practise your writing, to see whether you can complete the task within a given time.

2 **You recently wrote an article for a school magazine. Write an email to your friend about it. Write about 120–160 words.**

In your email you should:

- describe what you wrote about

- explain why you chose that topic

- say what you found challenging, and why.

Listening

3 **You will hear an interview with Haruto Tanaka, an artist who creates a special type of comic book called manga. For each question, choose the correct answer, A, B or C. You will hear the interview twice.**

a Haruto says that he decided to become a professional manga artist

    A after winning a competition.

    B during his studies at art school.

    C because his parents encouraged him to.

b What does Haruto find challenging about his job?

    A being criticised by readers

    B working with demanding editors

    C meeting very tight deadlines

c What does Haruto say about the manga series he's working on now?

    A All the main characters have western names.

    B Some events in the story are based on real life.

    C He wants it to be less serious than the last one.

d According to Haruto, the most important thing to do when starting out as a manga artist is

    A to get tips from experienced artists.

    B to produce something short first.

    C to practise by drawing a lot.

REFLECTION

1 Work in small groups and look at the image and quotation at the start of this unit. Discuss why you think the light bulb is used in the image. What do you think it represents?

What do you think the George R.R. Martin meant by 'A reader lives a thousand lives' in his quotation? Give examples from your own reading.

2 Working with a partner, use these questions to help you reflect on your progress as a learner while working on this unit.

a In the Think about it lesson, you practised different listening skills, one focusing on listening for ideas, the other listening for specific words and phrases. Which one did you find easier? Can you use these two listening skills in other school subjects? Give examples.

b In the Sociology and education lesson, you read two different types of texts and practised guessing the meaning of some words from the text, where they appeared. Are you getting better at this skill? What helped you guess the meaning of some of the words in this lesson?

c In the Talk about it lesson, you practised taking part in a group discussion. Did you prefer leading the discussion or someone else leading it? Why?

d In the Improve your writing lesson, you reviewed and practised using narrative forms. How confident are you about using these forms in your writing? What can you do to practise these forms even more? Do you have a favourite grammar book you use to practise English grammar? Why or why not?

e In the Project challenge lesson, you participated in a creative task. What did you enjoy about this task? What skills do you think you improved by doing this task? Would you like to do these types of tasks more often? Why or why not?

f In the Practise and prepare lesson, you learnt about the importance of timing your writing. How long do you take to write 120–160 words? If you think you take too long to complete a writing task, what can you do to speed up your writing?

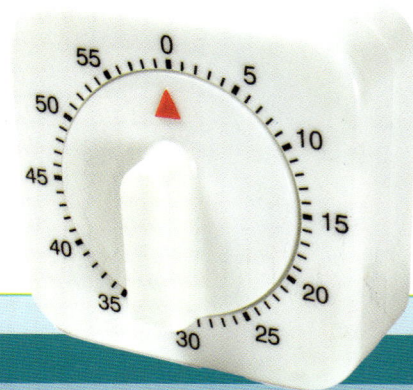

SUMMARY CHECKLIST

I can…

- [ ] follow a longer talk and understand main ideas and I can also follow a shorter story and identify specific information.
- [ ] understand different text types and understand the connections between ideas.
- [ ] participate effectively in a group discussion and take the discussion forward.
- [ ] write a short story and use the right techniques to create the desired effect on the reader.
- [ ] use a range of narrative forms correctly in either the simple or continuous form.

10 Looking ahead

IN THIS UNIT YOU WILL...

- **listen** to a talk about future career advice
- **read** an article about culture shock
- **take part** in an interview and **ask for** and **give** clarification
- **write** a formal email requesting more information
- **practise** using indirect questions to sound more polite
- **research** and **evaluate** different options.

GETTING STARTED

"The future depends on what you do today."
(Mahatma Gandhi, Indian activist and politician)

What do you think young people can do to prepare for their future?

Watch this!

Think about it: Choosing a future career

- **What do you think is important to consider when choosing a future career?**

Speaking

1   Work in pairs. Look at the vocabulary box. Use a reliable dictionary to check the meaning of any words or phrases you don't know. Would any of these aspects be important to you when choosing a job? Why?

a decent salary	job satisfaction
apprenticeship	long-term prospects
co-workers	the competition
flexible working hours	workforce
fulfilling	workload
high-pressured	work overtime

2   Now discuss the questions below.
   a   What jobs do your relatives do?
   b   Would you like to do the same jobs? Why or why not?
   c   What do you want to do after you leave your current school? Why?
   d   Do you think it's easy or difficult for young people to get their first job? Why?
   e   Have you been given any future career advice? If so, what was the advice about?

3   Look at the word box below with phrases we use to describe the personality and skills people need in different jobs. What do they mean? Use a reliable dictionary, if necessary.

a people person	imaginative
calm under pressure	outgoing
have a passion for	think on your feet

Listening

4   You are going to listen to a talk given by a career adviser to a group of students. First, copy the table. Then listen to the talk and complete the missing information. Write one or two words only in each gap.

Stage 1: Reflecting
• _____ [1] (e.g. deciding when to work)
• your interests
• _____ [2]
• _____ [3] (e.g. creativity)

Stage 2: _____ [4]
• what _____ [5] and _____ [6] necessary
• _____ [7]
• long-term prospects
• _____ [8]

Stage 3: _____ [9]
• first steps after school
• _____ [10] and qualifications (e.g. a _____ [11])
• alternative routes
• _____ [12] (e.g. in journalism)

5   Listen to the talk again and write down one more detail for each bullet point.

6   Work in small groups. Imagine you've just been to the talk about how to choose your future career but one of your classmates hasn't. Choose one of the three stages from the talk and use your notes from Exercise 4 to write a short summary of that stage. Then read your summary to the rest of the class.

STUDY TIP

Noticing collocations in texts

When reading or listening to a text, it is useful to notice what two words go together to make a phrase. We call these phrases collocations. For example, *interview* is often used with *job* to make the phrase *job interview*. We wouldn't say *profession interview* or *job questioning*. By using the correct words together when you speak or write, you will sound more natural. To check whether two words often go together, you can use a learner's dictionary or a collocation dictionary. There are also digital versions of these dictionaries.

---

7   Work in pairs. Listen to some nouns from the talk about choosing your career path. Write them down and match each one to a verb from the box to make a collocation. Some nouns can be used with more than one verb.

apply for	carry out	fulfil
attend	complete	gain
boost	earn	pursue

Speaking

8   Work in the same pairs. Choose five collocations from Exercise 7 and make sentences using them.

9   Work with another pair. Read out your sentences to them, but leave out either the noun or the verb that makes up the collocation. Can the other pair give you the correct word that completes the sentence?

For example: *When you attend a _____, make sure you are not late and dress smartly*. (the missing noun is 'job interview')

10 Work in small groups. As part of your career advice week, you have decided to prepare a poster with some useful tips for your classmates about how to choose your career. Use the information from the talk and decide on eight tips you want to include. Try to use some of the collocations from Exercise 7 and other vocabulary you have learnt in this lesson. Create your poster and share it with the rest of the class.

Psychology and social science: Culture shock

• **What aspects of everyday life might people find difficult when studying or working abroad?**

Reading

1 Work in pairs to discuss 'Culture shock'. What do you think the answers to these questions might be?

   a   What is culture shock?

   b   Who usually experiences culture shock, and when?

   c   What can cause culture shock?

2 Read the first paragraph of the article about culture shock on the next page. What are the answers to the questions in Exercise 1? Were you right?

3 Look at the Academic language box and check the meaning of any words or phrases you don't know in a reliable dictionary

ACADEMIC LANGUAGE

Psychology and social science

adapt	integrate
adaptation	negotiate
adjust	negotiation
adjustment	out of your comfort zone
anxiety	provide support and
a sense of belonging	guidance
disconnected	set of values
distant	welcome new
frustration	experiences

4 Which vocabulary from the Academic language box describes feelings? In pairs, discuss why someone who is experiencing culture shock might feel this way.

READING TIP

Using subheadings to locate information

If a text has subheadings, use them to quickly locate the information you're looking for.

5 Read the rest of the article and answer these questions.

   a   How do people feel at each stage of culture shock, and why?

   b   Is the feeling at each stage stated directly or implied?

   c   Why do people find the four factors difficult to cope with? Find one reason for each factor.

   d   Why do you think the three tips might help people cope with culture shock? Give one reason for each tip.

6 Read the comment written by an international student. In pairs, discuss which stages of culture shock she describes. What did she find particularly hard?

Being in a new place without your friends and family is definitely challenging and makes you feel out of your comfort zone. But it also gives you the opportunity to learn more about yourself! Thanks to this experience, I discovered how resilient I am and I've made new friends for life – which wasn't always easy. Back home people seem 'warmer' so I sometimes felt lonely in the new place. The school where I'm studying has given me lots of support and a chance to share my experiences with other international students struggling with very similar issues.

(A Mozambican student in the Netherlands)

7 In small groups, discuss what students coming to study in your country might find difficult. Think about the four factors from the article. Write down your ideas.

8 Write a short article for your school magazine giving advice to international students studying at your school. Use your ideas from Exercise 7 and the words and phrases from the Academic language box. Write about 120–160 words.

International students and culture shock

What is culture shock?

Culture shock describes the impact of moving from a familiar culture to one that is unfamiliar. It includes the shock of a new environment, meeting lots of new people and learning the ways things are done in a new country. It also includes the shock of being separated from the important people in your life, such as family, friends, colleagues and teachers: people you would normally turn to for support and guidance at times of uncertainty.

How many stages of culture shock are there?

There are usually five different stages – honeymoon, negotiation, adjustment, adaptation and re-entry shock.

1 Honeymoon stage

This stage can last for several weeks or months. This is the happy phase when you're fascinated by all the exciting and different aspects of your new life – from the sights and smells to the pace of life and cultural habits.

2 Negotiation stage

This stage is characterised by frustration and anxiety. This usually appears three months into your stay. As you are constantly faced with difficulties or uncomfortable situations that may offend you or make you feel disconnected, the excitement slowly disappears. You also start to miss your friends and family and idealise your life back home. You may not find the locals so friendly anymore, find it hard to integrate and may experience feelings of confusion, and even anger.

3 Adjustment stage

People usually move into this stage after about six to twelve months. Your life gradually starts to get better as the routine sets in and the local way of life, food and customs begin to feel more familiar. You may also have made a few friends or learnt the language, helping you to adjust and better understand the new culture you live in. You may still experience some difficulties, but you're now able to handle them better.

4 Adaptation stage

You now feel comfortable in the new country and you have successfully adapted to the new way of life. You no longer feel isolated or lonely and are used to your new daily activities and friends. You've gained a strong sense of belonging and finally feel at home in your new environment.

5 Re-entry shock stage

This stage can happen once you return home after living abroad for a long time. Things may seem very different from when you left, putting you out of your comfort zone, and you can feel like you no longer belong there. Your home town, friends and even your family have changed and moved on without you and you may find that you have to go through the whole process of culture shock all over again!

Factors that can contribute to culture shock

Climate

Many students find the climate can affect them a lot. You may find the differences in the weather, for example dampness and dark skies, difficult to get used to.

Language

Listening and speaking in a new language is tiring. In class, some international students have trouble understanding the lectures and reading materials. People speak quickly and you may feel embarrassed to ask them to repeat what they said.

Social roles and behaviour

Different types of social behaviour may confuse, surprise or offend you because you will, quite naturally, be comparing this with what is acceptable or unacceptable in your home country. For example, you may find that people appear cold, distant or always in a hurry, or you may be surprised by the formal or less formal way people greet each other.

Viewpoints

Although you may first become aware of cultural differences in everyday situations concerning things like food or dress codes, you may also notice that people from other cultures may have very different opinions about the world from yours. Cultures are built on firmly established sets of values and beliefs.

How to deal with culture shock

- Before leaving, don't forget to pack a few of your favourite things (for example, a framed photo) to make you feel at home more quickly.

- Try to welcome the new experiences with an open mind; accept invitations to events, taste new food, offer to help out new friends and explore the traditions.

- Remember that culture shock is part of the experience of living overseas and is impossible to avoid.

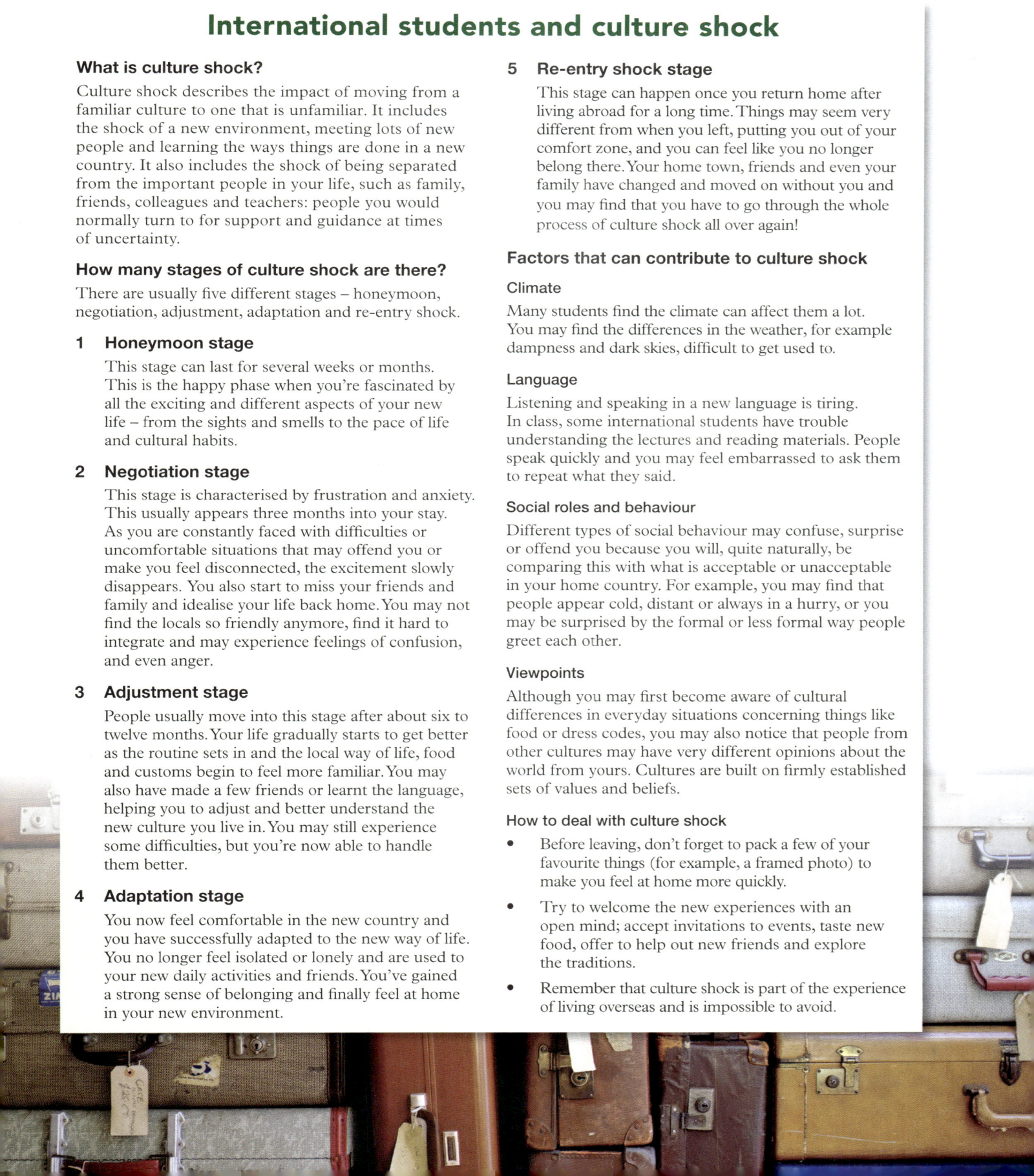

Talk about it: Make it or break it in interviews

• **What are the challenges of being interviewed?**

Watch this!

Listening

1   In small groups look at the activities below. Discuss whether you should or shouldn't do these things at a new school or job interview, and why.

> research the school or company that you are applying to
>
> practise answering questions
>
> get a good night's sleep
>
> eat very little
>
> arrive on time
>
> switch off your phone
>
> dress casually
>
> look down at the floor
>
> give extended answers
>
> sit up straight
>
> interrupt the interviewer
>
> complain about your current school/job

2   Listen to an adviser talking to students who want to study in the UK. She is talking about some dos and don'ts to follow during interviews. Which activities from Exercise 1 does she mention? Write the activities down.

3   Listen to the talk again. Put a tick next to the activities people should do during interviews and a cross next to those that people shouldn't do. In small groups, look at the activities that you ticked and discuss how important they are.

> **SPEAKING TIP**
>
> **Saying how important something is**
>
> When you want to say how important something is, you can say:
>
> • *I feel it's vital to…* (very important)
>
> • *It might be useful to…* (quite important)
>
> • *I don't think it's absolutely necessary to…* (not very important)

4   Listen to two interviews, one with a student named Peter and one with a student named Nawon. Whose do you think is better, and why? Compare your answers in pairs.

5   Listen to the second interview again. What does Nawon say to make her answers extended? Give examples.

6 Listen to the questions from the first interview. Your teacher will pause the recording after each question. Work in pairs and try to give more extended and appropriate answers than Peter did in his interview.

7 In the second interview, Mr Kowalski and Nawon both use some useful phrases to ask for clarification, give clarification and give themselves time to think. Copy the table below. Listen to the interview again and write the phrases in the correct category.

Ask for clarification	
Give clarification	
Give themselves time to think	

8 In pairs, practise answering these questions. Use the phrases from Exercise 7.

a   Can you tell me a bit about yourself?

b   What's your favourite subject? Why?

c   What are your strengths as a student?

d   What are your weaknesses?

e   What extracurricular activities have you done?

f   What are your long-term goals?

g   Can you give me three adjectives that best describe you as a person?

USE OF ENGLISH

Time adverbials used with the past simple and present perfect

Remember that when we talk about our life and experience in English, we often use the present perfect simple and present perfect continuous. We can use words like *since*, *for*, *once*, *just*, *already*, *not yet* and *so far* with these forms.

*I've been practising music **since I was five years old**.*

We use the past simple when we say when exactly the situations happened (for example, in 2020, last summer, a week ago, when I was 10).

*I **did** some voluntary work last year **during my summer holidays**.*

9 Work in pairs to interview each other about the topics below. In your answers, use either the present perfect or the past simple with appropriate time adverbials.

- your hobbies
- learning English
- your travel experience
- your current school

Speaking

10 Work in small groups. Do a role-play of an interview for a place in a new school.

- Decide who the interviewer and student will be.
- Select some questions from Exercise 8.
- Act out your role-play.

Remember to use the language you have learnt in this lesson. The rest of the group should listen and give feedback at the end about what the interviewee did well and whether they need to improve anything. Then exchange roles.

SOCIAL RESPONSIBILITIES

Being culturally aware

Many young people nowadays study or work abroad. Therefore, it is important to know what is acceptable in different social situations. Before you go for an interview for a place at a school or for a job, make sure you do some research on how to behave, for example how you should greet your interviewer and what the correct dress code is. You shouldn't expect that everything will be exactly the same as in your country.

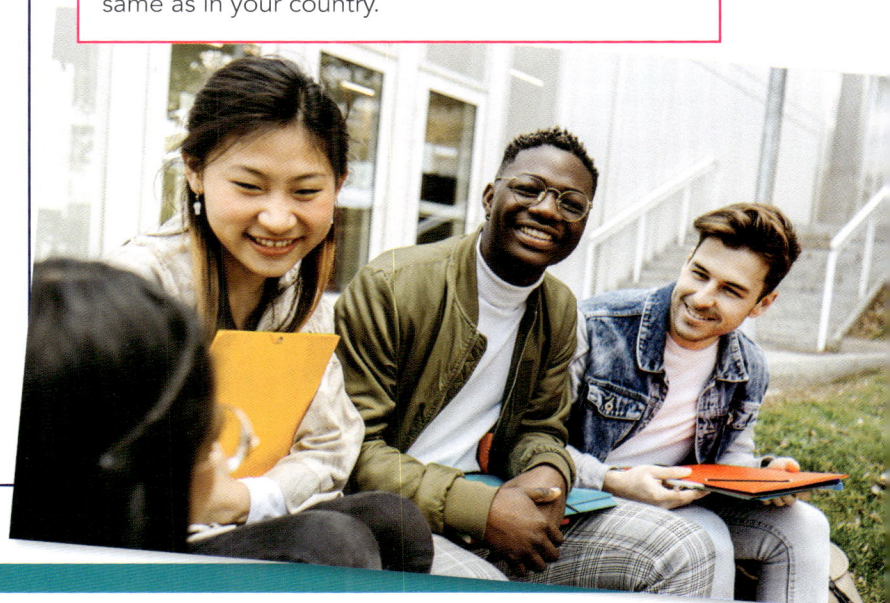

Improve your writing: A formal email requesting information

1 Work in pairs. Imagine you want to study at a language school to improve your English. Discuss what information you would like to know before enrolling at a language school. Write down your ideas.

2 Read the advert below for a language school called **Flying Colours**. Can you find all the information you discussed in Exercise 1? What information is missing?

Flying Colours Language School

Learn English with us!

We're based in Birmingham, United Kingdom

We offer:

• beginner to advanced classes
• six-month part-time courses
• three-month full-time courses.

Enrolment starts on 3 January

Our teachers are all highly qualified.

For more details, visit our website or contact us directly on flying-colours@omail.com

3 Read the email opposite, written by a student from China who is interested in studying at the language school. What information does he enquire about? Is it the same information you wanted to know?

4 Work in pairs and look at the email again. Answer these questions.

   a What register is the email written in?

   b Why do we need to use this register for this email?

   c What are the features of this register? Find examples of these features in the email.

USE OF ENGLISH

Indirect questions

To sound more polite in more formal situations, we use indirect questions to ask about something.

*I was wondering if you could help me. **Could you tell me** what time the presentation starts?*

These structures are more appropriate in formal situations. We call them indirect questions, but not all indirect questions are really questions. Look at direct and indirect questions and compare the word order. When we change yes/no direct questions into indirect, we use *if* or *whether*. For other questions we keep the same question word (for example, *what time*).

Direct questions

Can you help me? What time does the presentation start?

These questions can be used when talking to a friend or someone we know. If we use these questions with someone we don't know, or someone in charge (for example, a headteacher), they might sound slightly impolite as they're too direct.

5 Read through the model email to find more examples of indirect questions.

From: Lixin.Liu@greenfield.academy.com

To: flying-colours@omail.com

Dear Sir/Madam,

I saw your advertisement for courses at your language school on your social media page and I am interested in applying for one of your English courses. However, I would like to enquire about a few things.

Currently, I am studying at Greenfield Academy in Dalian, a city in China, where I also live with my parents. I would be grateful if you could let me know whether you provide accommodation for overseas students.

I have been studying English for nine years now and have reached upper-intermediate level. For this reason, I have decided I would like to take the IGCSE English exam next year. Your advertisement does not mention any exam classes, so I would like to enquire whether any of your classes focus on exam preparation, especially the IGCSE English exam. I would also like to know how many students there usually are per class. As I also focus on English studies at my current school, including life in English-speaking countries, it would be hugely beneficial for me to explore the United Kingdom. I was wondering if your school organised any trips or any other activities for students.

Last but not least, I could not find how much your school charges for individual courses. Could you possibly email me the fees for your courses and what your fees cover (for example, learning materials)?

Thank you in advance for your help.

I look forward to receiving your reply.

Yours faithfully,

Lixin Liu

---

6   **Work in pairs. Make these questions indirect to make them sound more formal and polite. Use the examples in the Use of English box to help you.**

a   How much are the course fees?

b   What do I need to bring with me?

c   What's your phone number?

d   Is there anything else I need to send with my application?

e   Will you be giving the talk about different career paths?

f   How do I get to your office?

g   When did you send me the last email?

h   Are you available for a meeting next Monday?

7   **Work in pairs to do a role-play. Imagine you want to find out more from the school secretary about a school interview you have next week. Phone the school and ask about the following:**

- **what time it starts / finishes**
- **where to go when you arrive**
- **what to bring**
- **how to get there from the city centre.**

8 Read the email below, which was written by a student to enquire about their interview at a new school. Discuss in pairs what you think the student did well and what they need to improve.

From: katrin.ferreira@starling.college.ac.uk

To: info@chaffinch.academy.ac.uk

Dear Sir/Madam,

I'm writing to ask about my interview that I have next week. I need more details.

I know what time the interview starts, but what time does it finish? My mum will be picking me up so I need to know. Also, where is the interview exactly? I've never been to your school before.

Also, do I need to bring anything with me? It'd be great if you could tell me so that I can put everything together before the interview next week.

And finally, how can I get to your school from the city centre? I'll be coming by public transport.

Thanks.

Can't wait to hear from you.

All the best,
Katrin Ferreira

---

9 Read the feedback given by Katrin's teacher. Did you identify the same issues?

You cover all the points from the task in your email. Your grammar and spelling are really good. Well done.

However, your email sounds too informal and would therefore be inappropriate for this situation. Remember, you're writing to a school secretary, a person you don't know, so you have to choose different vocabulary to the language you would use with your friends. Can you please rewrite your email and make it sound more formal? To do this you should:

- avoid using multi-word verbs that sound quite informal
- use words that sound more formal (for example, require instead of need)
- use full forms rather than contractions
- use indirect rather than direct questions.

Good luck!

10 In the feedback in Exercise 9, the teacher mentions using more formal-sounding words. Look at the formal words and phrases (a–k). Can you match them to the more informal words and phrases (i–x)?

a   I look forward to (+ -ing)

b   I've been informed about…

c   I have difficulty… (+ -ing)

d   Yours faithfully,

e   collect

f   Last but not least,…

g   Thank you.

h   require

i   gather all the necessary things

j   I would appreciate it if…

k   I am unable to…

i	need something	vi	put everything together
ii	I know (what time)	vii	and finally
iii	pick up somebody	viii	thanks
iv	I can't (2x)	ix	can't wait
v	It'd be great	x	all the best

STUDY TIP

Rewriting your own writing

In order to improve your writing, it is very important that you look at your teacher's feedback on your first draft. You should then rewrite your first draft based on your teacher's feedback.

If you don't, you will just continue making the same mistakes over and over again. The longer you ignore your mistakes, the harder it will be to fix them later.

11 Imagine you are Katrin. In pairs, rewrite her email from Exercise 8 and make it sound more formal and polite. Remember to include the suggestions made by Katrin's teacher. Exchange the email with another pair. Read their email and check that it sounds formal and polite. Give each other feedback.

12 Read this advertisement about speakers who deliver talks to help young people with their skills and future careers. Decide what other information you would like to enquire about.

Choose your guest speaker

Whatever event you're thinking of organising, we have a guest speaker for you.

Choose your guest speaker
- work in the 21st century
- art and design
- being a successful leader
- how to get your first job
- the world of business
- science and technology

or go to our website www.speakers4U.com to see the full list.

So what are you waiting for?

Contact us at pick-your-speaker@yahoo.com to book your speaker.

13 Look at your notes from Exercise 12 and write an email requesting more information. Remember to use some of the formal phrases from Exercise 10. When you finish your email, use this checklist to make sure you have done everything important. Then exchange your email with a partner and use the checklist to give feedback on each other's emails. Write the final draft.

Did you…?
- ✓ write a formal email?
- ✓ divide your email into paragraphs?
- ✓ request more information?
- ✓ use indirect questions to sound more polite?
- ✓ use appropriate formal sounding phrases?
- ✓ proofread your email to check your grammar and spelling?

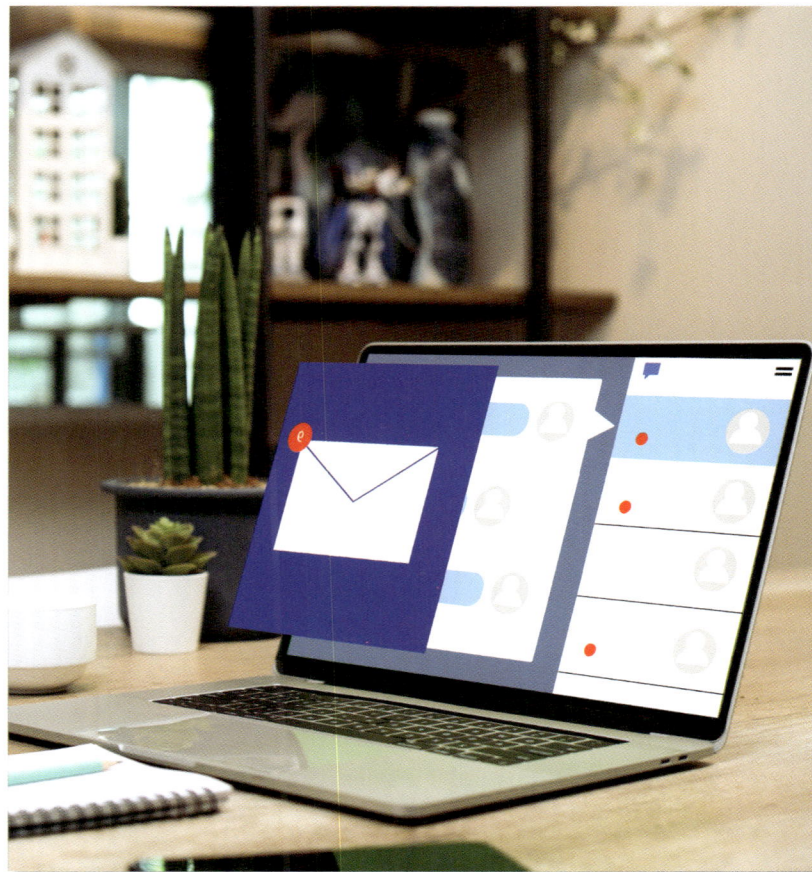

Project challenge

PROJECT OPTION 1

Carry out a survey and write an invitation email

You are going to do a class survey to find out what job(s) your classmates are interested in and why. Then you will write an invitation.

> What job are you interested in? _____
>
> If you're not successful in getting this job, what other job would you like to do? _____
>
> What would you like to find out about your future career? Choose a maximum of three ideas from:
>
> - what courses/qualifications are necessary
> - what extracurricular activities are necessary
> - if voluntary work is beneficial
> - skills needed to be a successful applicant
> - how popular the job is
> - typical working hours
> - typical responsibilities.

Step 1: Work in groups. Each member of your group should interview one student from another group. Use the questionnaire above to interview the student. Take notes of their answers.

Step 2: In your group, compare your findings. Discuss which job (for example, an accountant) or area of work (for example, advertising) other classmates are most interested in.

Step 3: In your group, do research online to find out who you could invite to talk about the career/job that your classmates are most interested in.

Step 4: As a group, write an email to invite your guest speaker. In your email you should mention:

- the reason for writing
- who you are
- when, for how long and for how many people the talk would be
- whether the speaker would prefer to give the talk at your school or virtually
- what you would like the speaker to talk about
- how the speaker can contact you.

Step 5: Prepare a poster to advertise the talk. Provide all the information that other students need to know, such as date, time and venue. Say who the speaker is and how this talk will help the students' future career choices.

Step 6: Present your poster to the class.

SOCIAL RESPONSIBILITIES

Gaining useful life skills

When you volunteer, you can learn and practise a lot of 21st-century skills, for example working in a team, time management and communication skills. These skills will be useful for your future studies and career.

SPEAKING TIP

Asking questions or commenting at the end of a presentation

At the end of a presentation, the audience is normally invited to ask questions or comment on what they have heard.

To ask questions, you can say:

Thank you that was very interesting, but could you tell us a bit more about…?

To comment, you can say:

I didn't know that…, so it was very interesting to hear about it.

PROJECT OPTION 2

Carry out research and give a presentation

You recently went to a career talk at which the speaker suggested that young people should try volunteering to gain work experience. You have decided to try virtual volunteering and want to persuade others to do the same.

Step 1: Work in groups. You are going to research virtual volunteering and take notes. Split your group into two.

- Group 1 should focus on researching what virtual volunteering is and what types young people can do.

- Group 2 should focus on researching the benefits of virtual volunteering and what skills students can improve doing this.

Step 2: Share your findings with the other group. Then decide:

- the three most interesting ideas for virtual volunteering

- what skills students can gain

- the five most important benefits of virtual volunteering.

Step 3: In your complete groups, use the information from step 2 to prepare a presentation about virtual volunteering.

In your presentation:

- introduce virtual volunteering

- provide examples of volunteering jobs

- inform students about the skills they can learn/practise

- highlight the benefits of virtual volunteering

- persuade students to try it.

Step 4: Practise your presentation and decide who will deliver each part.

Step 5: Deliver your presentation. At the end, allow time for other students from the audience to ask questions or comment.

Step 6: After the presentation, ask your classmates whether it persuaded them to try virtual volunteering, and why.

SELF AND PEER ASSESSMENT

Think about how well you, and your group, did in the project. Then complete the statements below.

a   Our group worked particularly well in the following activities:…

b   I really enjoyed working with… because he/she…

c   While doing this project, I learnt that I'm really good at… and I enjoy…

d   However, I need to practise… a bit more.

e   I learnt… and, in the future, this will help me…

Practise and prepare

Speaking

1 **For this exercise you are going to practise three different speaking tasks.**

Warm-up

To get used to speaking in English in parts 1–3, work in pairs to first answer the warm-up questions. Spend one to two minutes giving your answers.

- Can you tell me something about your best friend?
- What's your favourite music?
- What did you do last weekend?

Part 1: Interview

Answer the following questions as fully as possible. You have two to three minutes to complete this part.

- What job would you like to do in the future, and why?
- Can you tell me about a time you helped somebody, and what happened?
- Do you think that every young person should do some voluntary work? Why or why not?

Part 2: Short talk

Read the task below. You should spend one minute preparing what you want to say. Then give your talk for about two minutes.

Work experience

You would like to do a part-time job at the weekend in order to get some work experience. You are considering two options:

- helping in a local shop
- helping in an office

Explain the benefits of doing each option. Say which options you would prefer, and why.

Part 3: Discussion

Talk about the following ideas as fully as possible. You have three to four minutes to complete this part.

- There is an opinion that work experience is more important for young people's future than getting qualifications. What do you think?
- What do you think the advantages of studying or working in another country are? Why?
- 'Schools should teach all young people job interview skills.' Do you agree?
- In your opinion, should people in all jobs get paid the same salary? Why or why not?

Writing

2   **You recently gave a presentation at school and it was a success. Write an email to your friend about it. Write about 120–160 words.**

In your email you should:

- explain what the presentation was about

- describe how you prepared for the presentation

- say what you learnt from doing the presentation.

3   **Your school organised a talk with a career advisor and your teacher has asked you to write a report about the talk. In your report, say how helpful the talk was and recommend what else could be done to help students to decide on their future career. Here are some comments from other students in your class. These comments may give you some ideas, and you should also use some ideas of your own. Write about 120–160 words.**

I wish there was more advice about university interviews.

I learnt some useful tips for a job interview.

I wanted to find out more about particular jobs.

I'm glad we could ask some questions at the end.

REFLECTION

1 Look at the quotation at the start of this unit and the quotation below. Work in pairs to discuss how similar or different the ideas in both quotations are.

"The future belongs to those who believe in the beauty of their dreams." (Eleanor Roosevelt, an American human rights activist)

2 Working with a partner, use these questions to help you reflect on your progress as a learner while working on this unit.

a In the Think about it lesson, you learnt useful tips about what people should do when deciding on their future career. Which stage do you think you are at now yourself? Which tips did you find particularly useful, and why?

b In the Psychology and social science lesson, you practised reading a text for specific information. Which one did you find more challenging to find, and why? How can you practise this reading skill further?

c In the Talk about it lesson, you practised taking part in an interview. How confident do you feel now about answering questions in interviews? What else do you think you still need to practise?

d In the Improve your writing lesson, you practised writing in a formal register. How confident do you feel about this register?

e Also in the Improve your writing lesson, you practised using indirect questions. In what real-life situations do you think you will be able to use these questions? Give examples.

f In the Project challenge lesson, you practised persuading people to do something. Do you think you were successful? How do you know? Could you use this skill in other subjects? Give examples.

g In the Practise and prepare lesson, you completed speaking and writing tests. How do you feel about your progress in these two skills? After completing ten units in this book, do you think your performance in these two skills has improved? Why or why not?

SUMMARY CHECKLIST

I can…

☐ follow a longer talk and complete a table with missing information.

☐ follow an article and look for specific information.

☐ take part in an interview and ask for and give clarification.

☐ write a formal email and request information using indirect questions.

☐ research different options and evaluate how useful they are.

Literature

A poem

ABOUT THE AUTHOR

Elise Paschen

Elise Paschen is an American poet and co-founder of an organisation that aims to bring people closer to poetry by displaying poems in urban environments. She has won many poetry awards and her poetry covers a wide range of topics, from love and conflict to animals and nature, as well as life and death. She has both published and edited poetry books and encourages others to write through her teaching at the School of Art Institute in Chicago. As with many of Paschen's poems, 'The Tree Agreement' is based on her own personal experience. It focuses on a tree in her backyard and nature in the urban environment.

1   A weed is defined as a wild plant growing in a place where it is not wanted. Work with a partner to think of examples where a plant may be considered a weed when it grows in one place but not in another.

2   Work with your partner. Make a list of the advantages and disadvantages of having trees in an urban environment.

3   Read and listen to the first verse of the poem 'The Tree Agreement' by Elise Paschen. Does the neighbour see the tree as providing advantages or disadvantages? Do you think the poet agrees? Discuss your reasons with your partner.

> **The Tree Agreement**
> The neighbor calls the Siberian Elm
> a "weed" tree, demands we hack
> it down, says the leaves overwhelm
> his property, the square backyard.

Siberian elm

4 Now read and listen to the whole poem. Was your prediction in Exercise 3 about how the poet feels correct?

The Tree Agreement

The neighbor calls the Siberian Elm
a "weed" tree, demands we hack
it down, says the leaves overwhelm
his property, the square backyard.

5 He's collar-and-tie. A weed tree?
Branches screen buildings, subway tracks,
his patch of yard. We disagree,
claim back the sap, heartwood, wild bark.

He declares the tree "hazardous".
10 We shelter under leaf-hoard, crossway
for squirrels, branch house for sparrows, jays.
The balcony soaks up the shade.

Chatter-song drowns out cars below.
Sun branches down. Leaves overwhelm.
15 The tree will stay. We tell him "no".
Root deep through pavement, Elm.

Note: This text uses American-English spellings.

Squirrel

Sparrow

Jay

² **hack:** to cut in a rough or violent manner

³ **overwhelm:** to use a lot of force in order to win or control a situation

⁷ **patch:** a small area of ground

⁸ **sap:** the liquid inside a plant

⁸ **heartwood:** the inner circles of the trunk of a tree

⁹ **hazardous:** dangerous

¹⁰ **shelter:** to protect yourself or others from danger or unpleasant conditions

¹⁰ **hoard:** a large amount of something, often collected secretly to be used later

¹⁰ **crossway:** a path used to connect two places

READING TIP

Enjambment

The way in which the words of a poem are arranged into lines is an important feature of poetry. Enjambment refers to an arrangement where an idea or thought runs from one line to the next and the reader is forced to make a slight pause mid-sentence. Enjambment is often used to create tension and drama or to add emphasis to certain words.

5 Listen to the first verse being read with enjambment and then without it. Work with a partner. What difference do you notice? What words receive more emphasis when read with the enjambment? Why do you think Elise may have wanted to create this effect?

The neighbor calls the Siberian Elm a "weed" tree, demands we hack it down, says the leaves overwhelm his property, the square backyard.

The neighbor calls the Siberian Elm a "weed" tree, demands we hack it down, says the leaves overwhelm his property, the square backyard.

6   **With your partner answer these questions about the rest of the poem.**

   a   The poet refers to the type of clothes the neighbour wears for his job
        by saying 'He's collar-and-tie.' What is she really trying to tell us about
        the neighbour?

   b   The word *screen* in line 6 tells the reader that the tree hides some ugly things
        from view. In what other ways does the poet benefit from the tree's presence?
        Are any of the benefits the same as the ones on your list from Exercise 2?

   c   It is not only the poet that benefits from the tree. How do the animals
        in the photos benefit from its presence?

   d   The use of the word *demands* rather than *asks* in line 2 gives the reader
        a stronger sense of the conflict between the poet and the neighbour.
        What word does the poet use in the third verse to create a strong
        impression of how the neighbour communicates? Does it strengthen
        the idea of conflict or weaken it?

   e   Does the poem give the impression that the poet was willing to reach
        a compromise with the neighbour? Explain your answer.

   f   In the last line of the poem, the tree is described as 'Root deep through
        pavement'. Does this create an image of it being temporary or permanent?
        How significant do you think it is that the poem ends with this image?

   g   The poem is about a disagreement about the tree, Why do you think Paschen
        has chosen the title 'The Tree Agreement'?

   h   Do you think the tree should stay or be cut down? Why?

7   **Read the tasks below and choose one. When writing your poem, consider using
     enjambments where appropriate. When possible, use vocabulary which creates
     a strong impression. Try finishing the poem with a line which restates the main
     idea of the poem.**

     1 Write a short poem about
        the nature in an urban
        environment.

     2 Write a short poem
        about a difference
        of opinions.

Nonfiction literature

1 Answer the question below with a number from 1 (very important)
to 5 (not at all important). Work with a partner and explain your answer.

How important is music to you?

2 You are going to read and listen to two extracts from the book *31 Songs*
by Nick Hornby. Read the About the author box and the background information
in the box below. With your partner, decide what number from 1–5 you think
Nick Hornby may give to the question in Exercise 1.

Background information

After noticing that his son, Danny, at only a few days old responded
to music, Nick Hornby was sure that Danny would have a special
relationship with music. Danny was later diagnosed with autism – a
brain condition that makes a person's brain work differently from those
without the condition. It can limit a person's ability to communicate and
their ability to understand other people's feelings. People with autism
often find unfamiliar social situations hard to manage and may find social
relationships in general difficult. They tend to repeat the same behaviours
and routines, which can help them to reduce their level of anxiety. In
Extract 1 Hornby describes the relationship Danny developed with music.
In Extract 2 he expresses his opinion about the importance of music.

ABOUT THE AUTHOR

Nick Hornby

Nick Hornby
is a British
writer whose writing
has received many
awards. Several
of his books have
been made into
films. He has a
passion for music,
and music is often a
central theme in his
books. *31 Songs* is
a collection of essays
about 31 songs,
each of which are
important to him
in some way.

3 Read and listen to the extracts. How accurate do you think your answer in
Exercise 2 was?

1 [As he grew and developed,] Danny continued to feel the music – he
feels it so much, in fact, that he invented his own word for it, which
is no mean feat when your inability to communicate defines your
world. One of the many fascinating things about his condition (and
5 yes, there's fascination there too, just as there is laughter and pleasure
and excitement, mixed in with heartbreak and worry) is that, though
he has very little language, he has managed to find words for things
he fears he might not be given unless he asks for them. In other
words, there are some things so desirable that they can burst through
10 the blanket of silence that smothers him, and music ('goggo', as he
calls it), ranks right up there, along with crisps, and swimming, and
biscuits, which is pretty much where I'd put it too.

³ **no mean feat:**
a great achievement

¹⁰ **smother:** to prevent
something from
developing properly

¹¹ **rank:** to give
a higher or
lower position
of importance
to something

Danny's relationship with music is an intense one. He has to listen before going to sleep at night; he sometimes wanders round with a portable cassette player, volume turned up as high as it will go, and occasionally he retreats to his bedroom, like a teenager, in order to listen with a concentration not permitted him elsewhere. I find it almost overwhelmingly moving, watching him when he does that – my little speechless boy, his head lowered to the speaker, all the better to absorb every note (and-who knows – maybe every word) of every song.

And he seems to be developing [new musical] tastes too.

[…]

[This] is good news, because he tends to get stuck, to focus wholeheartedly on the tastes he already has (for salt and vinegar crisps, and Postman Pat videos, and peanut-butter sandwiches), rather than developing new ones.

[…]

You may think of yourself as a creature of habit, but he's gone way beyond creature. He's the Beast, the Tyrannosaurus rex, of habit.

2 …If it's true that music does, as I've attempted to argue elsewhere, serve as a form of self-expression even to those of us who can express ourselves tolerably well in speech or in writing, how much more vital is it going to be for him, when he has so few other outlets?

That's why I love the relationship with music he has already, because it's how I know he has something in him that he wants others to articulate. In fact, thinking about it now, it's why I love the relationship that anyone has with music: because there's something in us that is beyond the reach of words, something that eludes and defies our best attempts to spit it out. It's the best part of us, probably, the richest and strangest part, and Danny's got it too, of course he has; you could argue that he's simply dispensed with all the earthbound rubbishy bits.

15 cassette player: an old-fashioned device used for listening to recorded music

18 overwhelmingly: too much to manage

19 all the better: even better, in order to

26 Postman Pat: children's cartoon character

29 creature of habit: someone who always does the same thing in the same way

34 outlet: a way to express emotions

37 articulate: to express thoughts and feeling clearly

39 elude: to avoid

40 defy: to refuse to obey or do something in the usual way

40 to spit something out: to say something quickly

42 dispense with something: to do without

43 earthbound: uninteresting

4 **Work with a partner. Answer these questions about the extracts.**

a In your own words, explain why the author says that the fact Danny has invented his own word for music is 'no mean feat'.

b What does the author mean when he says 'they can burst through the blanket of silence that smothers him'?

c In your own words, explain why Danny goes into his bedroom to listen to music.

d Why does the author mention salt and vinegar crisps, Postman Pat videos and peanut-butter sandwiches?

e The author describes his son as 'the Tyrannosaurus rex of habit'. What impression does this give of Danny's need for routine and tendency to repeat behaviours?

f In the author's opinion, why is music more important to Danny than to those of us who 'can express ourselves well in speech and writing'?

g The author claims that music can help express deep emotions that we are unable to express with words. To what extent do you agree? What emotions do people typically express through music?

READING TIP

Conversational tone

A conversational tone in literature refers to a style of writing in which it sounds as if the writer is talking out loud, or is in conversation with the reader. It uses features that occur naturally in real speech such as interruptions and additions.

Notice how 'One of the many fascinating things about his condition (and yes, there's fascination there too, just as there is laughter and pleasure and excitement, mixed in with heartbreak and worry) is that, though he has very little language…' sounds as if the writer may be responding to a gesture or comment from the reader that indicated some doubt on the reader's behalf about what has been said.

A conversational style is often used in nonfiction literature, especially when writers express their own opinions, so that the writer appears more genuine. This allows the reader to feel they have a personal connection with the writer.

---

5 **Read the extract again. What other examples can you find of features that are similar to real speech? Work with a partner to compare your answers.**

6 **Read the tasks below and choose one. Write in a conversational style, using features of real speech where appropriate.**

1 Are you, or is someone you know, a creature of habit? Describe a situation that illustrates this.

2 Describe in what way someone you know has an intense relationship with music. Describe how highly they may rank music, how it compares in ranking to other things that are important to them and how their passion for music makes them behave.

A memoir

1   Read the definition of an autobiography and the quote that describes a memoir.
    In what ways are autobiographies and memoirs similar and different?
    Work with a partner to discuss your answer.

> An autobiography is an account of someone's life written by the person
> themselves. The person's entire life from childhood to the moment of
> writing is usually covered and it is normally written in chronological order.
> Autobiographies are nonfiction and often written in mid to late age.

> I had no interest in writing… of everything that's ever happened to me.
> Instead I was drawn to exploring specific moments, certain people and
> relationships, and particular events which still resonate powerfully for me
> as I try to understand the boy I was, and the man I became.
>
> (*Broken Music: A Memoir* by Sting, musician)

ABOUT THE AUTHOR

Elizabeth Nyamayaro

Elizabeth Nyamayaro is famous for her humanitarian work,
especially the work she has done with UN Women. She was
left in a village in Zimbabwe with her grandmother as the
rest of the family left to look for work. The relationship that
developed between them had a lifelong impact on Nyamayaro.
Her village was often struck by disease and famine, and she
was unable to attend school in her early years, instead doing
housework and collecting food. It wasn't until she was
10 years old that her family had enough money to send her
to school. But by that age she already had a dream about
what she wanted to be and was determined to achieve it.
Her book *I am a Girl from Africa* describes the major events,
people and relationships that helped her to fulfil her dream.

2   You are going to read and listen to two extracts from a memoir called *I am a Girl
    from Africa* by Elizabeth Nyamayaro. To what extent does the title suggest that
    being African is an important part of Elizabeth's identity? Do you think she stays
    in Africa throughout her life? Explain your answer to your partner.

3 Read and listen to the extracts. Were your predictions from Exercise 2 correct?

1

> *Elizabeth, now a young adult, has arrived in a new place to pursue her dream of working for the United Nations. Gogo is Elizabeth's grandmother and the person who raised her.*

How I wish my Gogo could experience everything alongside me. When I pass a red phone booth, I wish she had a phone and that I had the money to call her. *Gogo, I made it! Gogo, I'm here!* I imagine saying to her. When I think about how proud she
5 would be, seeing me here, I feel as joyous as a child.

[...]

I weave through the streets in the direction I've been pointed, and now I feel the exhaustion setting in: the travel, the adrenaline, the fear, all the walking in the rain, and feeling lost and out of place.
10 When I finally reach the youth hostel, I am overcome with relief. ...
A freckled girl with a tiny nose and bright orange hair sits at the desk.

As I approach her, trying to look friendly and upbeat, I see her lips moving and hear sounds emerge, but I do not understand
15 a single word, so I stay silent. She shakes her head and speaks louder, but her words still sound like gibberish, no matter how loudly she speaks or how often she repeats herself. I can see by the look on her face that she thinks I am stupid. This makes me nervous. I assume that she is asking me where I am from,
20 so I panic and blurt out, "I am from Africa!"

[...]

She has not told me her name so I decide to call her Tiny Nose in my mind.

[...]

25 "Well then. Welcome to London, girl from Africa," she says, and hands me a room key.

[...]

It's fine with me if Tiny Nose calls me "Girl from Africa". I could not want to be anyone or anything else. The fact that I'm African
30 is all that matters, and that is enough. I am after all *Mwana Wevhu* – a child of the African soil.

---

[5] **joyous:** extremely happy

[7] **weave:** to go somewhere by moving around a lot of things, rather than directly

[11] **freckled:** having small brown circular marks on the skin, particularly on the face

[13] **upbeat:** full of hope and happiness

[16] **gibberish:** words that have no meaning

[20] **blurt out:** say something suddenly without thinking

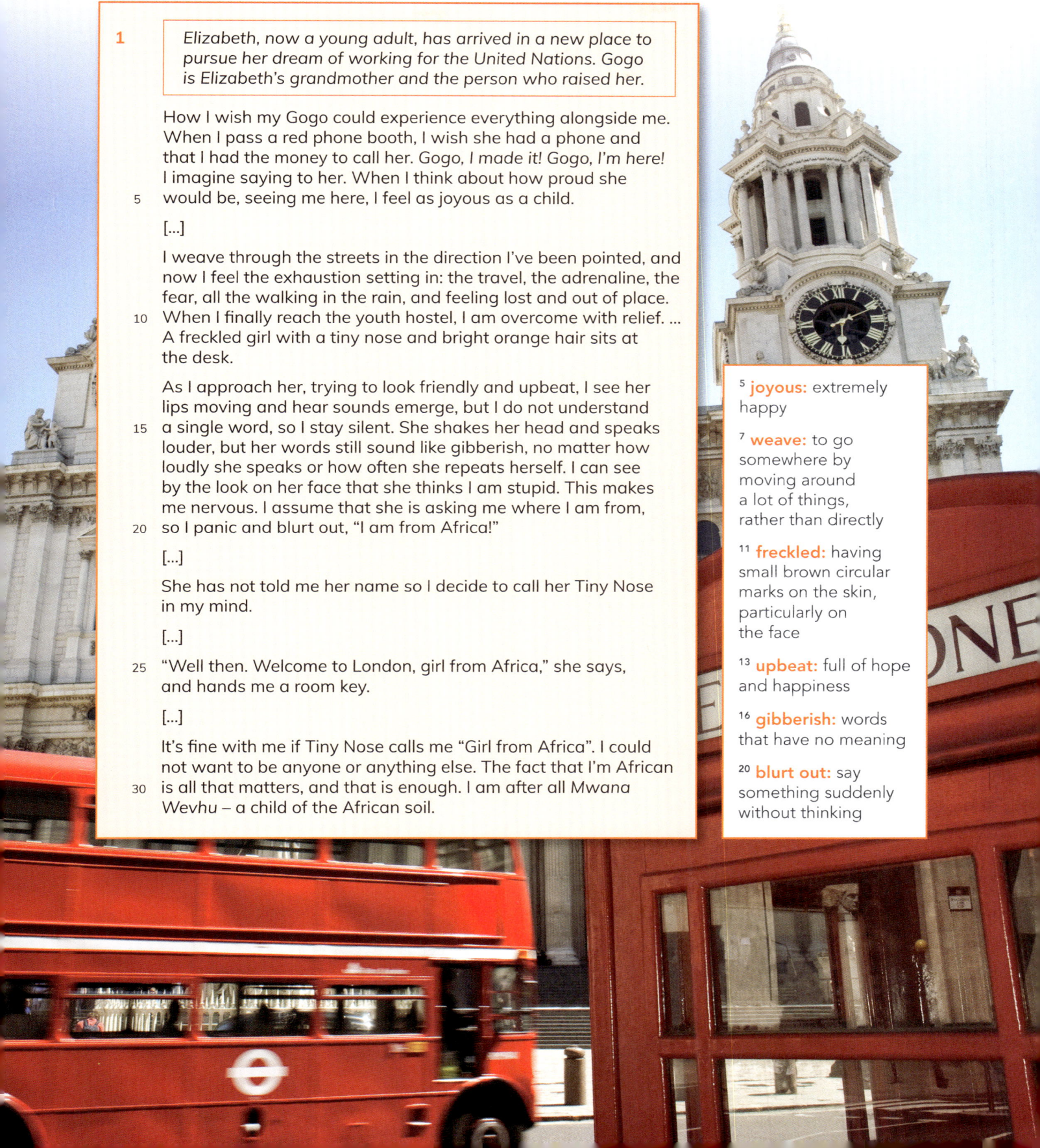

[...]

When night falls, I lie wide awake in my narrow bed, physically and emotionally exhausted.

35 [...]

I [remind] myself again who I am. I am *Mwana Wevhu*, a child of the African soil with big ideas and big dreams. I am a girl from Africa. And I am, as of this moment, one step closer to my dream.

2

> *There is a severe drought and many people in her village, Goromonzi, have died. Elizabeth's mother, who abandoned her as a young baby and who Elizabeth has no memory of, has arrived to take Elizabeth to live with her near Harare. Elizabeth is 10 years old. She calls her mother 'amai'.*

"Gogo, please! I need you. I need you so much!" I can feel my chest crack wide open at the thought of leaving her.

"Eeee, my dear child. Listen to me." Tears flow from her eyes. "You a have a special *shinga* – strength – that will always
5 protect you.

[...]

You, my dear child, you can always draw on your *shinga*, no matter the challenges you may face."

This does not soothe me; Gogo is my strength. "But I can't live
10 without you, Gogo." I bury my head in her chest and wail loudly.

Gogo takes my hand and places it on my heart, and holds it there. "Whenever you need me, I will always be right here with you inside your heart. Never forget that, my dear child. Never forget." My sad heart beats wildly against my hand.

15 Now I am terrified. *Where will this amai person take me? Will I ever see Gogo again?* "We have to go now," Amai says. She pulls me away from my beloved Gogo, and practically drags me out of the hut. And in that moment, my world falls apart.

"Where are we going?" I ask, and this *amai* person tells me in
20 a quick-quick way that we are going to the big city of Harare and then to Epworth, which is a township where she lives, near Harare. I know Harare is the capital city of Zimbabwe, so I listen carefully so that I will know how to get back to Goromonzi, back to my true home with Gogo.

[9] **soothe:** to make someone feel calm

[10] **wail:** to make a loud, high cry from pain or sadness

4 Look back at the quote in Exercise 1. With a partner discuss why Elizabeth might have chosen to include the moments, people and events that are described in the extracts, in her story. How do they help us to understand the girl she was and the woman she became?

Literary theme

Many literary books have a deeper meaning that underlies the plot and runs through the entire story. This is referred to as the literary theme of the book. It should not be confused with the subject matter, the difference being that the subject matter is clearly stated, while the literary theme is only implied. The literary theme requires the reader to reflect on and analyse the content. Common themes include friendship, life and death, identity, justice and love.

In *I am a girl from Africa*, the subject matter is Elizabeth's personal journey from her childhood village in Zimbabwe to her influential international career at the United Nations. The literary theme, however, is identity and the strength she takes from her roots.

5   **The title of the book is the first reference to the literary theme of the book. Read the extracts again and find other references to the theme of identity and heritage. Then compare your answer with a partner's.**

6   **With a partner, discuss the role of Elizabeth's grandmother, GoGo. How do you think she may be connected to the literary theme that runs throughout Elizabeth's story?**

7   **Answer these questions about the extracts with your partner.**

   a   *'Gogo, I made it! Gogo, I'm here!'* What does this statement (Extract 1, line 3) tell us about how easy or difficult Elizabeth's move to London was?

   b   When Elizabeth arrived at the hostel, she no longer felt 'joyous'(Extract 1, line 5) and instead had to try to appear 'upbeat' (line 13). Why do you think her mood had changed?

   c   How does the reader know that Gogo is also upset about Elizabeth's departure with Amai?

   d   Referring to the moment she was pulled out of her grandmother's hut, Elizabeth says 'in that moment, my world falls apart.' (Extract 2, line 18) What does she mean by this?

   e   Why do you think Elizabeth refers to her mother as 'this *amai* person' (Extract 2, line 15)? What does it tell us about her feelings towards her mother?

8   **Read tasks 1 and 2 and choose one to complete. When planning what to write, think about the literary theme that would run through the entire story and try to refer to it in your extract. Read your work to a partner and ask them what they think the literary theme may be.**

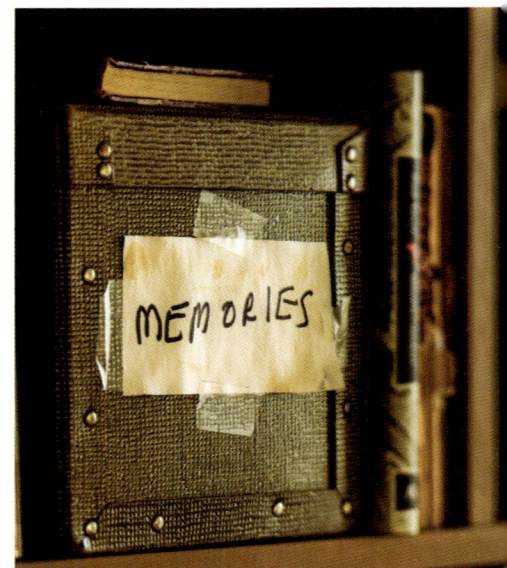

   1   **Write an extract from a memoir about yourself, or a relative or friend. Focus on a moment, person or event that helped to make you/them into the person you/they are now.**

   2   **Write an imaginary dialogue you might have with someone (real or fictitious) before heading off on a long journey that would present you with challenges.**

A novel

> **Background information**
> Brockwell Lido is an outdoor swimming pool in south London that first opened in 1937. It is open all year round and is an important, much-loved facility in the local community.

ABOUT THE AUTHOR

Libby Page

Libby Page describes herself as a writer, swimmer and optimist. Before becoming a full-time writer, she worked as a journalist. She is passionate about outdoor swimming and lives in London.

In *The Lido*, Page tell the story of an unlikely friendship that unfolds between an elderly lady, Rosemary, and a young journalist, Kate. Kate is writing about the possible closure of Brockwell Lido, the local public swimming pool. Rosemary is the lido's 'most loyal swimmer'. She has swum there her entire life and has many fond memories of swimming there as a child, and as an adult with her husband, George. The pool has been a constant part of Rosemary's life, but developers now plan to take it over and make it into a private gym. When Kate wants to interview Rosemary, Rosemary agrees but with the simple condition that Kate swims in the pool first. Only then does Rosemary slowly introduce Kate to the lido's loyal community.

1 Read the background information box and the About the author box.
   How do you think Rosemary may feel about the plans for the lido?
   Explain your answer to a partner.

2 Read and listen to two extracts from *The Lido* by Libby Page.
   Is your prediction from Exercise 1 correct?

> **1** Rosemary arrives at the lido at seven o'clock every morning. Once she is ready, she pushes open the changing room door and steps into the cold. She would dash if she could. Instead she walks to the edge, her feet arriving about three minutes after her mind. Her body is not
> 5 as strong as her will: growing old had forced her into patience.
>
> As she makes her way to the ladder she watches the other swimmers: a pool full of arms breaking the surface. Only the breaststrokers have faces that you can recognise.

> [8] **breaststroke:** a swimming style in which arms make circular movements in front of the body and knees are moved towards the body then kicked out.

Lowering herself down the ladder Rosemary feels like a tree in the
10 wind. Her branches creak. She lets go and is taken by the water,
letting its coldness surround her and getting used to the temperature
before kicking smoothly off the side. She begins her steady swim into
the mist. She can't see the deep end but knows that if she keeps
kicking she will eventually reach it. Rosemary is eighty-six but in the
15 water she is ageless.

[…]

Rosemary swims a steady breaststroke, dipping her head in and out
of the water and letting her ears fill with the pool. She can see her
fingers ahead of her wrinkling in the water, although she can't tell
20 how much is the water and how much is just her age. Her wrinkles
always surprise her. Young girls don't have wrinkles. She is a young
girl swimming in the morning under the watchful gaze of the big old
clock and the lifeguard who twiddles his whistle in his hand. She is
swimming before heading to her job in the library – she will have to
25 get changed quickly if she is to make it on time. Her hair will drip
behind her as she makes her way up and down the shelves of books.

'Have you swum the Channel yet, Rosy?' George will say when she
gets home in the evening.

'Still working on it.'

30 Now the library is closed though and George isn't here. She stops in
the shallow end and leans against the wall before walking slowly to
the ladder. She imagines this lido as a private, residents-only gym,
and although she is used to the cold water, a shiver runs through her.
When she climbs out she is no longer young and is painfully aware
35 of the existence of her knees. She never noticed that she had knees
when she was young; like her free bus card it is part of her life now
that she resents. She still always pays for her bus ticket, on principle.

2 The swimming club children are fearless. Rosemary watches them
wriggling like tadpoles up and down the lanes. They are young
40 enough to be completely unselfconscious as they stand on the edge
waiting to dive in. Jostling each other, they pull their brightly coloured
swimming caps tighter over their heads.

[…]

…their bravery still surprises her when they jump into the water.
45 When the instructor blows his whistle they dive one after the other like
knocked-over bottles, ever trusting that the water will greet them with
a smile and that their bodies will respond and know what to do once
they are submerged. Rosemary wishes she had that confidence in her
body – she can't always rely on it doing what she tells it to.

10 creak: to make a noise, usually when stiff material like wood is moved slightly

19 wrinkle: to develop lines on the skin due to old age or a long time spent in water

23 gaze: a long steady look at someone or something

23 twiddle: to move something repeatedly between your fingers for no reason

24 head (somewhere): to make a journey to a place

37 resent: to feel angry when forced to accept or do something

39 wriggle: to twist part of body quickly and repeatedly

39 tadpole: small aquatic creature that develops into a frog

39 lane (swimming pool): special marked strip of pool to separate swimmers

40 unselfconscious: unworried about what others may think about you

41 jostle: to push someone in order to move past them

48 submerged: below the surface of the water

3 **Work with your partner. Answer these questions about the extracts.**

a What does the writer mean when she says 'her feet arriving about three minutes after her mind'?

b The writer says Rosemary 'lets go and is taken by the water, letting its coldness surround her'. This gives the impression that Rosemary feels very calm in the water. Find another example which illustrates that Rosemary feels calm in the water.

c As Rosemary thinks about the wrinkles on her hands she remembers things from the past. What does she remember?

d Why do you think Rosemary resents her bus card?

e When describing the swimming club children, the author uses the words 'wriggling' and 'jostling', creating a feeling of movement and action. How does this compare to the way she describes Rosemary at the pool?

f In what way are the children's feelings about the pool similar to Rosemary's?

READING TIP

Characterisation

Characterisation refers to the way in which writers make their characters come alive in their writing. This can involve describing details from the characters' lives, their personal background, their thoughts and memories, their habits, routines and passions, their mannerisms and the way they move; all of which help inform the reader about the character and their role in the story.

When we read that 'Her body is not as strong as her will: growing old had forced her into patience', we get the impression that Rosemary is a determined person and that although she is not naturally patient, she is now. This information helps the reader believe Rosemary's determination and step-by-step approach later in the book when she tries to save the lido from closure.

---

4 **Copy the table below into your notebook. Read the extracts again and complete the table with details about Rosemary.**

Personal background	Thoughts and memories	Habits, routines and passions	Mannerisms and movements
86 years old swimmer worked in library was married to George			

5 **Read the tasks below and choose one.**

1 Think about one physical activity you do on a daily or weekly basis. How similar or different do you think it would feel for someone aged 86 to do the same activity? Write a short passage describing an older person doing the activity and include details about the person to develop your character.

2 Make a characterisation table about yourself or someone you know well. Include details that would help someone understand your/your friend's character. Extend the table if necessary to include more detail such as strengths and weaknesses, motivations and worries.

A play

1 **Read the About the author box. Work with a partner and discuss what you think the advantages and disadvantages would be of being related to a famous author.**

> ### ABOUT THE AUTHOR
>
> **Lou Harry**
>
> On his website, Lou Harry describes himself as 'a playwright who does journalism. A journalist who writes books. And a book writer who pens plays.'
>
> In his short one-act comedy, *Imagine Being Joyce Carol Oates' Aunt, Just for a Minute*, Lou Harry explores what it may be like to be the relative of a famous writer, in particular a writer who writes in a way that forces the reader to reflect and think deeply about certain issues.

2 **Read the background information box about Joyce Carol Oates. What additional advantages or disadvantages might there be in being related to a writer like her?**

> ### Background information
>
> The person Lou Harry has chosen to write about in his play is not invented – she is a real person. Joyce Carol Oates is an internationally successful novelist, playwriter and poet who has won many literary awards. One of her most distinguishing characteristics is the amount of literature she has written. She has written over 50 books, as well as plays, poetry and nonfiction. There have been periods of her writing career when she produced two or three books a year.
>
> Although she usually writes under her own name, she has also published books using the pseudonyms (false names) Rosamond Smith and Lauren Kelly.

3 **Look at the text without reading it. Which features can you see that show it is a play? When reading the play as a text, rather than using it to rehearse for a performance, why are these features important to the reader?**

Imagine Being Joyce Carol Oates' Aunt, Just for a Minute by Lou Harry

1   *Setting: A bookstore fiction section*

Lights up on CARRIE and KAREN, both in their 30s, facing an invisible fourth wall. Karen is scanning titles. Carrie has taken a Joyce Carol Oates book off the shelf. They do not know each other.

	CARRIE	*(to herself)* Can you imagine…?
5	**KAREN**	What?
	CARRIE	Oh, sorry.
	KAREN	I thought you were…never mind.
	CARRIE	Sorry, I was just… well… I mean, can you imagine what it would be like to be Joyce Carol Oates' aunt?
10	**KAREN**	Excuse me?
	CARRIE	Being Joyce Carol Oates' aunt. *(silence)* The writer. Joyce Carol Oates, the writer.
	KAREN	I know who Joyce Carol Oates is.
	CARRIE	I didn't mean to insult you.
	KAREN	You didn't insult me.
15	**CARRIE**	Good. If I did, I'm sorry. *(silence)* I mean, I can't imagine. *(silence)* The obligation must be overwhelming.
	KAREN	Obligation?
	CARRIE	The obligation of being her aunt. Of being Joyce Carol Oates' aunt.
	KAREN	She's a grown woman, right?
20	**CARRIE**	So?
	KAREN	She can take care of herself. I presume. Drive. Lift things.
	CARRIE	That's not what I'm saying. *(pause)*
	KAREN	Then what are you saying?
	CARRIE	Never mind *(pause)* Let's say it's Thanksgiving and the family is gathered around the table.
25	**KAREN**	The Oates family?
	CARRIE	Yes. So you're Joyce Carol Oates' aunt. What do you say?
	KAREN	Er… grace, maybe? I'm guessing.
	CARRIE	Not about that. About her books.
	KAREN	Her books?
30	**CARRIE**	Yes, she's a writer.

	KAREN	I know that. I told you I know that.
	CARRIE	A very prolific writer.
	KAREN	Yes, I know.
	CARRIE	I mean, a crazily prolific writer. Like a couple of books a year prolific.
35	**KAREN**	So?
	CARRIE	You can't keep up.
	KAREN	Do I have to?
	CARRIE	You're her aunt. Don't you think there's an expectation?
	KAREN	An expectation?
40	**CARRIE**	Yes, an expectation. Your niece is Joyce Carol Oates. Shouldn't you have read her latest book?
	KAREN	Okay.
	CARRIE	But it's not okay. How many books do you think an average person reads a year?

2	**KAREN**	If we were close, she'd know if I was reading her books. I'd tell her when I finished one. Thanksgiving dinner would carry no more expectations for literary conversation from me than any other meal. I could mention her latest book when she met me for lunch at Quiznos.
45		
		[...]
	KAREN	I don't even know if I'm going to Thanksgiving this year. It's never what you hope. What you expect. And spending the week before trying to cram the rest of her novel.
		[...]
50	**KAREN**	...With *Because It Is Bitter and Because It Is My Heart*. Got about half way through.
		[...]
		Never finished that one. Had to fake it.
	CARRIE	Fake it?
	KAREN	Joyce was in a particularly questioning mood that year. Needy? It was like she was still mentally rewriting the book even after it was out. Like there was something she wasn't satisfied with. Something she wanted us to solve for her. And, sorry, that is not what I'm at Thanksgiving to do. I have my own life, thank you very much. Jim and I were having serious problems that year and I thought... thought... that maybe I would find some support from the family. But, no, it was all about Joyce and the books and the reviews and playing the stupid game of trying to get her to talk about the next book, or any of the seventeen that she is in the middle of writing at any given moment, even though we all know that she won't say a word about it. Them. Of any of them. Like it's some state secret.
55		
60		

4 **Read and listen to the extracts from the play. Work with your partner. Answer these questions about the extracts.**

    a Why is the stage direction that states that the characters do not know each other important to the plot?

    b Why do you think Carrie thinks she might have insulted Karen in line 13 by implying Karen did not know who Joyce Carol Oates is?

    c In line 23 Karen asks 'Then what are you saying?' but Carrie doesn't answer. What was Carrie trying to say in line 16 when she said 'The obligation must be overwhelming'?

    d Karen says Joyce treats her unpublished books like a 'state secret' in line 61. What does she mean by this?

    e How do you think Karen feels about being Joyce Carol Oates' relative?

16 overwhelming: difficult to deal with

21 presume: to believe something is true because it is very likely

27 grace: something said before a meal to give thanks for the food

32 prolific: producing a great number of something

45 Quiznos: an American fast food restaurant

48 cram: to do a lot in a short period of time

52 fake: to pretend to feel or know something

61 state: a country or its government

READING TIP

Dialogue

In novels, authors can describe their characters and the characters' emotions in detail. In contrast, play writers rely mainly on dialogue to portray their characters, to convey mood and to explore the inner thoughts of the characters. What is said, how it is said, who says it and to whom are all important features in a play.

Notice in lines 8–9 how the writer uses an apology and hesitation to highlight that the question was originally an inner thought rather than a direct question.

---

5 **With a partner, answer these questions about how the dialogue has been written.**

    a At the beginning of the dialogue, there is a great deal of repetition and many short questions. To what extent do you think the writer has used these features to create a sense of confusion? Do you think it works?

    b Does the second extract convey the same mood as the first? How is the structure of the dialogue different to that of the first extract? What effect does this have on the mood?

6 **There are no stage directions for the tone of voice the characters should use in the dialogue. Work with a partner and add them to Extract 1. Work with another pair and read Extract 1 out loud, following the stage directions you added and compare both versions.**

7 **Read the tasks below and choose one.**

> **1** Invent a second act for the play with a scene at the Thanksgiving meal. Write the dialogue. Where appropriate, use short turns, long turns, repetition, questions and stage directions to create the correct atmosphere.

> Imagine you had a famous relative. Which famous person would you choose and why? What do you think you would talk to them about? What activities would you want to, and not want to do with them? Tell your partner.

⟩ Acknowledgements

The authors and publishers acknowledge the following sources of copyright material and are grateful for the permissions granted. While every effort has been made, it has not always been possible to identify the sources of all the material used, or to trace all copyright holders. If any omissions are brought to our notice, we will be happy to include the appropriate acknowledgements on reprinting.

Unit 1 Track 05 adapted from 'How to maintain a work-study-life balance', 12 October 2019, published by EDUroute s.r.o.; **Unit 5** Text adapted from 'The Girl Who Dreams to Live on Mars: Talk With Alyssa Carson' by Kaya Olsen, 4 March 2021, used with the permission of Moonshot Pirates (Alyssa shared this information during the Moonshot Pirates talk in February 2021); **Unit 6** Text adapted from 'Six ways robots are used today that you probably didn't know about' Jonathan Roberts, Queensland University of Technology, 5 May 2019, and adapted from 'What robots and AI may mean for university lecturers and students' Nisreen Ameen, Queen Mary University of London, 15 April 2019, both used with the permission of The Conversation; Chart A adapted from 'The evolution of digital device ownership in the UK', by Niall McCarthy, 2018, StatistaCharts, Ofcom via BBC; Chart B adapted from 'Average Screen Time Statistics For 2023', by Srishti, 2023, data provided on elitecontentmarketer.com; Chart C adapted from Ali H. Al-Badi, Sara Al Mahrouqi and Oualid Ali (2016), "The Influence of the Internet on Teenagers' Behaviour in Oman", Journal of Internet Social Networking & Virtual Communities, Vol. 2016 (2016), Article ID 171712, DOI: 10.5171/2016. 171712 Copyright © 2016. Ali H. Al-Badi, Sara Al Mahrouqi and Oualid Ali. Distributed under Creative Commons CC-BY 4.0; Chart D data adapted from 'Digital 2022: Global Overview Report', by Simon Kemp, 2022, Kepios, from Datareportal.com; **Unit 7** Track 36 adapted excerpt from 'Read the Stories of 40 Incredible Kids Who Have Changed the World', by Adam Schubak, 9 October 2020, Good Housekeeping, used with the permission of Hearst Magazine Media; Text adapted from 'What if plastic was never invented', by Goldie Poll, 2018, published on INSH, now Underknown; Text adapted from 'Struggles of Youth With Fast Fashion', by Angela Mao, 6 July 2020, published by Inkspire; **Unit 8** Text adapted from 'New Dating Method Shows Vikings Occupied Newfoundland in 1021 C.E.', by Brian Handwerk, 20 October 2021, Copyright 2023 Smithsonian Institution, Reprinted with permission from Smithsonian Enterprises. All rights reserved; Text adapted from 'Danish supermarket offers fresh take on expired food', by Sören Billing, 28 November 2016, used with the permission of The Local; **Unit 9** Track 46 adapted from 'Passion for books. Books for your passion', by Katie Yakovleva, published by AbeBooks Inc; Track 49 abridged from 'The Well', by Milgo Dahir-Hersi, published by World Stories (Kids Out); **Unit 10** Track 54 adapted from 'Careers Advice for Teenagers', used with the permission of Success At School; Text adapted from 'International students and cultural shock', published by University of Washington; **Literature 1** Text adapted from 'The Tree Agreement', by Elise Paschen from *The Nightlife*. Originally published in Poetry (January 2016). Copyright © 2016, 2017 by Elise Paschen. Reprinted with the permission of The Permissions Company, LLC on behalf of Story Line Press, an imprint of Red Hen Press, redhen.org; **Literature 2** Excerpts from *31 Songs*, by Nick Hornby, published by Penguin Adult. Copyright © Nick Hornby, 2003. Reprinted by permission of Penguin Books Limited; **Literature 3** Excerpts from *I am a Girl from Africa, a memoir* by Elizabeth Nyamayaro. Copyright © 2021 by Elizabeth Nyamayaro. Reprinted with the permission of Scribner, a division of Simon & Schuster, Inc. All rights reserved; **Literature 4** Excerpts from *The Lido* by Libby Page, reproduced with permission of Orion Books through PLSclear, *Mornings with Rosemary: A Novel* by Libby Page. Copyright © 2018 by Elisabeth Page. Originally published in 2018 as *The Lido* by Simon & Schuster. Reprinted with the permission of Marysue Rucci Books, a division of Simon & Schuster, Inc. All rights reserved; **Literature 5** Excerpt from *Imagine Being Joyce Carol Oates' Aunt, Just for a Minute*, by Lou Harry, 2014, from *Indy Writes Books: A Book Lover's Anthology*, used with the permission of Indy Reads.

Thanks to the following for permission to reproduce images:

Cover Weiguan Lin/GI; *Inside* **Unit 1** Ariel Skelly/GI; Javier Zayas Photography/GI; Thomas Barwick/GI; Willie B. Thomas/GI; Jag Images/GI; Carol Yepes/GI; Brian Hagiwara/GI; Kelly Mitchell/GI; Caterina Oltean/GI; Mikroman6/GI; Sam Edwards/GI; Apomares/GI; Sebastian Ramirez Morales/GI; Maskot/GI; Archive Holdings Inc/GI; Jag Images/GI; **Unit 2** Jordan Siemens/GI; Manoj Shah/GI; Leisa Tyler/GI; Holger Leue/GI; Mauro Rotisciani/GI; Santiago Urquijo/GI; northwoodsphoto/GI; Kevin Noble/GI; Chase Dekker Wild-Life Images/GI; Rebecca Harding/GI; Sarayut Thaneerat/GI; LWA/GI; Slonov/GI; Solstock/GI; Chris Conway/GI; Shy Al Britanni/GI; Georgeclerk/GI; Guido Mieth/GI; Brigitte Blättler/GI; Johner Images/GI; Alistair Berg/GI; **Unit 3** Maskot/GI; SDI Productions/GI; Peter Cade/GI; Werayuth Tessrimuang/GI; Peter Cade/GI; Lori Andrews/GI; Burcu Atalay Tankut/GI; Carlo A/GI; Thianchai Sitthikongsak/GI; Klaus Vedfelt/GI; Willie B. Thomas/GI; Universal History Archive/GI; Science Photo Library/GI; SDI Productions/GI; Wladimir Bulgar/GI; **Unit 4** Aliyev Alexei Sergeevich/GI; Ian Laker Photography/GI; 10255185_880/GI; Momo Productions/GI; Westend61/GI; Mediaphotos/GI; Runstudio/GI; Furtseff/GI; Jose Luis Pelaez Inc/GI; Fraser Hall/GI; Steve Heap/GI; Cultura Exclusive/Lost Horizon Images/GI; Hinterhaus Productions/GI; Tim Robberts/GI; filmstudio/GI; Cavan Images/GI; Donald Iain Smith/GI; Grant Faint/GI; Maskot/GI; Law Ho Ming/GI; Tom Grill/GI; Allan Baxter/GI; **Unit 5** James O'Neil/GI; Winfried Wisniewski/GI; Jodijacobson/GI; Evan Lipton/GI; Patrick J. Endres/GI; Grant Faint/GI; Winfried Wisniewski/GI; Mgokalp/GI; Gary Latham/GI; Kongkrit Sukying/GI; FG Trade/GI; Daniel Milchev/GI; NicolasMcComber/GI; Travelstoxphoto/GI; Chrissteer/GI; Tassii/GI; Cokada/GI; Gabriel Passarelli/GI; **Unit 6** Morsa Images/GI; D3sign/GI; Marioguti/GI; Mireya Acierto/GI; Solskin/GI; Capuski/GI; Javier Sanz/GI; Daniel De La Hoz/GI; Monty Rakusen/GI; Peter Cade/GI; Peter Dazeley/GI; Anchiy/GI; Tara Moore/GI; Momo Productions/GI; Westend61/GI; Maskot/GI; Drafter123/GI; Cavan Images/GI; Edwin Tan/GI; Mr.Cole_Photographer/GI; **Unit 7** Surasak Suwanmake/GI; Coldsnowstorm/GI; Rapideye/GI; Sarayut/GI; Peter Cade/GI; Ewg3d/GI; Frederic Cirou/GI; Pramote Polyamate/GI; Taiyou Nomachi/GI; Ryouchin/GI; Mixetto/GI; SDI Productions/GI; Clarissa Leahy/GI; Exxorian/GI; Eleonora Galli/GI; Miodrag ignjatovic/GI; Patchareeporn Sakoolchai/GI; Hiroshi Watanabe/GI; **Unit 8** Powerfocusfotografie/GI; Jose Luis Pelaez Inc/GI; Ultra.F/GI; Cavan Images/GI; Corey Ford/GI; Victor Habbick Visions/GI; Glasshouse Images/GI; Lorado/GI; Mark Garlick/GI; D3sign/GI; Peter Dazeley/GI; D3sign/GI; Klaus Vedfelt/GI; Solstock/GI; Compassionate Eye Foundation/GI; Nick Dolding/GI; Kitti Boonnitrod/GI; Westend61/GI; Aleksandarnakic/GI; Oscar Wong/GI; Shipskyy/GI; **Unit 9** Virojt Changyencham/GI; Lisbeth Hjort/GI; Andresr/GI; Ippei Naoi/GI; Dani Serrano/GI; Fred Stein Archive/GI; Chip Somodevilla/GI; Tara Moore/GI; Brais Seara/GI; Tom Penpark/GI; Dougal Waters/GI; George Pachantouris/GI; Henglein And Steets/GI; ATU Images/GI; Leonid Sneg/GI; Aaron Mccoy/GI; Schon/GI; Miguel Navarro/GI; Afriandi/GI; Don Mason/GI; Nora Carol Photography/GI; Portishead1/GI; Ajt/GI; **Unit 10** Sadeugra/GI; Thomas Barwick/GI; Luis Alvarez/GI; Mstudioimages/GI; Bruno Guerreiro/GI; Sturti/GI; Xavier Lorenzo/GI; Seksan Mongkhonkhamsao/GI; Weedezign/GI; Witthaya Prasongsin/GI; Ezra Bailey/GI; Vladimir Vladimirov/GI; Laindiapiaroa/GI; SDI Productions/GI; Nitat Termmee/GI; Calvindexter/GI; **Lit** Gregoria Gregoriou Crowe Fine Art And Creative Photography/GI; **Lit 1&2** Elise Paschen; Jozsef Zoltan Varga/GI; Alan Harris/GI; Mark L Stanley/GI; Marco Pozzi Photographer/GI; Colors Hunter - Chasseur De Couleurs/GI; **Lit 3&4** Elisabetta Villa/GI; Amtitus/GI; Oscar Sánchez Photography/GI; Daniel Grill/GI; Lit 5&6 Bryan Bedder/GI; Jeremy Walker/GI; Jan Hakan Dahlstrom/GI; **Lit 7&8** Steve Cadman Via Wikipedia CC-SA 2.0; Filadendron/GI; **Lit 9&10** Lou Harry; Nikada/GI

Key: GI = Getty Images